Praise for *The*

"As a modern-day prophet, Ken Bailey has demonstrated the gift of speaking God's Word with authority, boldness, and, most importantly, humility! 'Prophecy never had its origin in the will of man, but men spoke from God as they were carried along by the Holy Spirit.' II Peter 1:20-21. I have witnessed Ken's devotion and commitment to proclaiming God's Word for over thirty years. Ken is a modern-day Truth Teller!"
–Travis Smith, Longtime friend and Brother-in-Christ

"Ken Bailey is a prophet. He has been my friend and mentor over the past ten years. What I admire most about him is his character; the things he does when no one is around, and he doesn't realize I'm watching. Over the years he has given me words from God and they have always come to pass. He has also prophesied about world events and they have also come to pass. He often tells me about the visions God has given him about the end times. I can hear the pain in his voice, as he speaks about how it will be for some people who reject Jesus. Nevertheless, we always end the conversations with an evangelistic spirit and encourage each other to boldly tell as many people as we can about The Savior before those days arrive."
–William Green, former NFL running back, and first round pick

"The Lord led me to Ken through ALMS International (almsinternational.com). I had been praying for guidance and wisdom, for the Lord to lead me to smaller and efficient Spirit-filled mission organizations. Ken's love for reaching lost souls and feeding the poor is a major passion and priority of his. He REALLY loves Jesus and overflows with genuine joy and peace. I have never met anyone like him! Even my kids say he is the nicest person they have ever met. Ken has now become a Biblical mentor to me. My entire family is now actively involved with his current and future ALMS mission events that will be held around the world. Being a super conservative/skeptical Bible-believing Baptist, I am convinced Ken is indeed a last day's prophet and hearing directly from the Lord. He has prophesied about multiple specific events to my family that, shockingly, came true immediately. I have never witnessed someone with a prophetic gift like this before. This could only come from the Lord. In fact, my entire family witnessed miraculous signs and wonders with Ken when he visited us in Florida for a few days. He is telling the truth about his experiences."

–Rudolf Huettler, Electrical Engineer from Penn State University and now a personal friend of Ken

"As Paul writes in 1 Corinthians 12:28 that God has appointed prophets, Ken happens to be one who He has appointed. He has a sincere faith and a relentless pursuit to walk in God's will completely and totally. My wife and I have spent much time with him since his appointment as a prophet, and what we have witnessed and experienced during our time with Ken is hard to put into a few words, but it is very evident that God is active and very present with him. It never fails that God always shows up. Ken walks in signs, miracles, and wonders, and can be trusted as a voice of truth."

–Marshall Carrier, Cousin of Ken

"If you truly want to hear from God, ask Ken Bailey, as he is in constant conversation with the Lord. This book is absolutely God-Breathed. Ken is the true End Time Prophet. We are so grateful that God Miraculously brought Ken into our lives "For such a time as this"...
Amos 3:7, "For the Lord God does nothing without revealing His secret to His servants The Prophets."

–Bev Duncan, member of New Song Christian Fellowship, a church Ken pastored previously in Gunnison, CO

"I have known Ken just about all of my life. We are cousins who grew up together in Mission, Texas. I've watched Ken, from a distance, for many years, and most recently, up close on a mission trip that he led to Asia. Ken has a passion for Christ. He trusts God and is obedient at any and all costs. He will not compromise truth to make his life easier or to win the favor of man…he speaks truth and lives truth. Ken is a blessing and encouragement to my life."

–Bruce Carrier, Retired engineer, Pastor Advisory Team member at C4 Church

"This is an honor and Glory to Jesus. As an end-times prophet, before the Second Coming of Jesus Christ, Ken Bailey is the most dedicated servant I have witnessed, who is living out His calling. God's miraculous hand connected us during a soccer game in 2018, and my life has not been the same since. Ken has a close, intimate relationship with Jesus that has come through a costly daily process. He encourages every believer he meets to trust and obey Jesus, to live according to the Spirit, and to serve the true King of eternity!"

–Benjamin Sergo, A good friend and co-laborer in Jesus

"I first met Ken Bailey in a Holy Spirit vision as he was walking towards me. I have been present when the Holy Spirit has spoken to both of us. Ken has been tasked by God with presenting Prophecy warnings about the Nation and World concerning the End Times, and he does it with 100 percent accuracy."

–Roy Duncan, Elder, at New Song Christian Fellowship, Gunnison, CO

"I've known Ken Bailey for over fifty years. When my family moved to Mission, Texas, in 1971, the Baileys were the first church members that I met. I still remember the warmth and genuineness of this family, who were without pretense, and who immediately made me feel welcome. Most memorable, as we sat to share a meal, was the prayer of blessing that the father, Jack Bailey, made before we ate. Having grown up in church, I was used to hearing prayer that was often very formal and repetitious in language, especially if the Pastor was present. In contrast, Mr. Bailey's prayer over that meal was more like a son's conversation with a loving father. It was intimate, direct, and simple in language; a real conversation with the Father. This is the image of Jack Bailey that I carried when I learned that he had died. Sadly, as a self-absorbed teenager, I was woefully unaware of the deep impact that this father's death had on the Bailey family.

When my father, Jack Cash, passed away in 1986, I was pleasantly surprised to see Ken Bailey at the funeral. Although we had seen each other and loosely communicated over the years, it was a long drive from Colorado to Waco, Texas. I remember Ken sharing at that time that he simply had to come and honor the man who had meant so much to him after the death of his own father.

Fast forward to 2023, and I see Ken Bailey as a faithful follower and disciple of Jesus. I pray that his story and message impacts you personally, and also this crazy world in which we presently live."

–Wes Cash, Father, husband, grandfather, and follower of Jesus

"I met Ken Bailey in 2015, when I was his interpreter during his mission trip to Brazil. I took Ken to many homes, where he shared the gospel and led about 100 people to Christ. In these homes, I witnessed him casting out demons and praying for people to be healed, including my brother Gilson,

who had a severe case of Hepatitis C with a high risk of death. Ken is one of the men, chosen by God, who has the tools to bring not only physical and emotional healing, but also the gospel, to people all over the world."
–Genilson Holanda, Engineer in Brazil and friend of Ken

"Ken Bailey is a God-fearing man, believing in and following God wherever He leads him. For over twenty-three years, I have witnessed Ken in action, serving our Lord, on mission fields, in high school classrooms, gyms, FCA, the Navajo Reservation, and around the world. Leading people to the saving grace of Jesus Christ through the Holy Spirit, Ken is a Bible-preaching evangelist. Ken writes this book from the words God has given him."
–David Ward, Deacon, retired teacher/coach, personal friend, and Brother-in-Christ

The modern church loves to listen to sweet, motivational sermons and glossy preachers with high media ratings. And sitting in warm, comfortable chairs, the church began to forget that Jesus called us not to build a kingdom of this world to ennoble our lives with the achievements of modern technologies, but to bring the Gospel to people, which shows our love of Christ. We are not to pursue enrichment, or advancement, at the expense of faith in Him. I am not against wealth and prosperity. This is not about that. Moreover, in order to become rich or successful, you do not need to believe in God. I remember one picture, where in one church, in the Philippines, after heavy rains, people gathered in the church and praised God, standing knee-deep in water. My good friend and zealous brother in Christ, Ken, could be a successful, high-level, rich preacher. He has every tool for this. But he has chosen to stand, knee-deep in water, and praise the Lord! In humility and patience, he speaks with a loud voice in the Name of the Lord about our real calling as we see the last days approaching. Ken wants to see the church return to its mission—taking the gospel to the nations. Thank you for this, Ken. Don't be silent!"
–Ariel Ben David, pastor of the Messianic Community "Maayan" (the Well), Eilat, Israel

Ken is one of the greatest prophets of God in this generation. God sent him to prophesy about the future and end times in 2012, when Ken came to Uganda to do evangelism. It was our first time meeting him. He gave two prophetic words to my family and my ministry. The first was that God was going to use me in Uganda and I would also take the gospel to different nations of the world. As a young preacher, it sounded strange to me then, but now I have preached in eight countries beyond Uganda.

Secondly, Ken gave a prophetic word that in five years, there would be a radio station in the small town I was living in and it would be an opportunity for me and my family to preach the gospel. In 2017, a radio station was opened, and it has been a blessing to my family to preach the gospel to thousands of people in our region.

This proved to me that Ken is the current, greatest prophet that God has sent in this generation.

–Innocent Mubangizi, Evangelist from Uganda

"God led me to this man in 2021, when I saw a video of him on YouTube. The Holy Spirit told me, "This man is a humble servant of God, and an end time prophet. He does not preach a prosperity gospel, but teaches only the truth."

The Lord told me to contact him, and that he would come to Asia and help me feed and clothe the poor, orphaned, and widowed. He held a crusade here, and thousands of people turned from their idol worship, repented of their sins, and placed their faith in Christ. We have seen him minister in villages. He prayed for people to be healed from diseases and delivered from witchcraft, and they were. He always gives the glory to God and takes no credit for anything. He loves God and he loves people. We love him (Papa), and so do the people of our nation."

–Rishi, a pastor in Asia

"Read this book and discover what God is revealing to His servant the Prophet. I met Ken in a miraculous way on Facebook. He has a great love for the poor and needy. He has blessed my ministry with healing, love, and relief."

–Peter Waswa, Pastor/Evangelist in Kenya

"Ken Bailey has been a trusted friend and spiritual mentor in my life since college. As a young person, I appreciate his boldness to share God's Word and his dedication to serve the least of these around the world. I pray that this book draws you closer to Jesus Christ. Be encouraged by this timely message!"

–Morgan Aragon, friend and fellow follower of Jesus Christ

THE
END IS NOW
COMING

THE END IS NOW COMING

God's Urgent Warning to His Church and the Nations

KEN BAILEY

All Scripture quotations, unless otherwise indicated, are taken from the Holy Bible, New International Version®, NIV®. Copyright ©1973, 1978, 1984, 2011 by Biblica, Inc.™ Used by permission of Zondervan. All rights reserved worldwide. www.zondervan.com The "NIV" and "New International Version" are trademarks registered in the United States Patent and Trademark Office by Biblica, Inc.™

Verses marked NASB are taken from the New American Standard version of the Bible.

Some of the names of individuals mentioned in this book have been changed to protect their anonymity.

The End is Now Coming
Copyright © 2023 by Ken Bailey

All rights reserved. No part of this publication may be reproduced, stored or transmitted in any form or by any means: electronic, mechanical, digital, photocopy, recording, or any other—except for brief quotations in printed reviews, without permission from the publisher.

Visit the author's websites at: kenbaileyministries.com and almsinternational.com

ISBN (paperback): 979-8-9887687-0-8
ISBN (hardcover): 979-8-9887687-1-5
ISBN (ebook): 979-8-9887687-2-2

Book design and production by www.AuthorSuccess.com
Photo of Ken Bailey provided by Ken Bailey
Interior photos used by permission

I dedicate this book to my Lord and Savior—Jesus Christ
who loved me and gave Himself for me.

To Sue,
Thank you for your love and support on our
great journey with the Lord. I love you.

To Michelle and BJ,

How could a father be so blessed to have the most
amazing daughter and son in the world?
I love you both.

My FREE GIFT to You

Dear Reader,

I want to offer you a free gift. I have produced a powerful video of an encounter that I had with Jesus when I was in Asia.

This video has never been published. In it I share the true story of how the Lord performs several dramatic miracles and then appears to me in a vision.

I want you to have this incredible video. It will amaze you as you hear about God's awesome ability to do the impossible and how he rescues people in their time of greatest need.

I hope you will purchase my book—*The End is Now Coming*. Inside it I share many more stories of the astonishing miracles and visions that the Lord has given me and the urgent messages that God has asked me to share with you.

To get your free gift go to: www.kenbaileyministries.com/freevideo

Thanks for looking inside my book—**THE END IS NOW COMING**

Contents

Introduction 1

CHAPTER 1: From Joy To Agony: My Early Years With God 9
CHAPTER 2: Hearing God Speak: How It All Began 15
CHAPTER 3: The Prophetic Call of God 27
CHAPTER 4: Visions of Great Spiritual Warfare 50
CHAPTER 5: God Raises Up a Modern Day Prophet 55
CHAPTER 6: God is Shaking the Earth, the Nations,
   His Church, and You..68
CHAPTER 7: Signs, Wonders, and Miracles..79
CHAPTER 8: My Miraculous Vision of War, The Tribulation,
   and the Second Coming Of Christ 96
CHAPTER 9: The Shroud of Turin: Is It Jesus' Burial Cloth? 107
CHAPTER 10: God's Urgent Warning to the Church—Part I...............116
CHAPTER 11: God's Urgent Warning to the Church—Part II.............129
CHAPTER 12: Beware of False Prophets...144
CHAPTER 13: Does God Have Any True Prophets Today?...................156
CHAPTER 14: God's Urgent Warning to the Nations 165
CHAPTER 15: Another Jesus Revolution and a Word to
   Young People...179
CHAPTER 16: The Great Deception...187
CHAPTER 17: The New World Order 208
CHAPTER 18: Prodigal Sons and Daughters, Come Home to
   Your Father..229
CHAPTER 19: The End Is Now Coming.. 240

Epilogue 255
Notes 257
Acknowledgments... 259

Foreword

SUE BAILEY

Life is so much clearer when looking back, but there was a time when I thought my husband was going crazy, and I wasn't sure I wanted to continue this wild journey with him. He became very bold for Christ; he didn't consider the danger he was going into, just the people that he was sent to minister to. I often relate to Peter's wife. She watched her husband walk out of their home; never sure if he would return, but aware that Jesus had changed her husband into a man she did not recognize.

It would take years until I thanked Jesus for my amazing Christ-filled husband. During the struggle, I learned to trust Jesus, not myself. I realized that this transitional journey wasn't just for Ken, but for me as well.

I have known Ken for over forty years. You could say that I have had a front-row seat to the transformation God has taken Ken through. I have watched him fall deeply in love with God and become willing to give up more and more of his life. It wasn't that Ken was doing anything wrong, but he wanted to dedicate more time to the Lord, so he gave up golfing, fishing, and other time-consuming activities.

Ken wanted more time with Jesus. He would get up at night and lay on the floor and seek Him. Ken told me that the glory would come down on him, and he couldn't get enough. This glory didn't happen after just one night…it was years of seeking Him, and now Ken knew how Moses, Daniel, and many other Bible heroes felt. He had been with God and there was no going back.

Ken is the most God-loving man that I know. He has given up everything for the Lord. He does not want glory for himself, but only for God. The Lord is Ken's primary focus. He spends so much time seeking Him, talking to Him, and getting to know Him more deeply each day. He knows God in a way that very few people are willing to sacrifice the time and energy to reach.

Ken often says, "People are as close to God as they want to be!"

It's true. I sacrificed for a few nights, and I spent some time on my face seeking God, but my heart was not truly seeking Him. God knew this. God knows our hearts, and Ken's heart does belong to God!

People sometimes say that Ken wants attention. I can tell you that is not true. God has so many demanding works for Ken. Ken doesn't always want to share God's message or vision. He knows that it will not be popular, and people will accuse him of being a false prophet. But God wants him to obey.

The truth is that Ken doesn't even want to be a prophet. He just wants to be an ordinary guy that fits in with everyone else. But God has chosen Ken.

In the Bible, there is a verse that says, "For the eyes of the Lord move to and fro, throughout the earth, so that He may strongly support those whose heart is completely His." 2 Chronicles 16:9a

God's eyes rested on Ken one evening, and our lives have never been the same.

Ken made himself available to God, for whatever God wanted. He has laid his life down, and he does not want it back. He wants more of God; he wants to please God. He wants to hear the words from Jesus' lips, "Well done, good and faithful servant!"

God was not only speaking to Ken, but He was also giving him visions. Ken has shared visions with me, with friends, and with our church family. In the beginning, I was skeptical. I questioned the visions, but one by one, they all came true.

God told Ken about Covid, Russia attacking another country, digital money, and sadly, the decline of the United States, all before these events happened, and there are more. It happened; God really was speaking to him.

In Acts 2:17 the Bible says, "In the last days, God says, I will pour out my Spirit on all people; your sons and daughters will prophesy, your young men will see visions, your old men will dream dreams."

People are very uncomfortable with there being a Modern-Day Prophet. I know; I was one of those people. But God is all powerful–there is nothing that God cannot do. Our minds are limited.

We have to see it to believe it. I have seen it! God has included me in this biblical-like journey. I have seen God raise up a prophet for these last days. God has given him warnings and messages. Do not turn away because of your limited understanding.

Read about the prophets in your Bible, and God will open your eyes. He opened my eyes. He is consistent. He sends prophets to warn people during difficult times, like Noah, Moses, Daniel, and so many more. God is now sending Ken to warn people before He brings judgment upon the wicked.

I have always heard, "Enter through the narrow gate. For wide is the gate and broad is the road that leads to destruction, and many enter through it." (Matthew 7:13)

God has Ken climbing narrow trails on extreme mountains. Very few people would choose this route, but Ken has. He goes wherever God sends him, says whatever God tells him, and lives the life God has chosen for him.

I encourage you to read this book. It is the true story of a man who God has raised up to be His messenger in these last days. It contains unbelievable miracles and visions that will show you how powerful God is—even today.

Within these pages, are messages that Ken has received from God. They are for you.

Ken is telling you the truth, whether you believe him or not. God is warning you to get ready, for *The End is Now Coming*.

Sue Bailey,
Teacher, and Ken's wife

Prologue

It was Saturday morning, February 29, 2020. I was walking on the beach at South Padre Island with my wife, Sue, and a couple of friends.

I love to feel the sand under my feet and hear the sound that the waves make as they splash onto the shore. The seagulls were flying overhead, and kids were nearby, making sandcastles as they let their imaginations run wild.

It was a picture-perfect day. I felt so blessed. I couldn't think of any other place in the world that I would rather be.

After walking on the beach for about half an hour, out of nowhere, God began to speak to me. I know His voice, having heard Him so many times before. However, it was the voice that He uses with me when He wants me to do a very difficult thing for Him.

He said, "Ken, I want you to give a prophetic message in the church service tomorrow. I also want you to tell the congregation that you are a prophet. Have the sermon filmed and put it on social media and send it out to the nations.

I want the world to hear the message that I am going to speak through you. I want the nations to know that I have chosen you to be my prophet."

I immediately began to be troubled in my spirit. It had been a year and a half since the Lord had asked me to do something this demanding, and now He was asking me to do it again.

How could God do this to me? I was stunned at what He had just told me to do. I didn't want to do it.

I was the new pastor at a church in Texas. I had already grown to love the people in the community.

I knew if I obeyed the Lord, it could possibly cause me trouble. People who loved me now might turn against me, not wanting to hear prophetic messages in a traditional church.

As I continued walking on the beach, no one knew that God was talking to me. I visited with those who were with me, but inside, I was so angry at God for telling me to do this.

I thought to myself, "Who in their right mind would want to be a prophet? I sure didn't want to be one. Prophets are hated, mocked, and sometimes put to death. Count me out."

The Old Testament Prophet, Jonah, had nothing on me. I did want to see people repent, but telling church folks that I was a prophet might be worse than getting swallowed by a giant sea creature and spending three nights in its belly.

I was willing to be a secret prophet; a reluctant prophet. However, God had other plans.

I kept a smile on my face and did the best I could to get through the day. I didn't want to draw any attention to myself or tell the others what was happening.

Inside, I was dying a million deaths, knowing what I was going to have to do tomorrow. What I had looked forward to for so long, a great weekend at the beach, had now become a nightmare. I had lunch with everyone and then we loaded up and headed back home

Once we were home, I began to do what I did last time God asked me to do this. I began to argue with Him and try to talk Him out of making me do it. Maybe I could get the Lord to change His mind?

The pressure began to mount. It was now early evening and God just kept squeezing me. When I try to resist God's directives, it feels like He has me in a vice, where he clamps down on my chest and back and puts pressure on me until I agree to obey Him.

I couldn't breathe. I got sick to my stomach and didn't want to eat. I was miserable.

I knew that I was not going to get any sleep that night. I was so stressed out.

My wife went to bed, but I just paced back and forth, in another room, and I began to shout at God. I tried to keep my voice down so I wouldn't wake her up.

"God are you serious? Why are you doing this to me? Come on God. This is crazy. Don't make me give a prophetic sermon."

The vice just got tighter. God kept turning up the pressure on me.

I collapsed on the bed at midnight, in total exhaustion, and kept arguing. I got back up at 3 a.m. and continued shouting at the Lord.

I began to yell at Him, "I'm not going to give this prophetic sermon and tell them you have called me to be a prophet unless you give me a great sign. Maybe you didn't really tell me to do this while I was walking on the beach. You're gonna have to prove to me that you did."

I felt tormented. I had argued with God all night, begging Him to not make me give this sermon, and He wouldn't relent.

I wished I was dead. Maybe it would have been better for me to have never been born.

I wondered: Would God bring me the Great Sign that I demanded He give to me before the service started, so that there would be no doubt in my mind that He had actually spoken to me on the beach?

Had He really called me to be a prophet to the nations?

Would the Lord speak to me and give me a message to share with the World that day—March 1, 2020?

I knew I would soon get the answers to my questions. It was now 10 a.m. and the church service started at 10:45. We were living near the church, so Sue and I walked over to the chapel. I asked those who were present to come to the altar and pray for me. I told them that

God had asked me to give a difficult message and that I desperately needed their prayers.

I knelt at the altar, and they were all so gracious and prayed for me. When they were finished praying, I stood up and noticed that the baptistry was too full. We were going to have baptisms during the service, and I knew that some water would splash out if I didn't drain some off.

The church building was eighty years old, and the drain valve was located on an outside wall. I went outside to access it. It was now twenty-five minutes until the church service started.

I kept arguing with God. I still hadn't gotten the great sign from Him, which would confirm that I had to give the prophetic message and tell the people who attended that day that I was a prophet.

What was I going to do? Why hadn't God answered my prayer? How could He do this to me?

In extreme agony, I cried out to the Lord, "Oh God, why are you putting me through this? I need to hear from you Lord. I need a Great Sign from you."

Suddenly, I looked to my left and I saw a man who was walking quickly towards me. He was holding something in his hand …

◆◆◆

On March 1, 2020, God did a series of miracles for me that have changed my life.

I will never be the same. After you read this book and experience God, you'll never be the same!

Introduction

It was Thursday night, April 8, 2004. I was sitting at my office desk, in the county home that we were living in, out in east Texas. I began my normal time of prayer and praise with the Lord, when suddenly, I heard Him talking to me.

I was stunned. I couldn't see Him, but the God of the Universe began speaking to me. Then, for the first time in my life, the Lord took me into a vision.

It seemed like Jesus was standing right next to me as He spoke. His voice was gentle and loving; like a father speaking to his son.

He said, "Ken, I want you to surrender your life to me. It will cost you everything. I am calling you to make a costly commitment to me and follow me."

The Lord continued, "If you give your life to me, it will come at a great financial cost. I'll also move you far away from your children who are in college. If you follow me, you will never buy this home and the beautiful acres here where you want to continue living.

"Are you willing to follow me without knowing what you will do next or where I will be taking you? Will you let me have your life, to do whatever I want to do with it?"

Then the Lord stopped speaking to give me time to decide if I would accept His prophetic call.

I paused for a moment before answering Him. I thought of my love for Him and how I knew that it was the right thing to do with my life. I trusted Him.

Without hesitating, I said, "Lord, I will do it. Yes. I accept this costly commitment and your prophetic call on my life."

He then said the name "Bonhoeffer," and let me know that he was an author. He continued, "Go to Lifeway Christian Bookstore in Tyler, Texas, after you get off work tomorrow. I want you to resign from your current job in the morning. Write your resignation letter tonight."

Then the vision and the voice of the Lord stopped, but I could tell that He was very pleased that I had accepted His call.

I sat in awe, knowing Jesus had now called me to follow Him just as He had asked the disciples, and later Paul, to follow Him over 2,000 years earlier. These men made the radical choice to leave their jobs and families the moment that the Lord asked them to surrender their lives to Him.

After praising the Lord for a few minutes, I went to work. I immediately got on my computer and typed up my resignation letter. I would obey the Lord and resign in the morning, when I went to work at the school where I served as athletic director.

I then sat for a while longer and thought about how Jesus had just spoken to me and taken me into a vision for the very first time. I had never heard God speak so clearly and directly to me.

A man named Pat McGee had prophesied over me years before, telling me that a prophetic call from God was coming. Now I had received the call to be a prophet. It confirmed that Pat had truly heard from the Lord.

I was so excited. What did God have in store for my wife, Sue, and me in the days and years ahead? It was surreal.

I couldn't wait to go to the bookstore and see why God wanted me to know about a guy named Bonhoeffer. I knew one thing for sure. I was going to stay up again Friday night and see if God would speak to me again.

♦♦♦

Okay, you have now learned a little bit about me and that the Lord speaks to me. Now it is time for you to discover more about Almighty God and the messages that He has for you, which can be found within the pages of this book. They will help guide you in these difficult times that we are now living in as an evil, one world government begins to take control of the nations.

Fasten your seatbelt. Why? Because you are now going to go on a journey with God and experience His power and glory like never before. You will discover some incredible miracles that He has done and visions that He has given to prove that He is still speaking today and that He is in complete control of what is happening on the Earth.

As the world seems to be falling apart, you will discover that, in reality, things are actually falling into place. God's plans are being fulfilled, as written in the Bible.

The God of heaven and Earth is going to speak to you as you read this book. He has given me messages to share with you.

Let's begin our journey.

The Lord wants you to know that the end of life on Earth, as you know it today, is very near.

Evil is growing worse by the day. There is no place that you can go in public where you are free from being randomly attacked or shot by someone who is full of rage.

What in the world is going on? Our society is filled with violence, hate, racism, sexual immorality, lies, wars, fear, and chaos.

You need to be prepared for the sudden, life-changing events that are now coming upon the Earth. The battle between the forces of evil and the forces of good is coming to a dramatic climax. We are entering the period of time where the final battles between God and Satan will take place.

After the Bible, *The End is Now Coming* may be one of the most important books you will ever read. Within its pages, I share the powerful messages of what God has revealed to me about what is happening on the Earth now and why it is happening.

You will also learn about what is going to take place in the near future as God brings judgment upon this world. But there is hope, because I will also share with you how you can escape God's coming wrath.

Whether you are worried about the end times or not, I bet you have many of the following questions:

Why does it feel like we are losing our freedoms?

Is World War III about to begin or has it already started?

Where is God? Does He really exist? If He does, why is He letting all of this happen?

What is coming? What is going to happen to me? My family members?

In a world full of lies and propaganda, could God raise up a voice of truth? In these last days, will God raise up someone that you can trust; a prophet that is actually hearing from God? That has actually seen Jesus?

Is Jesus Christ really the same yesterday, today, and forever? If He is, can God call a man up to heaven today as He has done in the past?

Does God still do signs, wonders, and miracles? Can men and women still receive visions from God today, as they have in the past?

Is there really a place called heaven and a place called hell? If yes, how can I be certain that I will spend eternity in heaven?

Are the Antichrist and False Prophet, who are mentioned in the Bible, on the Earth now?

Is the End now Coming? Is this the end of the world as we currently know it?

All of these questions, and so many more, will be answered in the pages of this book. God is announcing to everyone that He has had enough of the wickedness, violence, and immorality that is on the

Earth. He is shouting, to anyone who will listen to Him, that just as in the days of Noah, He is warning people that He is soon going to bring His wrath to bear on the wickedness in society.

The Lord had Noah warn the people of his day that the end was coming. God, in His love, offered people a way to escape death from the flood waters that would come upon the Earth.

He didn't want anyone to perish! Instead, God desired that people would repent of their sins and, in an act of obedience, get on the ark, a rescue boat, and be saved from His imminent wrath. Sadly, no one heeded Noah's warning. Only Noah, his wife, their three sons and wives, and the animals were saved from the flood waters.

Today, once again, just as he did with Noah, God has asked me to warn the world that the end is now coming. I implore you to heed the Lord's warning.

Yet some people say that since we have the Bible that God no longer speaks. He no longer has prophets. This is not true. Even after Jesus ascended to heaven, God continued to have people who were chosen by Him to be His messengers; His prophets.

Let's look in the Bible in Acts 11:27-30:

> *During this time some prophets came down from Jerusalem to Antioch. One of them, named Agabus, stood up and through the Spirit predicted that a severe famine would spread over the entire Roman world. (This happened during the reign of Claudius.) The disciples, as each one was able, decided to provide help for the brothers and sisters living in Judea. This they did, sending their gift to the elders by Barnabas and Saul.*

So Paul, Barnabas, and the other disciples believed Agabus and took up an offering. Notice that the Lord gave the message of the famine to the Prophet, Agabus, not the disciples or the Apostle Paul.

Acts 21:10-11

10 After we had been there a number of days, a prophet named Agabus came down from Judea. 11 Coming over to us, he took Paul's belt, tied his own hands and feet with it and said, "The Holy Spirit says, 'In this way the Jewish leaders in Jerusalem will bind the owner of this belt and will hand him over to the Gentiles.'"

Once again, when God could speak directly to Paul, He chose to speak through the prophet Agabus. This shows the importance of New Testament prophets.

God is still speaking today. He has raised up prophets, in these last days, to be messengers for Him. In this book, *The End is Now Coming*, I will share the messages that God has spoken to me, to give to you, His church, and to the people of all the nations on Earth.

In this book, you will read the true story of how God raised me up, for such a time as this, to be a prophet and a voice of truth for Him. You'll read about the amazing miracles and visions that God has allowed me to experience and how they are also a huge blessing for you. All of them will strengthen your faith in God and perhaps convince you to believe what I am saying is true, *because it is true.*

In the remainder of the book, I'll share many of the messages He has given for His true, born-again followers and for everyone else in the world. These critical, urgent messages will inform you about what is happening now and what is soon going to take place as the end approaches. You will be given instructions on how to be prepared for the difficult days that lie ahead.

◆◆◆

Some of the benefits you'll receive by reading *The End is Now Coming*:

- You are going to read some actual last days messages from God. Along with your Bible, these Messages will prepare you for the evil events that are coming upon the Earth, as the one-world government is formed and the New World Order takes control.

- You will know how you can receive eternal life and how you can escape God's coming wrath that will take place in the seven-year tribulation that will soon begin. Your eternal destination is at stake.

- You will have God and His Words to help you in the days ahead. He has asked me to be His messenger, a voice of truth who you can trust, in a society full of people who are lying to you. God wants you to know what is happening in the world and not be deceived by the evil people who are pushing their wicked agendas and narratives on you and your family.

- You and your family members will not need to fear the future. Your faith will grow and you will know for certain that God is in control. You will understand that Bible Prophecy is not meant to scare you, but to prepare you for the future. You'll be prepared.

- Christ is coming soon and you'll know the signs of His coming. You can be ready to meet Him and not fear what awaits you after your life on the Earth is over.

It's all about JESUS. He is the one who performed the miracles and gave the messages that are recorded in this book. All the Glory and Honor go to Him and God, the Father.

Jesus is the Savior who died for your sins. He's the God who loves you.

The Lord is so good and He wants you to know what is going to happen in the days ahead. He wants to rescue you from your sins and have you spend eternity with Him in heaven.

In this violent, wicked world that is full of chaos, people are afraid. Maybe this describes you.

There has never been a more urgent time in your life where you desperately need to hear from God. He wants to speak to you.

After you read this book, there will be no doubt that you have heard God speak to you. You will find the answers you are looking for. You will find peace, love, and joy.

You'll know the truth and it will set you free. You will find Jesus. He is all you need.

The End is Now Coming is a love letter from God to you. God says, "Prodigal Sons and Daughters, come home to your Father.

"I know everything that you have ever done in your life and I Still Love You!"

CHAPTER 1

From Joy To Agony: My Early Years With God

Who would think that a small-town boy like me would be asked by God to one day be a messenger for Him to the world? As Nathaniel, one of Jesus's disciples once said, "Can anything good come out of Nazareth?"

In my case, "Can anything good come out of Mission, Texas?"

Before I begin to share with you about how God called me to be a last days servant of His, a prophet, I want to let you get to know me. I want to develop a relationship with you, so that you eventually begin to trust me. I know I'll have to earn your trust, and that's how it ought to be.

I want you to know that I was once a young man who had dreams of what he wanted to do with his life. I had everything all planned out.

Then one night, God showed up and that changed everything. The Lord asked me to abandon my plans for my life and undertake a great task that He wanted me to do: to bring His messages to you and the rest of the people in the world. I will share more about this later.

As you get to know me, I want you to see that I am a normal person, just like you. In fact, you may find out that we have some things in common.

My story has humble beginnings. I was raised in a blue-collar family. My dad, Jack, worked at a gasoline plant. My mother, Shirley, was a homemaker and cared for me, my sister Carol, and my brother Wayne.

My mother made sure we attended Sunday School and church each week. In fact, she made us go to church every time the doors were open. I mean *every time*.

Can you relate with me? Was it like this for you when you were growing up?

Up to the age of twelve, my life was so good. Then one day, I overheard a conversation that my parents were having. I found out everything was about to change.

I can remember my dad talking to my mother and telling her his head hurt. My dad was a hard-working man who never went to the doctor. He was a man's man and he was tough.

He was in so much pain that he started taking several aspirin a day for his headaches. He finally agreed to go see a doctor.

They ran some tests and discovered a large tumor inside his head. He decided that he would go to M.D. Anderson Hospital, in Houston, Texas, and have surgery to remove the tumor.

I'll never forget the words my dad told me when he left for the hospital. He said, "Son, I need to go have surgery and I'll see you in a couple of weeks."

When my dad left for the hospital, my mother went with him. Arrangements were made for my siblings and I to stay with our aunt and uncle, Tobi and Perk Carrier, at their home in Mission. I slept on their living room couch and I looked forward to my dad coming back home in a few weeks.

The Carriers had three sons, my cousins Bruce, Marshall, and Will. I was very close to them at that time and they are still a blessing to me today. I knew it would be fun to spend time with them and this would help me keep my mind off of my dad's surgery and my parents being gone.

I had a great time at the Carrier home, and they were so good to me. My aunt cooked some great meals and my uncle grilled hamburgers for us every Sunday after church. The Carriers would even make homemade ice cream. What more could a kid want?

My dad had the surgery to remove the tumor. We were told that the surgery went well, but they couldn't get all of it. He was sent to recovery in the ICU. Sadly, he wasn't going to come home after a couple of weeks and remained in the hospital.

It was March of my sixth-grade year, and I would go to school and get my mind off of my dad during the day. Then I would go home and start thinking about him again.

The nights were the hardest. I would lie down on the couch and pray. I was so stressed. I was twelve years old and living without my parents.

I would pray every night, and I started begging God to heal my dad and bring my parents home. A month went by, and every so often I would get to talk with my mom on the phone. It helped to hear her voice and get updates on my dad.

As the days passed by, I heard that my father got an infection and would be staying longer. I could hardly stand that news.

My brother, my sister, and I cleaned the church each week, along with help from the Carriers. This allowed us to bring in a little money for our family, since my dad wasn't working.

Two months went by and things just got worse for my father. I was scared now. Would he ever come home?

I begged my mom to come and get me and take me to see him. I asked my aunt and uncle to take me to see him. Everyone thought it was best for the Bailey kids to stay in school and not go to the hospital, in Houston, and see our dad.

As I went to bed each night, I would cry as I prayed even more fervently to God to heal my dad. I was a new Christian and I was calling out to the Lord, as best I knew how, to save my dad's life.

Next, we learned that he got pneumonia while he was in the hospital. Things just kept going from bad to worse. Shortly after that, we found out that he had gone into a coma.

As a kid, I didn't know what all of this meant, but I knew it wasn't good. I could tell my dad's health was going downhill fast and that he could possibly die.

It was now May and school was almost out. I begged and pleaded with my family to get me to the hospital in Houston. I had to see my dad. I wanted to hug him and tell him that I loved him.

Each day was very emotional for me. I could hardly function at school. My thoughts were on my dad nearly every moment of the day.

My nighttime prayers were this: "God, *please, please* save my dad's life. Let him live. If someone has to die, God, then let me die. Take my life. I am willing to die if you will let my dad live. I love him, God. I beg you to let him live."

I never heard God speak after I prayed; at least I don't think so. I just prayed and hoped God would let him live.

Finally, it was June 2, the last day of school. I barely got through the day. I had been thinking that if my mom wouldn't get me to Houston, and my aunt and uncle couldn't take me, I would get on a bus and go by myself.

When the school day ended, I rushed home to my aunt's house. It was now summertime and I was going to go see my dad, come hell or high water.

I was the first of the Bailey kids to make it home. I started walking up the sidewalk to the front door, and to my surprise, my Aunt Tobi was waiting for me at the door. I'll never forget her words. They still hurt to this day. She said, "Kenny, I hate to tell you this, but your dad died today."

It felt like someone had just stuck a knife into my chest! My aunt is an awesome Christian woman, and I love her dearly. She tried as gently as she could to break the news to me. She was hurting so badly herself. My dad, Jack, was her brother and he was just thirty-nine years old.

Without stopping or going to get a hug from my aunt, I went running around the left side of their home and I stood by the fence to their backyard. I wanted to be by myself.

I was as angry as I have ever been in my life. I began to scream at God. I cursed the Lord, out loud, for several minutes. I called him every cuss word a twelve-year-old boy could think of.

Have you ever been this angry at God? Have events in your life ripped your heart out at times? I'm guessing that you can relate with me here.

I had begged God, for months, to let my father live as I cried myself to sleep each night. As a young Christian boy, I had begged the Lord to spare my dad's life and He didn't do it.

I was angry at my family for not letting me go to the hospital and see my dad while he was still alive. I never got to tell him that I loved him and hug him that one last time.

I never got to tell him goodbye. I felt so cheated by my family and so cheated by God.

I wished I was dead. If this was how life was going to be, then I didn't want any part of it. At this point in my life, my dad was my world and he was gone.

I said, "What kind of God would take a twelve-year-old boy's daddy from him?"

My mother came home and soon we had the funeral for my father. My mom had never worked outside the home. Suddenly, she was forced to go to work and provide for her three children.

I still recall how my mother would sit on the couch at night and cry about not having enough money to pay the bills. I would sit next to her and try to console her. I was the oldest boy and felt some responsibility to help her.

I told her that I would mow lawns to earn money, so I didn't need any from her. I didn't know what else to say.

My mother worked hard to provide for us. I will always be grateful to her for that. She was now a widow and life was so difficult for her.

I had a pity party for two years. I was depressed, while trying to do life without my dad. Sports had been my world before his death, but now I didn't care to play them anymore. He wouldn't be there to watch me.

How could I go on in life? What was I going to do now?

Fortunately, I had a great pastor, named Jack Cash, that spent time with me. He taught me Bible verses and took me out to target shoot with a 22 rifle on many occasions.

Brother Cash, as we called him, loved to have an afternoon soda. There were times when I would be mowing or weeding the flower beds at church on a hot summer day. He would walk up to me and say, "Kenny, go across the street and buy us a bottle of bleach."

It was his funny way of referring to a soda; a Coke or Pepsi product.

There was a convenience store located across the highway from the church, and I would walk over and get us a cold soda. We'd both stop work and sit in the shade and drink them together. We would talk and he would always encourage me.

Brother Cash was such a loving, caring man of God. He knew that I was struggling to go on in life without a dad. He was a father figure to me and I'll always love him for being there for me during the most difficult years of my life.

He and some other people encouraged me, and I somehow got through junior high and high school. Now what was I going to do?

I still had some anger in my heart towards God. My dad was gone and I missed him so much. At this point in my life, you wouldn't think I would have much of a future with God and ever be very close to him. Maybe life without Him would be the better choice.

CHAPTER 2

Hearing God Speak: How It All Began

Now that you are getting to know me, you understand that my dad's death was the first major crisis in my life. It caused me to experience the agony of dealing with death while I was still very young. It made me realize that everything is not okay in this world.

I now knew that people died and went somewhere. I discovered that life could rip your heart out of your chest when someone you loved—a member of your family or a close friend—died. I didn't like death. It took my father from me.

I bet you have also dealt with the sting of death during your lifetime. What family members or friends have you lost? Who comes to your mind? Who helped you deal with your pain?

If you and I sat down to talk, I am sure you would move me to tears as you told me about someone that you loved who has passed away. You would tell me how much you loved them and why they were so special to you.

I pray that you have been able to go on with your life; that you got some love and support from others and that you are doing okay today. I pray that as I tell you, in the pages ahead, how you don't have to fear death if you are reconciled to God, that it will bring further comfort to you.

I still miss my dad, but I know I will see him again in heaven. We have a lot of catching up to do.

I hope that you will be in heaven with me. If you are, I want you to meet my dad and the rest of my family.

I will also want to know about what happened in your lifetime. I'm going to want to know your story and what special things God did for you over the years. I want to meet your relatives and friends. After all, time will be no more, and you will be my brother or sister for all eternity.

◆◆◆

I like communicating messages through the use of stories. I've learned this from Jesus, the greatest storyteller of all time.

While he was on the Earth, He shared many of His messages in stories; in parables. He told stories in a manner that people could relate to and that would help them remember His message. He was such a great communicator.

I want to share a few stories with you from my early adult years. I'll begin by telling you about how I started hearing God speaking to me.

After high school, I went off to attend college at Howard Payne University in Brownwood, Texas. My sister was attending the university, and I had grown to love it, too, during my visits to see her. I liked how friendly the people were, who worked there, and the young adults who attended the school.

After my freshman year was over, I decided to work as a summer staffer at Glorieta Baptist Conference Center near Santa Fe, New

Mexico. It was there that I met a young lady from California named Sue Roy.

We ended up dating for a year and a half and then we got married. We were both so young.

Not long afterwards, we had our first child, our precious daughter Michelle. Though we loved Howard Payne University, I wanted to pursue an undergraduate degree in a major that was not offered there.

Therefore, we decided to move to Abilene, Texas, and attend Hardin-Simmons University (HSU). They had a tri-college system where I could also take classes at Abilene Christian University (ACU) and McMurry University and transfer them over to HSU.

I took classes at ACU and picked up another major that I wanted to have. There are some great Christ followers who work at that institution. They have had a big influence on my life.

To provide for ourselves and our daughter, while we both finished college, Sue and I decided to accept positions as houseparents at a children's home. It was there that, two years later, we would welcome our wonderful son, BJ, into the world.

One night, as I walked down a hallway at the children's home, I stopped to check on a young man in his bedroom. He was lying on his bed trembling, as he held an eight-inch dagger over his chest!

I was alarmed at this and jumped into action. He was thinking about committing suicide. For obvious reasons of confidentiality, I won't mention his name.

I told him not to harm himself. I said, "I am here to help you."

He told me that he was depressed and that one of his parents had died.

He said he didn't have many friends at school and that life wasn't worth living. He continued to tremble and threaten to end his life with the knife, which he continued to hold just above his heart.

I told him that I knew his pain. He said, "You don't know what it is like to go through life and lose a parent and to feel so alone."

I replied to him, "I do know what it is like. My father died when

I was young and I had to grow up without him, so I know what you are feeling."

He was stunned. He asked, "You lost your dad?"

I said, "Yes, he died when I was twelve. I know how hard it is and the pain you are going through. There were times when I wished I was dead, but I made it. I want to come towards you and I want you to hand me that knife. I want to help you through this tough time. You are going to make it. I did, and you will, too."

I slowly stepped toward the bed, speaking calm and encouraging words, and the young man eventually gave me his knife. I still have it today.

He settled down and we talked for quite a while. Later, after he was okay, I left and went to my living quarters, which were located down the hallway from his room.

I immediately notified the appropriate people on our staff about the incident. They arranged for him to get some professional counseling the next day and in the months ahead. I am happy to let you know that this young man overcame his depression and became a healthy adult.

I finally went to bed, but I couldn't sleep. I kept thinking about what had just happened and how God used me to save this young man's life. Then, out of nowhere, I heard the Lord speak to me. He said, "Now do you understand that there was a purpose behind the pain that you experienced from your father passing away when you were a boy?

People comforted and helped you deal with your pain from the loss of your dad. Now you will be used by Me to help comfort other people as they deal with the loss of their loved ones and other hardships in their lives. I just used you to rescue this young man."

It was amazing to hear God speak so clearly to me. I realized that He had a plan for my life and that He even used suffering to accomplish His purposes.

Perhaps you have gone through some terrible times in your life;

some tragedies. Have you been harmed by someone or suffered some form of abuse? I want you to know that God loves you, and that He often takes our greatest heartaches in life to later do His greatest ministry work through us. At times, He'll use us and our experiences to help others overcome their pain.

Believe me, I still missed my dad and it has hurt so much to not have him with me. Yet now I knew that God was using everything that was happening in my life to shape me into someone He could use for His Kingdom. The Lord had shown me that He had a Divine Destiny for my life.

This was just the beginning of my service to the Lord as a rescuer. Over the years, the Lord has used me to stop several people from committing suicide.

I have been put in situations where I have rescued countless other people who needed someone to talk to; someone who could show them how to get their life back on track. Many of these people also needed to be saved, and I was more than happy to share the gospel with them and lead them to Christ.

As the months passed, I continued to grow spiritually. I also began to hear God's voice more easily and more frequently.

I often wondered what He had planned for my life. I knew what I wanted to do, but I still wasn't sure about what He wanted me to do after I finished college.

Sue and I both completed our bachelor's degrees at Hardin-Simmons University. HSU was a great school and we have such amazing memories from our time there.

We agreed that I should go to graduate school. The Lord led us to Baylor University in Waco, Texas. I accepted a graduate teaching assistant position there, where I would earn a small salary and have my tuition paid for as I completed my master's degree.

Our plan was to have Sue stay home with the children until they started kindergarten, and I would work part-time jobs while teaching and attending school at Baylor. She would babysit a few kids each week to earn some extra money for us.

I loved teaching college classes. It was an exciting environment being on a college campus and making so many great friends while I was in graduate school.

It was a great experience, getting to work at Baylor. However, I was so busy that I barely saw Sue and the kids, as my work and classes consumed all of my time. I was able to finish graduate school in just one year while teaching and having three other jobs. I'm exhausted just thinking about it now.

Sue also worked so hard to take care of our two kids and all the others she babysat. Without her, I wouldn't have been able to pull it off.

Now that I had finished my master's degree, I was ready to get my doctorate and become a university professor. My goal was to also write books and speak all over the world.

Sue and I loved young people, and I knew I wanted to inspire college students and influence them to live for Christ. I was pretty confident that I would spend my life at a Christian institution.

Sure enough, Moody Bible Institute in Chicago, Illinois, contacted me about coming to interview for a professor position that they had available. I was so excited. This was the moment I had worked so hard for.

I flew to Chicago and spent time with the staff at Moody. It was amazing; all that I hoped it would be. I loved Moody and the great people who worked there.

The interview team told me that if I was offered the position, they would pay for my doctorate. I found out that they also had Moody Press, their publishing house. If hired, I might be able to write and publish my books through them.

After our three days together, I was offered the position. My dream was going to come true.

I told the Moody staff that I would go home and pray and visit with my wife about this great opportunity. I was full of joy. It was what I had worked so hard for.

Sue could stay home with our children. She didn't want to miss any of their early years. She decided that she would begin her teaching career when both of our children were in school. I thought of how we could live in Wheaton and I could ride the train into Chicago, where Moody was located, to go to work each day.

One night, after I got back home, I was praying and the Lord told me to turn down the job. Even though I would be able to do some tremendous work for His kingdom there, He did not want me to go to work for Moody.

The Moody staff called me the next day and I let them know that I was going to turn down their job offer. I told them that the Lord had made it clear that He had another plan for my life. They were understanding and they asked me if I was firm on this decision.

I told them I was. I was then informed by them, and I quote, "Ken, you are the first person in the history of Moody Bible Institute to turn down a job at Moody once it was offered to them!"

I was surprised, and I apologized to them for not being able to come after I heard that comment. Nevertheless, I told them again that the Lord was very clear that I was not to take it.

I had turned down the very job that I had wanted all of my adult life. Yet, the Lord had made it very clear it was not about what I wanted to do in life that mattered. It was about doing what He wanted me to do.

Has your life turned out the way that you thought it would? Did you have your life all planned out, only to have things go completely different from what you thought it was going to be? We make our plans, but God is the one who is really in control.

The Lord told me that He wanted me to start my career by working at a school, and that He also wanted me to be a coach. I was to teach, coach, and start a Fellowship of Christian Athletes (FCA) program at a school.

Where would He take us? What school would offer me my first contract?

It didn't take long to get a job offer out in West Texas. I accepted an offer to teach and coach in a small, country school in Novice, Texas, which is located between Abilene and Brownwood.

Little did I know then that turning down Moody Bible Institute's unbelievable job offer would lead me into the prophetic call that God had on my life.

We packed our meager worldly possessions and made the move from Waco, Texas, back out to West Texas. Looking back, it is ironic that at my first job after graduate school, we would end up living in a rental house that was a church parsonage.

Ironic in the fact that there was a church in town that would soon need a pastor, and I would be offered the chance to take it. I wisely declined. As a rookie teacher and a year-round coach, I was way too busy with teaching, coaching, and FCA to be a pastor. Again, little did I know that years down the road, God did have plans for me to be a pastor.

During my first year of teaching, I was working so hard and for so many hours that Sue and our two kids would ride the school bus that I drove to the games just so they could spend some time with me. Sue would sit up front by me and sit on a five-gallon water jug just to get to talk with me. She was able to do this because we had thirty athletes and cheerleaders on the bus that loved to hold our two children.

We enjoyed our time in West Texas. It was a wonderful community full of good people who valued family life and living out in the country. I'm a country boy at heart, and so I felt right at home there!

Soon after we moved there, we met an incredible couple named Pat and Barbara McGee. Pat taught at the school, and he and Barbara were strong Christians. I immediately gravitated towards them.

Pat brought joy into every room he walked into and he was an outstanding teacher to boot. He was outgoing and full of the joy of the Lord. Barbara was a beautiful, godly woman that we grew to love.

Pat and I instantly became friends, and he was a strong supporter of the work that I did with the student-athletes. I needed his encouragement and wisdom, as I was a young teacher and coach out to prove myself.

Pat was pleased that our faith was so important to Sue and I, and he really liked the new FCA program that we launched to create a faith-based environment in our work with the local youth.

I will always treasure my time in West Texas because I got introduced to the power of the Holy Spirit in a very special way. It began when Pat asked me one day if I would like to attend a prophecy conference that was going to be held in Abilene.

Though I was busy, I jumped at the chance to go. It would also give me time, in the car, to visit with Pat each night as we made the forty-five-minute drive to the church where the event was held.

Why was I interested in Prophecy? Perk Carrier, my uncle, used to teach a class on Sunday nights at the church I attended back in Mission. He taught on end time events and Bible prophecy.

He covered the book of Revelation and the other New Testament passages containing Bible Prophecy. He spoke of the rapture and the tribulation. He taught about Israel and the books of the Old Testament prophets and prophecy.

His teaching about end time prophecy fascinated me. He spoke of Jesus coming back at the rapture, and he had us read and discuss Hal Lindsey's book, *The Late, Great, Planet Earth*.

God used my uncle to plant the seeds of prophecy in me. I fell in love with Israel. At the time, I didn't know that God was planning for me to go to Israel on many trips as an adult, and that I would later teach about Bible prophecy in Messianic churches there.

It's so clear, as I look back on my childhood, that God had planned all of this. I am simply in awe as I see the clear hand of God in my life over all these years. I was being raised by the Lord to be a prophet, and I didn't even know it at the time.

What else did God have planned for me? Time would tell, but I knew that there was a great adventure in store for me as I journeyed through life with this Awesome God.

What has God planned for you? Have you discovered your purpose, your mission, your talents? Are you living the life that God created with you in mind? If you are, then I like to say that you are in your "Sweet Spot."

If you're not, I want to encourage you to get alone with God and seek Him. He'll reveal to you what He wants you to do. As one of His followers, He's not trying to hide His will from you, and it is never too late to get started and on track.

I enjoyed attending the prophecy conference with Pat. We talked each night as we drove home about what we had heard from the speakers. It was incredible to hear what they were sharing about world events and how they indicated that Christ would soon return.

A week after the end of the prophecy conference, Pat spoke to me one day at school. He said, "Ken, the Lord has given me a word to share with you."

This was astonishing to me. I grew up in a conservative Southern Baptist church, and I had never heard of anyone getting a Word from God from another person. I was excited that I was going to get a message from the Lord that he had given to Pat.

I asked, "What did He say?"

Pat began to speak. He said, "Ken, the Lord told me that He has a prophetic call on your life. He is going to have you rescue people who have lost their way in this world. You are going to lead many people to Christ. He is going to have you restore broken people, and fix broken places, where He sends you.

"The Lord said that He is going to move you, many times, to a lot of different places. You will do the work He wants you to do and then

He will move you to the next town. He desires to have you serve Him with your life. In the future, a prophetic call from God is coming."

I was blown away by his words. God had spoken to me, through a friend, and had plans for my future. I got a prophetic message from God, for the first time in my life, from a man that was a spiritual giant in my eyes.

What did all of this mean? Would the words that Pat shared with me really come true?

How would I know who to rescue and where to go? Would I hear from God directly?

Would someone else, in the future, give me another Word from the Lord? I had all of these questions, and so many more, going through my mind.

I had studied prophecy since I was a teenager in my uncle's class. Now I had someone prophesy over me. I was moving more into the prophetic world. I wanted to hear God speak to me just as He had spoken to Samuel and the other prophets mentioned in the Bible.

After a couple of years in West Texas, God opened the door for us to move to Houston. An opportunity became available for me to go to work at Second Baptist Church and School. I would go from the country to the city, but I knew that God had called us to make this move.

It would allow me to work under the leadership of Dr. Ed Young. He was a powerful voice for the Lord, and I knew that God's anointing was on him.

What a blessing this was. I was excited about the education our children would receive and I was thrilled that I could openly share Christ at the school and church each day.

The students and staff were outstanding. I was blessed to be working with young people at the school and teaching junior high Sunday school for the church.

Hearing Dr. Young preach each week and having him stop by and talk to me was so special. I learned so much from him. He loved God and he loved people.

I was so pleased to find out that Dr. Young would go on the summer youth trip to the beach. The church bussed hundreds of kids to the beach each summer to get them away from the city and pour God's Word into them.

Dr. Young would go and spend time with high school students. He had a huge impact on their lives. How many pastors of megachurches did this each summer? That was so impressive to me.

As a young man, I had preached a few times at other places and I couldn't believe that Dr. Young did not have a bunch of notes or a sermon outline up at the podium when he preached. He had the sermon in him! He delivered it in such an amazing way as he calmly shared the word of God and told stories that related to the message of his sermon.

God was letting me learn from another storyteller. They don't come any better than Dr. Young!

I often thought, "How could a man be so gifted? He is on worldwide television and radio, and he doesn't even use notes."

I knew God was using Dr. Young to teach me leadership skills and prepare me for the work that He had for me in the future. What would that work be?

Would we soon be moving again? Did God have other people that He wanted me to go rescue and other broken places to fix? It didn't take long to get the answers to these questions.

CHAPTER 3

The Prophetic Call of God

As time went by, I wondered when I would get the call of God that had been prophesied over me by Pat McGee. God continued to move us and take us to different towns, where the Lord used me to rescue people and fix broken places. That part of Pat's message to me, from God, was certainly happening.

From Houston, the Lord moved us to the mountains of Colorado. There were many places where I could get out in nature and spend time alone with God. I began to hear His voice more frequently. He began to tell me, in the morning, that I would see someone that day who I did not plan to see. Sometimes He would tell me that I was going to get a call or text from someone before I did.

Sure enough, I would see the very person that He told me I would see. I'd run into them in town, or they would stop by our home. I also got texts and phone calls from the exact people who the Lord told me I would.

This was crazy. I shared what was happening to me with Sue. I began to tell her, ahead of time, that we would see a certain person that day, and we would. While we were riding in the car, I'd say to her that this person was going to text or call, and they did. God was training me to hear His voice, and I was in awe of this.

Over the years, I would spend time in the evening with Sue and the kids and we had a normal family life. After they went to bed, I would stay up late to spend time alone with the Lord. I would read my Bible and pray. I would sing songs to God and praise Him.

As my late nights with the Lord continued, I began to sense His presence in the room with me. I didn't see Him, but the delight of His presence filled my heart with a joy that I can't even begin to put into words.

I told Sue what I was experiencing at night. I shared that the only way I could describe the joy that I felt in His presence with me was to say, "The Glory came down."

After eight years in Colorado, God called us to go back to Texas. After we moved, I continued to stay up late at night with the Lord and I continued to hear Him speak to me. I heard Him whisper to me, "Ken, this pleases me that you are worshiping me; that you stay up late to be in my presence."

I was seeking Him and He was letting me find Him. I was intentionally giving up sleep at night to spend more time with God. He said in Jeremiah 29:13, *"Seek me and you will find me if you seek for me with all your heart."*

I wanted Him more than anything else in the world, including sleep.

Sue was happy for me that I was having these experiences with God. She wondered what it felt like being in His presence.

Then one night, my life changed forever! It was Thursday night, April 8, 2004. I was sitting at my office desk in the country home that we were living in, out in East Texas. I began my normal time of prayer and praise with the Lord, when suddenly, I heard Him talking to me.

I was stunned. I couldn't see Him, but the God of the Universe was speaking to me. Then, for the first time in my life, He took me into a vision where I clearly heard Him talking to me.

He said, "Ken, I want you to surrender your life to me. It will cost you everything. I am calling you to a costly commitment. I want you to follow me and give your life to me."

The Lord continued, "If you abandon your life and follow me it will wipe you out financially. It will cause you to lose the ability to live near your kids, who are in college. I will move you far away from both of them. If you follow me, you will never buy this home and the beautiful acres here where you want to continue living.

"It will require that you leave these students and people who you love here, in Martins Mill, Texas. I want you to go and follow me to a new work that I have for you.

"I am not going to tell you what you will do next or where I am taking you if you choose to say yes to my call. Are you willing to lose everything and give your life away to me?

"Will you let me have your life to do what I want to do with it?"

Then the Lord stopped speaking to give me time to decide if I would accept His prophetic call.

I took only a moment of time before answering Him. I thought of my love for Him and how I knew that it was the right thing to do. I trusted Him.

Without hesitating, I said, "Lord, I will do it. I will give you my life, right now, no matter how much it costs me. Yes, I accept this costly commitment and your call on my life!"

He then said the name Bonhoeffer, and told me, "Go to Lifeway Christian Bookstore in Tyler, Texas, after you get off work tomorrow.

I want you to resign from your current job in the morning. Write your resignation letter tonight."

Then the vision and the voice of the Lord stopped. I could tell that the Lord was very pleased that I had accepted His call.

I simply could not believe what had just happened. I was in awe of what the Lord had done.

Jesus had called me to follow Him, just as He had called the disciples, and later Paul, to follow Him. These men dropped everything that they were doing and followed Jesus from that moment on. They left their jobs and family when He called them to follow Him. Now I was being called by the Lord, in the same way, over 2,000 years later.

After praising the Lord and sitting there for a few minutes, I went to work. As I started typing my resignation letter, I leaned back and thought, "Oh wait a minute, Sue has no idea about what I am about to do. This decision, to resign and move again, is also going to have a big impact on her life."

From past experiences of hearing God speak to me, I believed she would support this decision that I was about to make. I decided that I would obey the Lord and resign in the morning when I went to school, where I worked as an athletic director.

Almighty God had just spoken to me and taken me into a vision for the very first time. I also had never heard God speak this much, so clearly and directly, to me.

Pat McGee had prophesied over me, years ago, that the prophetic call of God was coming. Now it was here, and it confirmed that Pat had truly heard from the Lord on the day that he spoke to me at school.

I was so excited. What did God have in store for Sue and I in the months and years ahead? It was surreal.

I didn't sleep much that night. Could you? My mind kept going over the words that Jesus had spoken to me.

When Sue woke up, I was excited to tell her all about the amazing vision and the words that the Lord had spoken to me. She told me that she trusted me, and that if God wanted us to leave, that she would also turn in her resignation. I was so grateful for her love and support.

I left the house and headed for work. When our superintendent arrived, I went and met with him in his office.

His name was Todd Williams. He had hired me three years earlier and had treated me so well over that time. I enjoyed working with him.

Todd was disappointed that Sue and I were resigning. However, he understood that we were being obedient to what we believed that the Lord wanted us to do.

I told him that the Lord had spoken to me and had told me to resign, and that He was moving us to another place. I handed him my resignation letter and walked out the door.

Sue had also made it known that she was resigning. Word of our resignations spread quickly throughout the school and town. The Baileys were leaving.

There are no secrets in small communities. Is it like that where you live? Everyone knows everyone else's business and word spreads around town like a wildfire that is out of control.

It was hard telling my students and athletes that I was leaving. I had grown to love those young people so much. I knew it would break some of their hearts. I knew some would be crushed and feel like I was abandoning them.

I wasn't. I was simply doing what the Lord had told me to do.

I had no idea what I was going to do next or where we would be moving to, but I trusted God. I wondered where He was going to move us to and what we were going to be doing?

God came calling. He asked me to surrender my life to Him and told me it would literally cost me everything.

Now that I had resigned, I had to be honest with myself. Would I really follow Him, or would I hold on to my life? Would I turn my back on the American dream, living in comfort, and lose my life and gain Christ? Was I willing to lose all of the money we had worked so hard to save?

Well, I somehow got through the day. I told Sue that the Lord had told me to go to the Lifeway Christian Bookstore. So, after school, we jumped in the car and headed there.

When we got to the bookstore, I looked for some books written by a guy named Bonhoeffer. I had never heard of him. I couldn't find any, so I talked to the woman who was working at the counter.

She got on her computer and did a search. She told me that they didn't have any books by him in stock. She offered to order one of his books, but I didn't know which one to order, so I declined.

I decided to go over to the bargain books table and see if there were any books that I might want to buy that were on sale. I found a book about the Columbine tragedy, and decided I would buy it. It was about Rachel Scott, and the title of the book was *Rachel Smiles*.

Sue and I lived in Colorado when the shooting at Columbine High School took place. We'll never forget that day and all of the innocent people that were killed.

After buying the book, we went and had dinner at a restaurant and then went back home. I had experienced my first vision the night before, so I decided I would stay up late again and see what God might do that night.

It was Friday night, April 9, 2004. I began to praise the Lord and worship Him. I thanked Him for the miracle that He had done the night before, in taking me into a vision and for speaking to me and calling me to give my life to Him and accept His prophetic call.

After a while, I decided that I would begin to read some of the book, *Rachel Smiles,* that I had just bought at the bookstore. At page twenty-six, I was shocked by what I found. The author, Darrell Scott, Rachel's dad, began to write about a man named Dietrich Bonhoeffer and how he was martyred for his faith after he had been arrested for helping in a plot to try and assassinate Adolf Hitler.

Rachel was then described as a martyr for her courage in not denying Christ in the face of death. As I read further, I was stunned. In the pages of *Rachel Smiles*, I was given the title of the book I would need to order that was written by Bonhoeffer. The book was titled *The Cost of Discipleship*. I couldn't believe it.

Then I heard the Lord speak to me. He said, "Ken, get on your computer and type in the name Dietrich Bonhoeffer." I obeyed the Lord, and I opened up a page on my computer about Bonhoeffer.

I began reading and found out that he had been a German theologian and pastor. He had demonstrated great courage in standing up against Hitler and the Nazi regime during World War II. He had been involved in an unsuccessful assassination attempt on Hitler. He was caught and put in a prison camp. Later, Hitler sent orders to the camp to have Bonhoeffer hung just a few days before allied troops freed the prisoners there.

Then the Lord spoke to me again and said, "Ken, look at the date of his death."

I found the date that Bonhoeffer died. It was April 9, 1945. I was blown away. At that very moment, it was April 9, 2004.

God was honoring Dietrich Bonhoeffer on the fifty-ninth anniversary of his death. I sat in silence and marveled at what God had just done. It was another miracle.

God was now tying my life to Bonhoeffer's forever. He wanted me to do what Bonhoeffer had done with his life. God was calling me to be a prophet. I was to speak out against the evil that I saw in the world and to take a stand against it no matter how much it might cost me personally. I sensed then that I might be martyred for my faith, as Bonhoeffer was, at some point in the future.

God was using Darrell's book about Rachel to honor those who were martyred at Columbine. He was also supernaturally performing a miracle in my life and using this book to bring Dietrich Bonhoeffer's name and writings to me.

I realized that the Lord had done two more miracles for me that day. He had taken me to the bookstore and led me to the bargain books table to buy a book about the Columbine tragedy. Little did I know that inside *Rachel Smiles* I would discover Dietrich Bonhoeffer and the name of the book that God wanted me to order—*The Cost of Discipleship*. The Lord had told me in the miracle the night before, when I had the vision, that He was calling me to a costly commitment.

I then had another miracle occur in finding out that Bonhoeffer was martyred, on that very day, April 9, and that the Lord had directed me to get on my computer so that I would find this out. How amazing it was to see God honor Bonhoeffer on the fifty-ninth anniversary of the day that he was martyred!

I also found out that Bonhoeffer was thirty-nine years old when he died. You may be shocked to learn this—my dad was thirty-nine years old when he died.

I now knew what book to get, and I soon ordered *The Cost of Discipleship*. I began to read it and I have continued to study Bonhoeffer's life and writings to this day.

A couple of the quotes that Bonhoeffer is famous for have had a great influence on my life. Here's one of them:

"When God calls a man, He bids him to come and die!"

Another quote from him was this:

"To be silent in the face of evil,
is evil itself and God will not hold us guiltless.
Not to speak is to speak.
Not to act is to act."[1]

God had called me the night before to die to myself and follow Him in a costly commitment. Now I knew why the Lord had tied my life to Bonhoeffer's.

If you visit my website at kenbaileyministries.com, you can view several videos where God has me speak out against people who are doing evil things in the world. It all started on this fateful night when God introduced me to Dietrich Bonhoeffer.

It was now late Friday night and I was wide awake. I couldn't believe what God had done in the past two nights. I had experienced several miracles, and God was calling me to be a prophetic voice for Him.

I praised the Lord for giving me those amazing miracles. I was so full of joy thinking about how great God is. He is still doing miracles today.

I just sat there in awe and wonder. How could God pull all of this together in this manner? I thought to myself, "Who is this God?"

I now had more questions than ever. What was God going to have me do next? Where was God going to move Sue and I to? I knew it was going to be far away from home and I knew it was going to be very costly.

Why did He choose me? I was so unworthy to be used by Him.

Have you ever stopped to think about how powerful God is? He holds the universe together and calls each star by name. To think that He takes time to talk to us is humbling. Who are we compared to our incredible, awesome God?

I decided to head to bed and get some sleep. I couldn't wait to tell Sue what had just happened when she woke up on Saturday morning.

After a good night of sleep, I shared with Sue what had taken place; that God had shown me, in the book *Rachel Smiles*, Bonhoeffer's name and the book title. She was so happy that God had done more miracles for me. She was a witness to me buying the book the afternoon before and that there had been no Bonhoeffer books in the bookstore.

The odds of all that happened on these back-to-back nights are off the charts. I realized, once again, that nothing is impossible for God. How great is our God?

Within a month of resigning, I had four job offers. I knew immediately that two of them were not related to the vision and God's call on my life. I let them go. It came down to taking a position at Colorado Springs Christian School or going out to San Diego to work at Shadow Mountain Community Church and Christian Unified School District.

Sue and I flew out to San Diego and visited the church and school there. We had a great time and loved the people who we met.

I had a chance to meet privately with Dr. David Jeremiah, the senior pastor at the church. I had so much admiration and respect for him. He was an outstanding teacher of the Word of God and he was a huge supporter of the school.

His children had attended the school and now his grandchildren were entering the school. We had a great visit and I told him it would be an honor to work with him.

The weather was amazing in San Diego; cool nights and warm days. There was a great staff at the church and school. What more could we ask for?

I was offered the position, but I told the school and Dr. Jeremiah that I wanted some time to pray about it and seek the Lord before possibly accepting the offer. They were kind enough to give me a couple of weeks.

The following weekend, Sue and I flew to Colorado Springs, Colorado. We were both asked to interview at Colorado Springs Christian Schools for positions that were open there. We had a tremendous visit and loved the staff at the school. We just seemed to click with the school administration.

It seemed like a dream job. Everything seemed to be running well at the school and I could just step in and help continue the great things they were doing there.

In my flesh, I wanted to accept this position. We had already lived in Colorado, and Sue and I both love the mountains. Accepting this offer would let us spend some time in the mountains, where we loved to hike, camp, and fish. We could work with some amazing people there as we served the Lord.

We flew back home to Texas. This would be a difficult decision.

We began to pray and seek the Lord's will on this. After a week went by, I got a call from Dr. Jeremiah. He wanted to know if I had made my decision yet. I told him that we were still praying and we were not ready to make a decision. He was gracious and gave me a little more time to think and pray about it.

A few more days went by, and then I clearly heard from the Lord. God was calling us to go to San Diego and work there. The Lord showed me that the San Diego offer was tied to the vision.

It was a costly commitment to move all the way out to San Diego. Housing was very expensive there. We would also be far away from our children who were in college.

I picked up the phone and called Dr. Jeremiah and told him we were coming and would accept the job offers. He was pleased with this, and it felt good to finally make the decision and move forward.

I then had to call Colorado Springs Christian School and declined their offer. That was a tough call to make because I knew I would have just loved working with those people.

Everything that was given to me, in the vision, was tied to going to San Diego. That would become evident as the years went by.

I never told anyone at the church or school in San Diego about the vision that I had from the Lord on April 8, 2004. The vision was the very reason that God took Sue and I and moved us to California to go and work with them.

After three weeks of searching that summer, we finally found a house that we were able to buy. The housing market was tight and prices were near all-time highs.

What was God's plan? What was He going to show me in California? What experiences would I have that were tied to His prophetic call on my life and to the vision?

We moved out to San Diego, and we got to work with the most amazing people who were on staff at the church and school. I am also so grateful for the time that I got to spend alone with Dr. Jeremiah. He was everything that I thought he would be; wise, gentle, and supportive. He was extremely busy, overseeing a megachurch staff and heading up the Turning Point Radio and Television Ministry.

Attending church and hearing his sermons was such a blessing to us. His preparation for his messages was so evident. He is such a great Bible teacher and God continues to use him in a mighty way.

I was blessed to go on a trip to Israel with him as part of a tour group. We had a great time there, and we got back home to San Diego about 2 a.m. on a Sunday morning. I'll never forget this. Without much sleep at all, Dr. Jeremiah got up a few hours later and preached at both services at Shadow Mountain Community Church. The sermon was powerful, and people had no idea that he was exhausted and had just gotten back from Israel.

I was fortunate to work with Dr. Jeremiah. I cherish the years we had together. Doc, as I referred to him, was so committed to excellence. He once told me, in one of our private meetings, "No one remembers who finished second."

In other words, he was going to always give God his best, and he wanted the church and school to serve the Lord with excellence.

I never heard him brag the entire time I was there. Let me assure you he had a lot of things he could have boasted about. He pastored a megachurch, was the author of many bestselling books, and his radio and television ministry was growing around the world. However, he only boasted about Christ.

While in San Diego, we rarely got to see our kids. They were back in Texas, and it was hard for us to get time to go back there and see them. That was difficult, but that was part of the vision that I had. What the Lord shared with me in the vision, and His call to a costly commitment to Him, was coming true.

I really enjoyed my time working at the church and school. However, after four years, I felt the Lord was leading us to leave San Diego. We wanted to get back to Colorado and also go on more mission trips to share the gospel around the world.

We had invested money in renovating our San Diego home, and we were hopeful that it would sell quickly, but that didn't happen.

At the same time, we put our house up for sale, the housing market in Southern California began to collapse. Due to the crisis in the mortgage industry from foreclosures that resulted from risky mortgages being issued for years, home prices dropped rapidly in most of Southern California.

After a long period of time, we sold our home and lost about $280,000. It wiped out nearly all of the money we had. Again, the words that the Lord had spoken to me in the vision were coming true. He said that if I followed him, He would cause us to be put through great financial hardships.

It hurt to lose this hard-earned money, but I knew God had a reason for it. I began to understand what He was allowing to happen in my life. God was crushing me!

He was allowing me to be tested in many areas of my life. He was crushing me and trying to get me to the point where He could use me for His kingdom work. I would have to die to myself to ever be of any use for Him. I would have to go through the refiner's fire.

I won't lie. It hurt. The Lord allowed me to start suffering at age twelve when my father died. He has been testing me ever since. Why? God was making it clear that He wanted total control of my life. He wanted me to get to the point where all I had was Him.

He was preparing me for greater work for His Kingdom, where I would have people come against me and persecute me when I served Him as a prophet. He was preparing me for a life that involves suffering for His name, as He did with the Prophets of old and the Apostle Paul, and so many other servants of His over the years.

The vision that I had where God called me to a costly commitment was being fulfilled. It was the first of many visions that I would have in the coming years.

I chose to follow Christ in a costly commitment, and I don't regret it. I surrendered to His prophetic call to be a voice of truth for Him, to the Church, the Nations, and leaders of the world.

I'll never go back to *comfortable Christianity*. I have chosen *costly discipleship*. That's where you find Jesus. That's where you find lasting joy.

May I ask you a couple of questions? Will you follow Christ and His call on your life? Will you lay down your life for Him or will you waste your life by holding onto to it and living for yourself?

I chose to surrender everything. However, I walk in unspeakable joy each day. Christ died for me. I must live for Him with every breath and heartbeat that I have left.

◆◆◆

The Lord opened the door for us to move back to Colorado. We were blessed to get to work with some great people in the community and school in the town of Simla. God made it clear to me that we were to only stay there for a short season of time; that a new work would come to us very quickly.

One Sunday, on the way home from church, the Lord spoke to me and took me into a vision. He said, "One day you will pastor a church in the mountains of Colorado."

I told Sue about it and wondered when that would occur.

Sure enough, God only allowed us to stay in Simla for two years. Sue and I loved the people there, but the Lord took us down the road to help rescue some more people.

The Lord next took us back to Texas, where we worked with some incredible staff and students in Nueces Canyon. God had me make some connections to do some work with a nonprofit organization that was based in the area.

Out of nowhere, Sue was contacted and got offered her dream job back in Colorado. The Lord told me to honor her and encourage her to accept it. She had sacrificed so much for me over the years, always being willing to move to the next town that the Lord wanted me to work in.

This time, we made a move for Sue. She loves living in the

mountains of Colorado. I worked as an associate pastor in Westcliffe, and started doing work for the youth ministry organization.

I spent a great deal of my time setting up events to reach junior high, high school, and college students with the gospel. Through our ministry work, we wanted to reach the youth of America for Christ and get them plugged into a local church, where they could grow in their faith and be discipled.

This work caused me to be on the road a lot and not get to spend much time at home with Sue. She understood, then and now, that God has this call on my life to take the gospel to the nations.

I was also blessed to get to do some international evangelism during this time. I went on a trip to Israel to meet with some messianic church leaders who lived in the city of Ashdod.

When I arrived in Israel, I went to the church and discovered that I was the first person to arrive for the evening church service. I sat in the back of the auditorium while the worship team was on stage rehearsing the songs that they would sing that night.

I did not speak Hebrew and I didn't know who the leaders of the church were, so I went to the Lord in prayer. I prayed silently, "Lord, would you please lead me to someone who speaks English so that I can talk with them and have them introduce me to the people that are the leaders of this church? Lord, you have put it on my heart to go and visit Holocaust survivors while I am in Israel. Would you lead me to someone who works with Holocaust survivors?"

As soon as I ended my silent prayer, the worship team finished their rehearsal. One of the men on stage began to walk straight towards me. He came up to me and started talking with me.

He said, "My name is Sebastian."

I replied, "My name is Ken Bailey. Do you speak English?"

He answered, "I do. I also speak Hebrew, French, and I'm learning Russian."

I was so excited. I found someone who spoke English! I told

Sebastian that I had come to meet with the church leadership and asked him if he would introduce me to them when they arrived. He told me he would.

We began to visit for a few minutes, and I decided that I would ask him another question. I asked, "Sebastian, do you know anyone who works with Holocaust survivors? I want to go visit them and take them some food and give them some money to help them buy food and medicine that they need but can't afford. They have suffered so much in their lifetime and I want to bless them and tell them that God loves them."

He said, "Ken, I work for a Holocaust ministry in Israel. I will be going out to visit Holocaust survivors this week. You can come with me."

During the week, we went to numerous apartments of Holocaust survivors and I got to meet with them. Some of them spoke Hebrew, Russian, or both. Seb was able to interpret for me and get me in to visit with these people. God had placed a love for them upon my heart.

I couldn't believe the miracle that was happening. I was beginning my ministry work in Ashdod, Israel. I had prayed a simple prayer in faith and God instantly answered the prayer.

On this trip I was also invited to speak on Bible prophecy at some Messianic congregations. God had planned for this to take place when my uncle taught me about prophecy so many years earlier.

As I continued on my trip, I traveled to Jerusalem. I always have miracles take place when I am in Jerusalem. As the locals say, "When you talk with God in Jerusalem, it's a local call."

I can always literally sense the covering of God over the country when I have stepped off the plane in Israel. When I am in Jerusalem, I sense His presence with me in a very special way.

I like to stay in the Old City when I am in Jerusalem. I checked into my hotel room and went for a walk over to the Mamilla Mall, which is located nearby. I like to go walking there and I sometimes stop and eat at one of the restaurants.

After walking for a while, the Lord spoke to me very clearly. He said, "Call Chris Karelse."

I did not know anyone by that name. Since the Lord is always connecting me to new people, I called the last guys that I was with in Rishon LeZion, Israel, and asked them if they knew anyone named Chris?

They said they did. They knew a guy named Chris Karelse. They told me that he lived in the Netherlands. They sent me his phone number.

I was totally surprised. This was crazy. In obedience to the Lord, I called Chris, knowing that he lived in the Netherlands. He answered the phone.

I knew it was going to sound crazy to him, but I told him the truth. I said, "I am walking in the Mamilla Mall, in Jerusalem, and God just told me to call you!"

He was totally surprised. He said, "That's amazing. I am not at home in the Netherlands. I am also in Jerusalem and I'm staying at a place that is only ten minutes away."

It was 5 p.m., so I invited him to come over and have dinner with me. He accepted my dinner invitation.

I hung up the phone and I just stood there taking in what had just happened. The God of the universe had just spoken to me and told me to call a guy I didn't know who lives in Holland, and now we were going to have dinner together. "Who Is This God?"

Chris and I met, and we marveled at the miracle that God had done to have us meet each other. When the Lord has a divine appointment for you, He will even do miracles to make sure that it happens.

After a wonderful meal together and time of sharing, we have been great friends ever since. We have done some ministry work together in Israel, Holland, and America. God had a divine appointment for both of us that night.

On this trip to Israel, I also got to meet some men who pastored messianic congregations in Israel. These congregations are composed of Jewish people who believe that Jesus is the Messiah, and many of them have immigrated from countries that were once a part of the Soviet Union.

I have become very good friends with these men. One day, on another one of my trips to Israel, one of them offered to take me to the place where the Old Testament prophet, Samuel, had lived in his lifetime. He told me that, even today, another man who claimed to be a prophet lived there.

I was so excited to go there. I knew in my Spirit that the Lord had something planned for me while I was on the property.

We traveled to Samuel's old property. I met the man who currently lived there. He was kind enough to let me spend a few hours with him and I got to know him a little bit.

I knew God was calling me to this place to be anointed. I thought it would be by the man who was living there, since I had been told that he was a prophet.

After we had some introductory conversation, he suddenly spoke out to me, with a loud, angry voice. He said, "You came here because you want me to anoint you."

I told him, "Yes!"

He said, "I am not going to anoint you! Why are you in Israel?"

I told him about our nonprofit, Alms International, which my wife and I had founded to feed and clothe poor people around the world. I went on to tell him that we helped to provide food and financial assistance for Holocaust survivors, new immigrants to Israel, single mothers with children, and we also fed hungry children.

He was pleased with this and calmed down. He then prophesied a blessing over Alms International and said that one day it would have a huge presence in Israel and help many people in the country. Time will tell if He delivered a true word from God to me.

He got tired and told me he was going to take a nap. I went over to a cave that is located on the property and found that there was a pool of spring-fed water inside of it. I took off my pants and I went into the water in my boxer shorts, then an amazing miracle took place. God spoke to me and confirmed that He was anointing me, while I was in the water, to complete the prophetic work that He had called me to do.

I will be forever grateful to be chosen to be a servant of God and then have the awesome privilege of being anointed in the pool on the property where the prophet Samuel used to live. Only God could do this.

After that amazing trip to Israel, I finished up my youth ministry work and I wondered what God had in store for me next? Soon, there came an opportunity to look at the possibility of going to work with Jonathan Cahn.

Sue and I flew out to New Jersey to meet with Jonathan and his wife Renata. We were able to tour the church campus and attend a church service.

Jonathan is such a gifted speaker, and he gave an excellent message. We had a wonderful time with both of them while we were there. I absolutely wanted to go to work with them and their team.

Many years had now gone by since the Lord had called me to be a prophet and to surrender my life completely to Him. However, the Lord had told me it was not yet time for me to go "public" and announce my prophetic ministry. So, I did not tell Jonathan that I was a prophet, but Jonathan knew that there was something going on with me in the spirit realm. He said, "Ken, you are the first person that I wanted to hire who I invited to my home."

While at his home, he took me to see his office where he writes his books. His book, *The Harbinger*, was already on the *New York Times* bestseller list.

After asking Jonathan some very direct questions about his ministry work and his motive for doing it, the Lord showed me that he was pure. He never once boasted, although he had a growing church and he was a very successful author.

He patiently answered all of my questions and went on to offer me the position. That speaks volumes about who he and Renata are. They are humble servants of God, and the Lord is using them in a mighty way.

Jonathan offered me a position to come on staff as his church administrator and then to eventually to become his personal assistant. This was an awesome opportunity for me, and Sue would be able to work at a school in the area.

I asked Jonathan for a week to go home and seek the Lord about this. Over the years, the Lord has taught me to never take a position right on the spot when emotions are running high. I had to hear what God wanted me to do and not respond in the flesh.

I went home and talked to Sue. I began to fast and pray. I absolutely wanted to go to work with Jonathan and serve the Lord with him.

I had started taking people to Israel on tour trips, and Jonathan let me know that I could continue to do that. He was so generous and so kind.

While I prayed and fasted for several days, Jonathan and I kept in touch by email. One night, the Lord spoke to me and He said, "Ken, I know you want to go and work with Jonathan. I understand that. However, I want you to turn down the job. I want you to start speaking for me. It is now time for you to begin your prophetic ministry."

Honestly, I was crushed. Yes, I wanted to obey the Lord no matter how much that would cost me, and I did.

I had quickly come to love Jonathan and Renata, and I wanted to go and work with them. I knew we would have such a great time working together.

Sadly, I emailed Jonathan and let him know that I could not take the position. He was disappointed that I turned down the job, and it broke my heart to tell him I couldn't come. He thought we would really work well together. So did I; yet it wasn't God's plan at that moment. Perhaps one day we will do some ministry work together.

What was I going to do now? Where did God want me to speak? What messages was He going to give me to deliver to people around the world?

I had sent my resume to a church in Gunnison, Colorado. I knew that they had already offered the position to some other candidates before I contacted them. After a couple of months of waiting, I was contacted by them and invited to come and preach.

Eventually, I was asked to become their pastor. After much prayer, I accepted the offer. God confirmed to me that this was the pastor position He had told me about in the vision that I had a few years earlier.

Do you remember the vision that I mentioned where God told me that I would pastor a church in the mountains of Colorado one day? God was now causing that vision to become a reality.

A pattern was now taking place. God was giving me visions and they were coming true. He was telling me, in advance, what I was going to do.

There are times when I have conversations with friends and I have told them about my career and what God has had me do in the past. When I tell them about the opportunities I have walked away from, they are amazed.

Let me review them for you:

I had a chance to go to work for Moody Bible Institute as I was coming out of graduate school and the Lord had me turn it down.

I had the opportunity to work at Second Baptist Church and Christian School, under the leadership of Dr. Ed Young. I was there for four years and then the Lord had me leave and move to Colorado.

I got to work at Shadow Mountain Community Church and the Christian school there, with Dr. David Jeremiah, for four years, and then the Lord had me leave there. I could have stayed at both of these places and retired comfortably. That wasn't God's plan.

I tell them about the chance I had to go to work with Jonathan Cahn, and the Lord telling me to turn down the offer because he wanted me to be a prophetic voice for Him. Yet again, God had other plans for my life.

Once I have shared these career opportunities with friends, they often tell me, "Those are all dreams jobs. If I got one of them, I would have stayed the rest of my life."

I also hear, "You are crazy to have left these jobs or to have turned down those job offers. Have you lost your mind? Why would you do this?"

The answer is very simple. I have surrendered my life to Almighty God and He has told me to leave these jobs, or decline the amazing job offers, because He has another work He wants me to do. It all goes back to my costly commitment to follow the Lord, no matter what.

God is also fulfilling the first prophetic message that I received, where I was told that I would have to move a lot in my lifetime as I served the Lord. Do I miss the people that I worked with and those that I had to decline a job offer from and I was not allowed to work with? Yes.

I have thought, many times, about the other experiences I missed out on because I followed the Lord. However, know that I am at total peace about all of these decisions, since God has clearly led me to these other places. I would have been out of His will if I had done anything else.

Because of my obedience in these decisions, the Lord has continued to use me as a vessel for Him. He has blessed me more than I can ever put into words.

God told me that He wanted me to start speaking and give prophetic messages. His word was quickly confirmed. I began to get many visions and messages from the Lord. I am in awe of what He started doing and what He is still doing today.

I began to experience signs, wonders, and miracles almost every day, and I'll share many of these with you in a later chapter in this book. I also began to have many more visions as I began my pastoral work in Colorado.

CHAPTER 4

Visions of Great Spiritual Warfare

I grew to love the people at the church that I pastored in Colorado. Many of them believed that we were living in the last days before the rapture of the church. As a result, the Lord had me share many Bible prophecy messages in the sermons that I preached there.

Then the Lord began to give me prophetic visions. Let me share a couple of them with you:

> One evening, in the fall of 2018, the Lord took me into a vision. I was outside on a dark night and I was looking up at the stars. Suddenly, I saw a bunch of serpents, black vipers, coming towards the Earth. They were all tangled up, bound together like a ball made from rubber bands, and only their heads and necks were free to move and hiss.

All of these serpents looked like angry black cobras. They were entangled and coming, on what seemed like a planet, straight towards the Earth; straight towards me.

You would think that I would have been terrified. I wasn't. I was totally calm as they sped towards the Earth, having been cast down out of heaven.

A light, out of heaven, was shining on the left side of this ball of vipers. I could see that the snakes were trying to free themselves, but they couldn't. They were angry, hissing, and trying to bite, all in vain. They were bound together and they were coming to the Earth.

The vision ended and the Lord revealed to me what I had just seen. I saw the fulfillment of Revelation 12:7-12:

> *Then war broke out in heaven. Michael and his angels fought against the dragon, and the dragon and his angels fought back. But he was not strong enough, and they lost their place in heaven. The great dragon was hurled down—that ancient serpent called the devil, or Satan, who leads the whole world astray. He was hurled to the earth, and his angels with him.*
>
> *hen I heard a loud voice in heaven say: "Now have come the salvation and the power and the kingdom of our God, and the authority of his Messiah. For the accuser of our brothers and sisters, who accuses them before our God day and night, has been hurled down.*
>
> *They triumphed over him by the blood of the Lamb and by the word of their testimony; they did not love their lives so much as to shrink from death. Therefore rejoice, you heavens and you who dwell in them! But woe to the earth and the sea, because the devil has gone down to you! He is filled with fury, because he knows that his time is short."*

I was wide awake and astonished that the Lord had taken me into this vision of Revelation 12. Heaven celebrated that Satan and the fallen angels had been cast down, but I knew things were now going to get bad on the Earth.

The last few years have proven what the Lord warned me about ahead of time of how bad things were going to get. We have had some of the worst natural disasters in recorded history. We have had the evil coronavirus, vaccine mandates, and lockdowns unleashed on the Earth.

We have had a terrible war break out between Russia and Ukraine, and rumors of coming wars. We have civil unrest and violence in cities all over the world.

We have severe famines across the Earth and rising fuel and food prices. We have unspeakable violence and immorality that show us that conditions are as they were in the days of Noah and Lot. Jesus said these would be some of the many signs we would see in the last days.

We have all these evil agendas being put forth; transgender lies, gender lies, Critical Race Theory lies, and so much more. Can you believe that you live in a world where people tell you a boy can be a girl and a girl can be a boy? That you have to apologize for your skin color or race, when the God of the Universe made you that way? When people say they are for girls and women, but let men, who claim to be women, take over girls' and women's sports and use their locker rooms?

Can you not see the evil caused by Satan and his demon followers? Evil is advancing on the Earth and God has me warn you that more is coming.

Only a few days later, the Lord took me into another vision. This time I was in a church building. I was standing up at the front of the auditorium, and suddenly, red streaks of lightning started coming down from heaven.

The lightning branched off when it came near the people sitting in the auditorium. It appeared to strike them on their shoulders. They were not afraid or harmed as the lightning struck them.

As the vision ended, the Lord spoke to me and told me that this vision was to fulfill the words written in Joel 2:28-32 and Acts 2:17-21.

"In the last days, God says, I will pour out my Spirit on all people. Your sons and daughters will prophesy, your young men will see visions, your old men will dream dreams.

Even on my servants, both men and women, I will pour out my Spirit in those days, and they will prophesy.

I will show wonders in the heavens above and signs on the earth below, blood and fire and billows of smoke.

The sun will be turned to darkness and the moon to blood before the coming of the great and glorious day of the Lord.

And everyone who calls on the name of the Lord will be saved.

The Lord said, "Ken, you saw red streaks of lightning as I poured out my Spirit on the Earth for these last days. It was red in color in the vision, to honor my Son, who shed His blood for mankind's sins.

"I have poured out my Spirit, this final time in the church age, so that my sons and daughters have the power to come against the devil and the fallen angels that you saw in the previous vision of the vipers. I have poured out my Spirit on the church, and believers will have the power to be my witnesses in the world in these last days.

"The Greatest Spiritual Warfare in the history of mankind has now come to the Earth. My followers will have Holy Spirit power to finish taking the gospel to the nations, while they are under a fierce attack."

Look at the current condition of the world and you will see that economies are collapsing and that the world is plunging into darkness. There is violence everywhere. There is now the possibility that you can be shot at the grocery store, movie theater, schools, or even church; World War III is on the horizon, and many would say that it has already started, as many nations are now at war or rumored to be going to war.

Without a doubt, we are experiencing tremendous spiritual warfare. But friend, if you have repented of your sins and placed your faith in

Christ, you don't need to be afraid. Jesus said it would get like this at the end. He also told us that He would be with us even to the end of the world.

Difficult times are coming to the Earth; famine, war, and violence. More medical tyranny, phony climate crisis tyranny, and economic tyranny will be enforced by the globalists and the New World Order.

It is all part of the beast system, and with it will come great persecution of Christians. Don't live in fear. I have great news for you. If you are a Christian, God will be with you in whatever challenges that come our way.

We will escape the wrath of God that will soon come to the Earth. All born-again believers will be raptured before the tribulation begins.

CHAPTER 5

God Raises Up a Modern Day Prophet

I shared part of this story with you in the prologue. Now I want to share the whole story with you, and let you see how powerful God is, as He completed a series of miracles for me that are simply staggering!

♦♦♦

I was excited. We were going down to the beach at South Padre Island, located by Corpus Christi, Texas, to get away for a night.

For months, I had been wanting to spend some time with Rudy, one of our deacons at the church. I wanted to hear his life story and get to know him better.

I had decided to start spending time with each of the deacons at the church to build a deeper relationship with them and their families. Today, Rudy would ride down to the beach with my wife, Sue, and I, and we would be able to visit with him in the car.

The drive was all that I had hoped it would be. He began to tell us about his life of being raised in the community where I was the new pastor. It was so obvious to me that he loved God and he loved his family.

Upon arriving, we had dinner with Rudy and a couple of other people. It was a wonderful evening of food and fellowship. As the night ended, I was already excited about getting some time at the beach the next day.

I slept well and got up early to watch the sunrise. It was now Saturday morning, February 29, 2020. We had coffee together and then headed for the beach.

I love the beach; the sounds of the waves crashing on the shore, the birds in the air, and the smell of the salt water. I enjoy watching children make sandcastles, and it is so peaceful to walk barefoot in the sand.

As we walked on the beach the Lord began to speak to me. I knew His voice, having heard Him so many times before. However, it was the voice that He uses with me when He wants me to do a very difficult thing for Him.

I immediately began to be troubled in my spirit. It had been a year and a half since the Lord had asked me to do something this difficult, and now He was asking me to do it again.

I say "asking me" loosely. The Lord commands me to speak the message that He gives to me. He tells me to get ready to speak for Him, and I know that He is going to put pressure on me until I do.

Here's what happens. God starts to squeeze me after He asks me to do something for Him. I literally feel like I am in a large vice that is secured to my chest and my back. If I argue and try to disobey the Lord, or delay obeying, He just tightens the vice more and squeezes me to the point that I can't breathe.

I don't want to eat, I can't sleep, and I am just miserable because I am not obeying Him yet.

What was God telling me that He wanted me to do? The Lord began to tell me that He wanted me to give a prophetic message in the church service the next day, March 1, 2020. He also wanted me to tell the people that I was a prophet.

At that time, I was doing a sermon series on marriage and dating, and I had already prepared a sermon for Sunday. I was overwhelmed when the Lord spoke to me at about 11:25 a.m., while we were walking on the beach, and He told me to give a prophetic message.

Before I go on, you need to know that I sometimes argue with God when He asks me to do these difficult things for Him. I knew very well that if I obeyed Him, it would rock this conservative, Baptist church and could lead to me being forced to resign. There aren't many churches or people that want prophetic messages, and most certainly don't believe that there are any true, authentic prophets on the Earth today.

I want to be transparent with you and let you know what it is really like for me in the prophetic realm. At times, there are very demanding tasks that the Lord asks me to do for Him, and in my flesh, I don't want to do them because I know how much persecution they will bring to me.

I never want to be a false prophet and hurt the Kingdom of God, so I always want to be sure God has clearly spoken to me. However, sometimes I have heard God's voice and I just don't want to do the difficult assignment that He has given me to do. When this happens, I am simply not fully surrendered to Him, as I should be, and this is sinful on my part.

I argue with the Lord and I try to get out of doing what He wants me to do. So, this time I decided that I would do a very "spiritual thing" (sarcasm intended) and see if I might be able to avoid giving the prophetic message.

Rudy was walking by me and I stopped and said to him, "I believe the Lord might be asking me to give a difficult message at church tomorrow. I already have my sermon on marriage and dating ready to give. Would you pray and see what you believe the Lord would have me do?"

Rudy agreed. I was happy about that. He knew that the marriage series we were in was going well and that it was having an impact on people. It was my hope that he would come back to me and say, "Preach the sermon you have ready and sometime, in the future, you can give the difficult sermon."

Then I could tell God, "I sought godly counsel and Rudy thinks I should just give the marriage sermon. I'll share that prophetic message some other time, God."

A few minutes later, as we continued walking on the beach, he said, "I think you should give the difficult message."

I was devastated. Here I was trying to trick God and get out of it, and now I would have to give the prophetic message and tell people that I was a prophet.

The pressure began to mount. No one else knew what I was going through as we walked on the beach. I just kept it to myself until we got home.

We went and had lunch together, and then Sue, Rudy, and I made the drive back home. I was friendly in the car, but inside, I was feeling sick to my stomach knowing what I would have to do.

We had such a great time with Rudy on the trip to the beach. He is a wonderful Christian man and a gentle giant.

We got back home and the pressure continued to increase. It was now 5 p.m. and the squeeze was on.

Tomorrow, with a short amount of time to prepare, I would have to give an incredibly difficult sermon. The Lord was commanding me to give a prophetic message to the nations. He wanted the message filmed and then sent out on social media to the world.

I had a choice. Would I obey God and give the prophetic message and tell the church that God had called me to be a prophet? Would I share with the world that many years ago, in a vision, God had asked me to die to myself and be a prophetic voice for Him? Who would believe me?

I died a million deaths, but I obeyed him back then. Surely, our loving God would not ask me to do it again and make me go through the agony of giving a prophetic message, and then, on top of that, tell people I was a prophet. At least that's what I hoped would happen.

I told my wife, Sue, that the Lord was pressuring me to give a prophetic message. She felt bad for me and later told me that she hoped I wouldn't do it.

She had been with me when the Lord had required me to do it before. She was certain it would cause problems for us at the church and that I very well might need to step down from being the pastor.

We had only been at this church in Texas for four months, and neither one of us wanted to move again. We loved the people there.

Sue went to bed, and I stayed up to argue with God and to half-heartedly prepare the prophetic sermon. God began to tell me that He was going to shake the Earth, His Church, and everyone in the world. I made some notes of what He was telling me, but I didn't want to give this message.

I started shouting at the Lord, under my breath, so I wouldn't wake Sue up. "God, you can't make me do this! Are you serious, God? This will blow the church up and people, who love me now, will turn against me."

The Lord just tightened the vice and continued to pressure me to obey Him. You may know what I am talking about. Perhaps God has told you to do something difficult and you have felt him pressure you until you obey Him.

You may think that there is no way God would pressure someone to obey Him. No loving God would do this. May I humbly remind you of the stories of Jonah, Jeremiah, and Moses.

Read what God spoke to Jeremiah.

Jeremiah 1:17
"Get yourself ready! Stand up and say to them whatever I command you. Do not be terrified by them, or I will terrify you before them."

The Lord can be demanding when He wants a reluctant prophet to do something. I knew God would discipline me severely if I did not obey Him, and He would be just in doing it since *delayed obedience is disobedience.*

How could He make me do this? I did not choose to be a prophet. He chose me.

I have never wanted to be a prophet and I sure didn't want to be one now. Yet, I had no choice.

I knew that if I obeyed the Lord, I was going suffer anguish at church the next day. Honestly, I had a terrible, sinful attitude towards doing what God wanted me to do. I was only focused on how this was going to affect me and I was acting so selfishly at this moment.

At midnight I laid down on the bed, tossing and turning until 3 a.m. I couldn't sleep. I just kept crying out to God to let this cup pass from me and to let me do the marriage sermon.

Totally exhausted, I got up and started pacing in the room. Then I sat at my desk, and I wrote down some more of the key points that the Lord wanted me to give in the prophetic message.

God told me that judgment was coming upon the Earth. He was calling people to repent of their sins and telling me to warn them of the consequences if they didn't.

I then shouted at God, for the next four hours, just loud enough to not wake Sue. I began to tell Him, "You have got to give me a great sign before the service starts, proving to me that you are clearly speaking to me to give the prophetic message and tell them I am a prophet. I need proof that you really are telling me to do this."

At 7 a.m. Sue got up. She watched me pacing the floor, talking out loud to God, arguing with Him to not make me give the sermon.

If you have read your Bible, you know that prophets are hated, treated badly, put in prison, and often put to death. I sure didn't want to be a prophet, though I had been one since the Lord's prophetic call came to me in 2004.

I continued shouting at God, "I feel like Moses at the burning bush. I don't want to do this. I just want to pastor a church, take people on mission trips, love on people, teach the Word, and lead people to Christ.

"Why are you making me do this? I don't want to do it. God, please choose someone else for this task. You already have people, known worldwide, that can do it.

"Go tell Francis Chan to give this message. Franklin Graham or David Platt would be way better than me. God, have Jonathan Cahn give the message or David Jeremiah. They are well-known and well-respected, and people around the world will listen to them more than they will believe me."

God just tightened the vice again and kept the pressure on. I kept arguing while I showered and shaved for church. I can't begin to tell you how badly I wished I could have crawled into a cave or just died.

I was in agony; *EXTREME AGONY!* Except for my father's death, this was the worst day of my life. I wished I had never been born. I mean that.

I would rather have been dead. Who would want to give this message? Who in their right mind would ever want to be a prophet?

Sue and I were staying in a small, temporary office building and using it as a residence while the church parsonage was being remodeled. It was located right across the street from the church. At 10 a.m. we walked over to the building.

I was so angry at God; so hurt and stressed out. I still had no great sign from Him. I must confess to you that I was not being totally obedient in getting ready to give the prophetic message He was asking me to give. I had only written half of the prophetic message down and I brought my marriage sermon with me when I walked over to the church. Maybe God would relent at the last second.

I walked into the small chapel where the church held worship services. Sue went with me. Rudy was also there, filling up the baptistry with water for the baptisms we would have that day.

We were going to baptize some more people this morning. It was the fifth Sunday in a row that we were blessed to baptize new believers. The Holy Spirit was moving in the community. An awakening was underway.

I asked Rudy, Sue, and those in the auditorium to pray for me. I told them God was asking me to give a difficult message. I knelt at the altar, and they were all kind enough to pray for me.

I had never been under this much stress in my life. Great spiritual warfare was happening. Satan was coming after me and he was determined to stop this move of God that had begun in our community.

After the time of prayer, I got up and noticed that the baptistry was a little too full and that water would likely spill out on the carpet when I did the baptisms. The church building was eighty years old, and the drain valve was located on an outside wall. I went outside to drain some water off. It was now twenty-five minutes until the church service started.

I kept arguing with God under my breath. I still hadn't gotten the great sign from Him which confirmed that I had to give the prophetic message and tell the people who attended that day that I was a prophet.

Suddenly, Rudy came outside and he walked up to me very quickly. He says, "Ken, you've got to see this. While we were praying for you, at the altar, the Holy Spirit spoke to me. I started to walk back to the adult Sunday school class and the Spirit spoke to me again and said, 'Take the Sunday school quarterly to Ken and show him what the lesson is about today.'"

Rudy handed me a new Sunday school quarterly, which was being used by the adult Sunday school class.

I opened the quarterly and I was totally stunned. The title of the lesson, for March 1, 2020, was "A Prophet like Moses." Our adult Sunday school members, at that very moment, were inside the church studying this very lesson.

I then read the next part of the lesson which said, GOLDEN TEXT—*"I will raise them up a Prophet from among their brethren, like unto thee, and will put my words in his mouth; and he shall speak unto them all that I shall command him." (Deuteronomy 18:18)*. KJV

This was a miracle. God was confirming to me that He was raising me up to be a prophet from among the people there, and that He was going to put His words in my mouth to speak to the nations that day.

The adult Sunday school class, while reading and studying this lesson in their classroom, had no idea what was going on outside of the church. Rudy was one of the class teachers, and he had read the lesson in preparation to teach the class that day, and then brought the quarterly directly to me.

I couldn't believe it. God had Rudy bring me *the great sign*, confirming that He was raising me up as a prophet from among them that very day. There was no doubt in my mind now that I was to speak a prophetic message, to the people at church and to the nations, which the Lord would give to me. I was to tell the congregation and the world that I was a prophet.

I hugged him and thanked him for listening to the Holy Spirit by bringing me the quarterly with this message in it. The Lord told me to take a picture of Rudy holding the quarterly to capture the moment and this miracle. I told him, "I will never forget this day for the rest of my life, and I thank God that He used you to be the one who would bring this to me."

SCRIPTURE LESSON TEXT

DEUT. 18:9 When thou art come into the land which the Lord thy God giveth thee, thou shalt not learn to do after the abominations of those nations.

10 There shall not be found among you *any one* that maketh his son or his daughter to pass through the fire, *or* that useth divination, *or* an observer of times, or an enchanter, or a witch,

11 Or a charmer, or a consulter with familiar spirits, or a wizard, or a necromancer.

12 For all that do these things *are* an abomination unto the Lord: and because of these abominations the Lord thy God doth drive them out from before thee.

13 Thou shalt be perfect with the Lord thy God.

14 For these nations, which thou shalt possess, hearkened unto observers of times, and unto diviners: but as for thee, the Lord thy God hath not suffered thee so *to do*.

15 The Lord thy God will raise up unto thee a Prophet from the midst of thee, of thy brethren, like unto me; unto him ye shall hearken;

16 According to all that thou desiredst of the Lord thy God in Horeb in the day of the assembly, saying, Let me not hear again the voice of the Lord my God, neither let me see this great fire any more, that I die not.

17 And the Lord said unto me, They have well *spoken that* which they have spoken.

18 I will raise them up a Prophet from among their brethren, like unto thee, and will put my words in his mouth; and he shall speak unto them all that I shall command him.

19 And it shall come to pass, *that* whosoever will not hearken unto my words which he shall speak in my name, I will require *it* of him.

20 But the prophet, which shall presume to speak a word in my name, which I have not commanded him to speak, or that shall speak in the name of other gods, even that prophet shall die.

21 And if thou say in thine heart, How shall we know the word which the Lord hath not spoken?

22 When a prophet speaketh in the name of the Lord, if the thing follow not, nor come to pass, that *is* the thing which the Lord hath not spoken, *but* the prophet hath spoken it presumptuously: thou shalt not be afraid of him.

A Prophet like Moses

Lesson Text: Deuteronomy 18:9-22

Related Scriptures: John 1:43-46; Acts 3:22-26;
Hebrews 3:1-6; Jeremiah 28:1-9

TIME: 1405 B.C.   PLACE: plains of Moab

GOLDEN TEXT—"I will raise them up a Prophet from among their brethren, like unto thee, and will put my words in his mouth; and he shall speak unto them all that I shall command him" (Deuteronomy 18:18).

A photo of the title page and the Golden Text used in the lesson.[3]

Lesson Exposition

Our lessons this quarter all deal with messianic prophecies from the Old Testament.

Moses was now nearing the end of his leadership of Israel. Since the day he returned from the wilderness after his encounter with the Angel of the Lord in the burning bush, Israel had been guided by his counsel and had depended on him for virtually everything. Joshua would take over the main portion of Israel's leadership needs, but he was more of a general than a prophet as Moses was.

THE ABOMINATIONS OF THE NATIONS—Deut. 18:9-14

Abominations enumerated (Deut. 18:9-11). Appearing as a sudden shift in subject matter, verse 9 begins a detailed prohibition of the practices that characterized the peoples of Canaan. The message is very clear: the Israelites must be very careful not to allow themselves to be influenced or enticed into imitating these practices.

Passing a child through the fire (vs. 10) is a reference to both actual child sacrifice and to various ceremonies of dedication to false gods in which a child is merely passed over a sacred flame as a symbolic gesture. Either practice is detestable and forbidden among God's people.

"Divination" (vs. 10) involves fortune-telling by interpreting random events, whether it be by cards, dice, tea leaves, animal entrails, crystal balls, lines on the palm of the hand, or the stars and planets. An "observer of times" would be someone who purports to have psychic abilities to predict the future. An "enchanter" is one who interprets various omens as signs of future events. A "witch" is one who casts spells that influence people or events.

A "charmer" (vs. 11) specializes in causing people to do things against their will or altering their thinking about something. A "consulter with familiar spirits" is basically what we would call a medium. The distinction between a "wizard" and a "necromancer" is one of specialization, the latter focusing on one who speaks with the dead.

Consequences of the abominations (Deut. 18:12-14). The seriousness of these sinful activities is emphasized by the Lord in verse 12, for

From the Sunday School Quarterly—March, April, May 2020.[2]

I then said something else to Rudy, at that moment. Out of nowhere I said, "You have to help me get to Asia so I can minister there."

Little did I know that this was a prophetic word that came out of my mouth that would manifest two years later.

Once again, I asked myself, "Who is this God?"

I was speechless. How could God orchestrate all of this?

I realized that the quarterly had been written long ago. It was then printed and shipped to the church.

God timed it so that the arrival of the quarterly would meet my demand that He would have to give me a great sign showing me that I had to give the prophetic message. How could He arrange all of this and time it so perfectly? How did He know that I would ask Him for a great sign?

Genesis 18:14 says, *"Is anything too hard for the Lord?"*

I know the answer now. It is no. Nothing is too difficult for the Lord. Against astronomical odds, He did this miracle for me.

It is obvious that God worked a series of extraordinary miracles, all at the same time, to confirm that He had spoken to me and that I was a last day's prophet like Moses; that He was raising me up from among my brothers and sisters. He was going to have me deliver a prophetic message on March 1, 2020, and He was going to put His words in my mouth for me to speak to the nations.

It all happened just as God had planned it. The Holy Spirit had spoken to Rudy at just the right time to be the person who would deliver this great sign to me. If he hadn't been obedient to the Holy Spirit's voice by bringing the quarterly to me, I may have not given the message that the Lord had commanded me to give.

Rudy had no idea that I had been up all night and all morning arguing with God. He didn't know that I had been yelling at God or that I felt like Moses at the burning bush, and that I was being made to do something that I didn't want to do.

He didn't know that I was a prophet. Rudy also didn't know that I had been shouting at God to give me a great sign to prove His voice was real and that He was commanding me to give the prophetic message and announce to the world that I was a prophet.

Now, with just fifteen minutes until church started, I had the great sign from God that I had asked for. I would have to pull myself together and give a prophetic message, a sermon that I didn't want to give, and to also tell the people that I was a prophet.

Looking back, I realized God knew that the Coronavirus was spreading across the world. He knew that my message would go out on video prior to lockdowns, mask mandates, Israel's next election, and Him shaking the nations.

I was still in agony, knowing that I would now have to walk inside the church and do what the Lord had confirmed that I had to do. I took out a pen and wrote a few more words on the sermon that I had prepared.

I had no idea how I was going to get through this service. I still wished I was dead or had never been born.

Would I be courageous and obey Him and do what He said I had to do now that I had the great sign? Would I be a coward and not obey Him?

I had been telling the congregation, in my previous sermons, that Satan was going to come against this move of the Holy Spirit. I said that in order to have a genuine revival, there had to be a Satanic attack that came against it.

That day, that attack came. Satan was furious that so many people were getting saved, and he wanted to put an end to this outpouring of the Holy Spirit in our midst.

I realized that I was under a great spiritual attack from Satan. It was an all-out assault by Satan on me and the church. I knew it, but no one else did.

I was aware that this message could eventually lead to me stepping down as pastor. No one in this church had ever heard a sermon like the one I was about to give, and no one, in the eighty-year history of this church, had been told by their pastor that he was a prophet.

CHAPTER 6

God Is Shaking the Earth, the Nations, His Church, and You

Our church services had been going longer. We had started introducing contemporary worship songs along with our hymns. I had also added a time of congregational prayer, where people had a chance to testify about answered prayers and great things God had done in their lives.

I was full of joy as I saw the Spirit moving, and I didn't care that the services went longer. We didn't put God on the clock, and as a result, He often moved in a powerful way. It was like living in the book of Acts, because we were letting the Holy Spirit have control of our time together.

I was also told by the Lord to have communion. All of this made for a lengthy, but precious, Spirit-led church service on March 1, 2020.

It is a day that I will never forget because of the miracles that I saw God do in bringing me the great sign and how He spoke to me, telling me what to say even as I was giving the message. The Lord said, in the Sunday school quarterly, in Deuteronomy 18:18, *"I will put my words in his mouth and he shall speak to them, all that I command him."*

That is exactly what happened.

The service began. The hymns and worship songs blessed me as our congregation sang with great enthusiasm to the Lord.

The baptisms were amazing. I always enjoy baptisms and seeing the faces of loved ones and friends who are so proud of the one who is being baptized.

During communion, the Lord had instructed me to only drink the cup. He had told me to do this a few years earlier in a service, the first time He had me tell a church that I was a prophet.

Why does He require me to do this? The Lord is telling me that it is a bitter cup that He has set before me. It is bitter because He is warning me that if I drink it in obedience to what He is asking me to do, it will come with much suffering and persecution. I am being asked by the Lord to drink the bitter cup and show Him that I will be obedient, no matter what it costs me.

The Lord drank the bitter cup of taking a brutal beating and dying on the cross for my sins when He didn't have to. Would I drink the cup and be willing to suffer for Him and His Kingdom?

I trembled and drank the cup. I told the Lord that I would obey Him and give the very difficult message that He had asked me to give. I love Him and I owe Him a debt that I can never repay. At times, in my flesh, I only wish it were easier to follow Him as His servant, a prophet.

Before I went to the podium to deliver the message, I went to the front pew and knelt in prayer. I began to weep as I prayed out loud and I asked God to help me get through the service and for Him to speak through me.

I got up and took my notes and Bible to the podium. I looked to see that the service was being filmed, as the Lord had asked me to do. It was, but as I was about to start speaking, I heard a whisper come to me that said, "Have Sue film the sermon."

I ignored this, thinking that I must be talking to myself or that it was a distraction from Satan.

The Lord had given me the title of the message, "God is Shaking the Earth, the Nations, His Church, and You."

I was going to begin my sermon by reading in Amos 3:6-8 and emphasizing verse 7, where God says, "Surely the Sovereign Lord does nothing without revealing his plan to his servants the prophets."

I didn't want to say, straight up, that I was a prophet. Instead, I wanted to infer gently that God was speaking through me and that I was a servant of His; a prophet, as it states in verse 7. Surely God would be okay with me doing it this way; at least I hoped so.

Out of nowhere, the Lord whispered to me at the podium, "Start in Amos 3:1. I want you to call out Israel for her sins."

I obeyed and began reading Amos 3:1-2:

> *"Hear this word, people of Israel, the word the Lord has spoken against you—against the whole family I brought up out of Egypt: You only have I chosen of all the families of the earth; therefore I will punish you for all your sins."*

The Lord whispered, "Call out Israel and tell them that I have this against them: You have great immorality in the nation, with Tel Aviv now claiming that it is the LGBTQ capital of the world, with one in every seven adults claiming to be gay or lesbian. Tell Israel they have sinned greatly, as they continue to reject my Son, Jesus, and do not believe He is the Messiah. Tell Israel, because of your sins, you can't even form a government when you hold an election."

As I was going to keep reading scripture, the Lord said, "Call out New York City for its sins."

The Lord said, say this, "New York City, where are you? After 9/11, you came to church for a short time and then you turned away from me again. You never repented."

I couldn't believe it. God was speaking through me, putting the very words He wanted me to say into my mouth, even as I was standing at the podium. None of this was written on my sermon notes.

The word of the Lord just came to me as it did with the Old Testament prophets. This was exactly what the lesson in the Sunday school quarterly stated would happen this day, from Deuteronomy 18:15-19. God would put His words in my mouth and I would speak them.

As I continued giving the message, I read Amos 3:6-8.

> *"When a trumpet sounds in a city, do not the people tremble? When disaster comes to a city, has not the Lord caused it? Surely the Sovereign Lord does nothing without revealing His plan to His servants the prophets. The lion has roared–who will not fear? The Sovereign Lord has spoken–who can but prophesy?"*

As I spoke, I was hoping that the audience would understand what I was saying as I delivered this prophetic message. I was telling them that the Lord had called me to be His servant, a prophet, and that I was giving them a prophetic message.

I did not want to stop the sermon and just tell people that I was a prophet. I hoped that they would connect the dots during the sermon.

I went on to say that some of my spiritual gifts were prophetic in nature. I said that I saw storm clouds on the horizon. Difficult times were coming to them and the nations.

I stated that I wanted to alert them that things were going to get worse in the world and I wanted them to be prepared. The main point of the message was that God is now going to shake the Earth, the Nations, His Church, and You. God was going to shake everything.

I said, "The church is asleep around the world. The Lord is trying to wake us up. He is trying to make people see that they need to get saved before He brings His wrath upon the Earth."

I showed a short video clip of a pastor preaching a message, that the rapture could occur at any moment. Suddenly, in the video, the rapture happens and it shows the people, in a church auditorium, who were left behind. It stunned those who were in attendance in our service.

Honestly, I wondered if the Lord might not rapture us during my sermon. It jolted the people in our auditorium who were watching the video. There was such a powerful presence of the Holy Spirit in our service.

I continued my sermon and I talked of how God had poured His Spirit out at our church, and we were seeing signs and wonders. No doubt there was a big movement of the Holy Spirit among us.

I quoted Acts 2:17-21:

In the last days, God says, I will pour out my Spirit on all people. Your sons and daughters will prophesy, your young men will see visions, your old men will dream dreams.

Even on my servants, both men and women, I will pour out my Spirit in those days, and they will prophesy. I will show wonders in the heavens above and signs on the earth below, blood and fire and billows of smoke. The sun will be turned to darkness and the moon to blood before the coming of the great and glorious day of the Lord. And everyone who calls on the name of the Lord will be saved.

Then the Lord had me mention how most people want a one-hour church service. They just want to give God a little bit of their time on Sunday morning. Yet we are happy to attend a two-hour movie or a three-hour sporting event. The Lord had me say, "We love pleasure and entertainment more than we love Him."

I then talked about how people were full of fear. I said there would be even greater fear spreading across the world in the weeks ahead.

I shared how God was shaking the Earth through record hurricanes, tsunamis, fires, earthquakes, tornadoes, volcanoes, famines, and plagues of locusts. He then used the virus to shake everything.

I told of how God was exposing all secret sin and that judgment began with the people of God. I shared I Peter 4:17:

For it is time for judgment to begin with God's household; and if it begins with us, what will the outcome be for those who do not obey the gospel of God?

I mentioned the sexual misconduct of Catholic priests and Protestant pastors and how God was now exposing their sins that they had tried so hard to cover up.

God revealed this to me and said, "What you cover up, I will uncover. What you uncover, I will cover up.

"Secret sin that you try to hide will be exposed. Secret sin that you confess and repent from will be covered up with My grace, love, and mercy. You will be forgiven if you confess and repent of your sins."

I shared the following passages of scripture:

I John 1:9
If we confess our sins, he is faithful and just and will forgive us our sins and purify us from all unrighteousness.

James 5:16
Therefore confess your sins to each other and pray for each other so that you may be healed. The prayer of a righteous person is powerful and effective.

I then said, "God is shaking each of us. He wants us to walk in holiness."

God said in the message, "I am coming soon for a pure and spotless bride, and I will shake my church and followers so that they will turn from their wicked ways."

The Lord had me tell the nations that individuals who are walking in purity before Him had nothing to fear. He would watch over them and take care of them.

He said, "I am sick of the sin in this world, and I am getting ready to bring my wrath on these wicked people. Repent of your secret sins."

Somehow, I got through the sermon and walked down the aisle to exit the church. As I passed Rudy, he spoke to me and said, "you got through it." He was encouraging me as I walked out of the auditorium in total exhaustion.

I appreciated that so much. God had gotten me through the most difficult message I had ever given.

◆◆◆

I still have the printed sermon that I used to deliver this message. It is unbelievable to read what God told me to say and what came to pass after I gave the message. World events happened that totally validated the prophetic message the Lord told me to give on March 1, 2020.

Little did I know that my words from God were so prophetic, as Covid struck the world and a pandemic was declared just two weeks later. Things got much worse just as God had me share in the message.

This sermon was given on March 1, 2020. Two days later, on March 3, Israel held its third election, trying to form a government, and they failed again. God had prophesied though me and it continued, as Israel failed again in a fourth election, on March 23, 2021, to form a government.

God is judging the nation of Israel. They were hit hard by Covid, and the country was shut down a few times, which badly hurt their tourist business and economy. There continues to be turmoil in the political realm in Israel and terrorist attacks on Israel from its Arab neighbors.

God prophesied through me, ahead of time, that disaster was coming to New York City, America, and the world. New York City would go on to become an epicenter for Covid deaths in the U.S.

How tragic. God was saying that He was going to bring judgment to America. He did. It continues today.

America is now experiencing God's judgment. Our country was locked down and people went to their homes. Countless deaths have been recorded. Schools and businesses were closed, which resulted in many companies going bankrupt.

Vaccine and mask mandates swept the nation. There were countless adverse reactions and deaths from the vaccine mandates. Children suffered greatly from having to learn from home and from having to wear masks and take vaccines that harmed or killed some of them.

Stock markets across the world began to plunge. The price of oil went to zero as there was a glut of oil on the market and no buyers. This resulted in corporations giving their oil away because they didn't have any more places to store it until they could eventually sell it.

Many churches closed their doors. They were not considered essential. In many states you could go to the liquor store, Walmart, and other places, but the government would not allow you to attend church. Wicked leaders used the crisis to grab power and many are still holding on to it to this day.

People began to panic. There was fear everywhere in the days and weeks after the Lord had me give the sermon. God was shaking everything. Looking back, we all know that He did. He is still shaking us today.

When I think about what happened, on March 1, 2020, I want to make something very clear. I received the great sign from God in that Sunday school quarterly that God was raising me up as a prophet and that He would put His words in my mouth for me to speak.

Please know that I am quite aware that Jesus is the one who ultimately and totally fulfilled Deuteronomy 18:15-19. This is shown in the New Testament, in Acts 3:21-23:

Heaven must receive him until the time comes for God to restore everything, as he promised long ago through his holy prophets. For Moses said, "The Lord your God will raise up for you a prophet like me from among your own people; you must listen to everything he tells you. Anyone who does not listen to him will be completely cut off from their people."

However, God first used that passage for Joshua, when it was written 3,400 years ago, and He used it again for me; another man who He has raised up to be a prophet. I am humbled. I am not worthy. He has shown me grace.

I also want you to know that I am no longer a reluctant prophet. I have apologized to God for shouting at Him and for my selfish desire to do life my way. It is His call on my life to serve Him humbly as a last day's prophet, and I will do it.

He bought me with His precious blood. I will now do whatever He tells me to do without delay. He died for me. I will live, "All In," fully surrendered to Him.

♦♦♦

Why did the Lord do these incredible miracles and have Rudy bring me the Sunday school quarterly that contained the scripture from Deuteronomy Chapter 18? God did this to confirm that He had chosen and appointed me to be His servant; a prophet.

As I have already mentioned, God has asked me to be a "voice of truth" for Him to the nations. However, there was a voice of truth before me several decades earlier.

During World War II, the Lord had Dietrich Bonhoeffer, a German pastor and theologian, speak out against the evil work of Adolph Hitler and the Nazi regime. Bonhoeffer warned Germany and the world of how evil Hitler was, but very few people listened to him.

Like Bonhoeffer, God has called me to speak out against the evil in the world today. I am amazed at how the Lord has tied my life to both Moses and Bonhoeffer in incredible, confirming miracles.

God will do miraculous things to prove that He has called someone to a position. Look at what Paul says in II Corinthians 12:12:

> *I persevered in demonstrating among you the marks of a true apostle, including signs, wonders and miracles.*

God proves to the world, through signs, wonders, and miracles, that He has raised someone up to do a work for Him. God is showing you and the people of the world that He has raised me up to be a last days prophet for Him by the evidence that I include in this book.

It is my hope that you are now beginning to trust me as you see the miracles that God is doing on my behalf. Again, all of this is for God's glory. I can take no credit for anything.

My former pastor and boss, Dr. David Jeremiah, wrote these words in his commentary, on p. 13, of *The Jeremiah Study Bible*:

> *Genesis 6:13 commentary*—"*Noah labored unremarkably, for the first two-thirds of his life and was approaching "retirement age," when the call of God came. Throughout history, God has often raised up a champion for the cause of righteousness in a time of widespread immorality.*"[4]

Like God did with Noah, the early part of my life was unremarkable, and I am now approaching the age of retirement. He has asked me to stand against the great immorality and the antichrist system that has come upon the world.

The Lord has also commanded me to tell all of you, just as Noah did, that He is soon going to bring judgment against the wicked people who are on the Earth. God had Noah warn people that He was going to flood the Earth and destroy evil people. Then it happened.

Today, once again, God warns everyone that He is soon going to bring His wrath upon the immoral and wicked in what He calls the tribulation; a coming seven-year period of unprecedented war, death, deception, and judgment.

The Lord wants to rescue you and others from being deceived by evil world leaders and the global elite, who are trying to take over and form a one world government. The Lord is being loving in warning you, and everyone who is alive, that *THE END IS NOW COMING*.

Through these miracles, the Lord also wants you to know how great He is and that He still speaks and does miraculous things today. He knows that these miracles you are reading about can strengthen your faith as you go through the difficult days that are coming.

I pray that as you take an honest look at the condition of the world around you, that you are aware that something is terribly wrong. You see that you no longer live in the world that you grew up in and that there are evil people on the Earth today who want to usher in a new world order.

CHAPTER 7

Signs, Wonders, and Miracles

I simply can't believe all of the signs, wonders, and miracles God has done in my life. All Glory to Him.

There is not enough space to include all of them in this book. I'll pick out a few of these riveting miracles and share them here.

I want you to see how awesome God is. He is so powerful. He has no equal in all the universe.

Some people believe that miracles have ceased since Christ went to heaven and the last of his disciples died around the end of the first century. This is simply not true.

Almighty God is just as powerful today as He has always been. I pray that you fall more in love with Him as you continue reading this book. After you read this chapter, I think you will.

The Galatians 2:20 Miracle

At times, when I have done something very difficult and given a message that the Lord wanted me to give, He will reward me with a miracle. After I obeyed the Lord and gave the March 1, 2020, prophetic sermon, the Lord blessed me with a miracle a few days later.

On Wednesday evening, March 4, just three days after giving the prophetic message, I had a special encounter with the Lord. Late that night, my wife, Sue, went to lie down on the bed to go to sleep.

At 11 p.m., I decided I would lie beside her and let her rest her head on my left shoulder. She likes to snuggle with me and then go to sleep. As I was laying there, the Lord began to speak to me.

The Lord asked me a question. "Ken, can a person be demon possessed?"

Honestly, I must confess that I was a little annoyed when He asked me this. Surely, He knew that my answer would be yes.

I said, "Lord, of course someone can be demon possessed. You, Lord, cast out many demons while you were on the Earth."

He asked, "Ken, do you know the verse Galatians 2:20?"

I said, "Sure Lord, I know the verse."

The Lord said, "Say it to me."

I whispered the verse to the Lord so that I didn't wake up Sue.

> Galatians 2:20
> *I've been crucified with Christ, therefore I no longer live. Jesus Christ now lives in me and the life I now live in the flesh, I live by faith in the Son of God who loved me and gave Himself for me.*

The Lord said, "Say it to me again, but say it very slowly."

So, I slowly said the verse again. Just as I finished saying, "Jesus Christ now lives in me," the Lord said, "Stop."

Then He said, "Ken, I live inside you."

Then the Lord said something to me that shocked me, that I had never heard anyone say before. He said, "Ken, you are Christ-possessed. Just as a person can be demon possessed, someone can also be Christ-possessed. I possess you Ken and I live inside you."

That was why Paul said, "Jesus Christ now lives in me."

Paul was Christ-possessed.

Immediately after that, I began to have a wave of "joy unspeakable" surge and pulsate through my body. It went from the top of my head to the tip of my toes. It continued for over thirty minutes.

I just had to wake Sue up and share this moment with her. I wanted her to know what was happening; what God was doing for me at that very moment.

Sue woke up and listened to me tell her what the Lord had just told me about Galatians 2:20 and how I was now Christ-possessed. As I told her about the wave of joy moving through my body, she said, "It's because I am lying next to you."

Her half-awake, humorous comment instantly caused us to laugh, and the pulse continued as she went back to sleep.

This joy that I experienced was not goosebumps on the surface of my skin. It was inside my body, in my spirit, in the core of my being. You might even say it was in my bones.

The Lord gave me a taste of heaven by giving me this pulse of joy. Perhaps in heaven, it will feel like that pulse all the time. I can't begin to put it into words of how great it felt to experience this joy as the Lord rewarded me for obeying Him in giving the prophetic sermon that I had begged Him to not make me give.

If only I would realize that when God gives me a difficult task to do for Him, it is really for my good and His Glory. I pray that in the future, I will instantly obey Him when He asks me to do something difficult and my selfish nature wants to try to talk Him out of having me do it.

My friend, you can also be Christ-possessed if you will fully surrender your life to Him. Each day, get up, deny yourself, and take up your cross and follow Him. Jesus died for you. Will you live for Him? Are you crucified with Christ?

Miracles in Brazil

I'll never forget the mission trip that I took to Brazil in July of 2015. My wife, Sue, and I were invited to go with International Commission, a nonprofit organization that takes people on short-term mission trips to various countries.

We joined nineteen other churches in Santo Andre, Brazil, a suburb of Sao Paulo. The organization had worked for many months to prepare for an evangelistic outreach to the city. It would be a time of working with one of the local churches to do door-to-door evangelism.

Sue and I were blessed to be assigned to the Batista Monte Sinai Church. The pastoral staff, led by Manual Santos and his son, Alex Santos, were such a joy to work with. The numerous church volunteers became our friends, and we grew to love the people of the church.

I was assigned an interpreter by the church to work with me as I went out to do evangelism in various homes during my time there. His name was Genilson Holanda. Genilson spoke English pretty well and was such a big help to me.

Each morning, we would eat breakfast and then head out for a busy day of making visits to various homes. Once at a home, we would share the gospel with those we met.

I love people, so when I walk into a home, I like to make people feel comfortable. I smile a lot and try to get people to laugh as I make fun of myself while I get to know those who are in the room with me.

This puts people at ease and, in most cases, they quickly become comfortable talking and laughing with me. After a while, I ask if I can share the gospel with them because I want to have them in heaven with me for all eternity. The answer has always been yes.

I made many home visits during this mission trip, and many people came to a saving faith in Christ. This brought me great joy.

I also got to know my interpreter very well, as we spent day after day together. Genilson is a wonderful man who loves God deeply. He had taken time off of work to be a part of this evangelistic outreach with his church. I grew to love him and his family.

Genilson would tell me about who I was going to meet before I went into the house. Each home visit had been planned, so I had a general idea of who lived at a home before I would go in.

He told me about his own family, and how some of them were not believers and did not attend church. As our time together went by, he told me that he had scheduled my last home visit to be with his own mother and brother. He told me that neither one of them were Christians.

He said that he had shared the gospel with them many times and that they always rejected the message of salvation. He didn't have much hope that they would ever be saved, but he wanted me to speak to them.

He also told me that his brother, Gilson, was very sick and that doctors had told him that he had less than a year left to live. He did not tell me what disease or medical issues he had been diagnosed with.

On my final afternoon of evangelism work in Brazil, Genilson took me to his mother's home. As I walked in the door, his brother, Gilson, rushed up to me and said, "You have to pray for me to be healed!"

I was surprised that he was so aggressive in wanting me to immediately pray for his healing. At that point, he was desperate. He was dying.

I then responded by saying, "First, I must share with you and your mom about Jesus, and tell you about the opportunity that you have to spend eternity in heaven. Then, I will pray for your healing afterwards."

He didn't like my answer. Without delay, I went right over and met his mother. She was kind and gracious to me. Genilson interpreted for us and I enjoyed meeting her and visiting with her for a moment.

She sat down on her couch and Gilson sat next to her. Genilson and I sat in chairs across from them.

I began to share the gospel. I explained how God had sent His only Son down to the Earth to live a sinless life and pay the penalty for all our sins.

I explained how Jesus was beaten, whipped to the point of death, and died a cruel death on a cross, and that He was buried and rose again on the third day. He defeated sin and death. He died in our place and gave us the opportunity to repent of our sins and place our faith in His atoning death on the cross.

As I shared this good news with them, the Holy Spirit was convicting both of them of their sins and their need for a Savior. After presenting the gospel, I asked them if they would like to pray and call on the Lord to forgive them of their sins and save them?

Both said yes. We prayed. They repented and placed their faith in the gospel, and both of them were born again that day.

Genilson was shocked. He was so full of joy, knowing that his mother and brother had received eternal life. He got up, with tears in his eyes, and hugged them. Then he hugged me. As only God can do, his mother and brother would now be with him in heaven for all eternity.

We celebrated for a couple of minutes, just as the angels did in heaven. It was so special to get to see Genilson's great joy over what had just taken place.

I then felt led by the Holy Spirit to pray for Gilson's physical healing. Before I pray for someone and ask the Lord to heal them, I tell them and anyone else in the room that is listening what is going to happen.

I tell the person that one of three things is going to occur. I say, "God may heal you immediately; even as I am praying or when I finish praying. God may choose to heal you, over time, in the coming days, weeks or months. Finally, God may choose to not heal you at all."

I go on to explain that for reasons unknown to us, God chooses to heal some people and to not heal others. Yet, we know that all healings are temporary. Our bodies eventually wear out and we pass away.

After explaining what was going to happen, I knelt in front of Gilson. I placed my hand on him and began to pray, in faith, that God would heal him.

While praying, I sensed that healing power was going out of me to Gilson. When I finished, I calmly got up and I told Gilson that I felt healing power go out of my hand to him.

I didn't know if Gilson was healed that moment, or if he would ever be healed. I talked with him and his mother for a few more minutes, and then Genilson and I left his mother's home.

When the mission trip ended, my wife and I flew back home to Colorado. We talked of the great things that took place during our time in Brazil and how so many people had come to faith in Christ.

One evening, shortly after we had returned home, my wife and I were sitting in our upstairs living room. My phone rang and I answered it. I was greeted by a person who was screaming my name, "Ken, Ken, this is Genilson!"

Since he was screaming, my first reaction was to think that maybe someone had died. Maybe Gilson had died and not been healed.

He went on screaming, in excitement, and said, "You won't believe it! My brother, Gilson, has been healed. You prayed for him and God has healed him. It's a miracle. The news is spreading all over the area and across Brazil. Gilson has been healed."

Gilson had been to his doctor and they had run tests to get an update on his condition. They couldn't believe the results. They were stunned that they verified that he had somehow been healed.

My wife, Sue, was sitting there with me, listening to the conversation. When the call ended, we celebrated this great news. Not only had Gilson been born again, but God had now healed him physically.

Over time, I went on to find out that Gilson had a severe case of hepatitis C and it had been infecting his liver. He was told by the doctors that he only had a short time left to live.

As of this writing eight years later, Gilson is still alive and doing well. I thank God for healing him.

Here is Genilson's short summary of his time with me in Brazil and his brother's miraculous healing.

◆◆◆

During an International Crusade program in July of 2015, promoted by Baptist Brazilian Association, we had a very great opportunity to receive, in our local church, a couple of God, Pastor Ken Bailey and his wife Sue.

Although we had been praying for this project for at least six months, we could not imagine how blessed this amazing visit would be. Nevertheless, Christ showed us again that he has every single thing under His control and sent His servant, Ken, not "only" to share gospel messages, but also to show us His merciful action through miracles, healing people with diseases, casting out demons, changing minds, and preparing hearts to receive Him as the Lord and Savior of their lives.

Despite almost all visits and church services having been previously planned, many of them had to be rescheduled for several reasons, and others included to meet each person's availability and new demands. One of these visits was at my mother's home, where my brother was living.

He was very sick, suffering from chronic hepatitis C, and was undergoing intensive treatment trying to reduce inflammation of the liver. But even with proper medical follow up, there wasn't a good body response, and so his risk of dying was imminent. Besides that, he had been fired from his job and was now unemployed and fighting in the law court against medical insurance regarding the right to receive a very expensive medicine recommended by doctors.

In this disadvantaged scenario, Pastor Ken came and prayed to God, asking for healing, and immediately we told him that Christ still wanted my brother alive and serving Christ. Well, a week after Ken left Brazil, my brother, Gilson, received the latest exam results which showed that he was completely healed, exceeding any medical expectation. God had answered Ken's prayer and healed my brother. In addition, my mother was also led to Christ.

Another blessed visit we made was to my father-in-law. He was going through a very tough time due to bladder cancer, which spread throughout his body. However, after this amazing visit with Ken, he received Jesus Christ as his Savior and he experienced a peace beyond our understanding, and then died a year later in May of 2016.

In a nutshell, about fifty families had been visited and more than 100 people led to God, recognizing Him as the only Lord and Savior!!!

It was really incredible, what God had done in that week by His messengers Pastor Ken and Sue, to whom we have great gratitude and debt of love.

God Bless you!

Genilson Holanda

♦♦♦

All glory, honor, and credit for Gilson's healing go to the Lord. I simply offered up the prayer in faith. God did it all. Gilson says that God used me as a tool to bring healing to him.

Friend, it is my hope that this amazing miracle encourages you. God is still doing miracles and healing people today.

The Miracle at Monarch Mountain

On Sunday, September 6, 2020, I had Roy Duncan, Bev Duncan, and Ben Sergo come over to visit Sue and I at our home in Gunnison, Colorado. At the end of our time together, the Lord said to me, "Look at the time on your phone."

It was 3:16 p.m. He told me to show it to these four people, who were with me, and to tell them that the time, 3:16, represents John 3:16, when the Lord shows it to me.

John 3:16
For God so loved the world that he gave his one and only Son, that whoever believes in him shall not perish but have eternal life.

This applies to me when I see that time during the day or during the night. The Lord also confirms to me that He is speaking to me when I see 3:16, and how important it is to Him that I take the gospel to the nations. I must tell nonbelievers that He came and died so that they might have the chance to repent of their sins, believe the gospel, and receive the gift of eternal life.

On Tuesday, September 8, just two days later, I was at the Duncan home and the Lord had me share some prophetic videos that I had made the day before. They were filmed by Jonathan and Josh Owen while we were on location outside of Buena Vista, Colorado. Roy, Bev, and Ben were there, but Sue was teaching school.

After showing them the videos of the message to Governors and God's Miraculous call on Ken Bailey's life, the Lord said, "Look at your phone and see the time."

I did, and it was 3:16 p.m. again. He told me to show them and tell them that this was a sign and wonder to them. Amazingly, in forty-eight hours, He had shown them 3:16 twice and spoken to me while I was with them.

I told the Lord before going to bed on September 11, 2020, that I was so tired, and I didn't think I was going to the Let Us Worship event that was being held by Sean Feucht at Memorial Park in Colorado Springs the next day. I was exhausted and so I told the Lord that I was not even going to set an alarm.

I told him, "If you don't wake me up early enough for me to get there on time, I will know you want me to stay home and rest. If you want me to go, you will have to wake me up early. If you do, even though I am exhausted, I will go and make the seven-hour round-trip drive to the event. I will go and minister to people there."

The Lord woke me up at 3:16 a.m. I was stunned. It was the third time the Lord had spoken to me in just five days and shown me that it was 3:16.

Friend, sometimes the Lord wants you to serve Him in a costly way, even when you are experiencing exhaustion. He got me up after only three hours and sixteen minutes of rest. 3:16 equals John 3:16 for me, and the Lord wanted me to go do Kingdom work and seek to save those who are lost.

I got up and began to make the drive to Colorado Springs. I was praying and talking to the Lord as I headed to the event. I was heading east on Highway 50 towards Monarch Pass. Around 5:30 a.m., while driving, the Lord began to speak to me and encourage me. He told me that He was pleased with me that I was going to the event even though I was exhausted. He said, "You will meet Sean today and give him the message you typed up to give to him."

I was so exhausted from getting very little sleep. I began to doubt that I was hearing the Lord speak to me. I told Him, "Lord, I'm not sure that I am really hearing from you this morning. I am so tired, I'm just not sure that you are really speaking to me."

He said, "Ken, I will prove to you that I am speaking to you right now and I will bring a name to you and you will never need to doubt again that I, the Lord, your God, am speaking to you!"

I said, "Ok Lord, what is the name?"

He replied, "Nathan Jones."

This upset me. I started arguing with God. I shouted at Him, "Nathan Jones. Are you kidding me? I'll never have that name come to me."

I said, "God, are you serious? I haven't talked to him in years. We met one time, long ago. I don't even have his phone number. Please God, give me another name. There's no way that name will ever come to me."

I continued to argue with God. I said, "Really God, I'll never get that name. His name will never come to me. Come on God, there's no way this is going to happen. Now I know I must not be hearing from you."

The Lord was so good. After I argued with Him for several more minutes about how it would never happen, He calmly said to me, "Ken, when the name Nathan Jones comes to you, *and it will*, you will know that I am speaking to you and you can trust my voice. From now on, you should never doubt that I am speaking to you. I will do this miracle and confirm to you again, that I have been speaking to you all of these years, and that you are really hearing my voice."

A chill went through my body, after the Lord said the words, "*and it will.*" I'll never forget those words.

Over the past thirty years, God has spoken to me a countless number of times. Nevertheless, it was early in the morning, and I was so tired and I wasn't sure that I was really hearing Him speak to me. Perhaps, in my state of exhaustion, I was just hearing chatter in my head and I was speaking to myself.

I drove on to Colorado Springs. I arrived at the event early and was able to stand up front on what ended up being the second row. The crowd began to gather. Sean and the band were on stage warming up.

Suddenly the Lord spoke to me. "After rehearsal, Sean will walk off the stage. When he does, go over and speak to him briefly and give him the note you wrote for him."

Sure enough, rehearsal ended and Sean walked off the stage. God spoke to me again saying, "Go now."

I walked over to Sean and had a short conversation with him. I knew he was busy and there would be many people who would want to speak to him. I introduced myself and I told him that this worship service and outreach event was all planned by God. I told him that God wanted these events to occur all over the world. He agreed.

We talked a few more minutes and then I gave him the note that I had written to him. I told him that I knew he didn't have time to read it now, just to put it in his pocket and read it later.

I don't know if Sean ever read the note. I never heard from him, and that's okay. I was just being obedient to what the Lord told me to do.

Now I knew that at least part of what God had spoken to me earlier in the morning was true. He had told me that I would meet Sean and that had come to pass.

Even before the event started, people that I didn't even know started coming up to me and asking me to pray for them. This was surprising. What was drawing them to come to me and ask for prayer? God had planned it all.

I drove back home after the event was over. I got in late and collapsed into bed and went to sleep.

Out of nowhere, on the next day, September 13, 2020, Bridgette Ballew Vieh, a friend who lived across the street from me while I was growing up in Mission, Texas, contacted me on Messenger. We had not talked to each other in over forty-eight years. Here is our exchange:

◆◆◆

Sept. 13, 2020—Messenger. SUN 8:42 PM. MST

Hi Kenny.

This is Bridgette Ballew Vieh. We were neighbors in Mission. I heard that you were involved with FCA and told my friend that you and your family helped my family get connected at Conway Baptist church. I hope you, your sister and brother, and your mom are well. I never heard anything again about you all after elementary school—it is all a blur. I really cared for you all deeply—God bless you and your family.

My response:

Hi Bridgette,

I have never forgotten you guys. I have thought about you many times over the years. Wayne is married with five grown kids and lives in Midland. Carol is married with three grown kids and lives in North Los Angeles. I have done a bunch of work with FCA. I was a teacher, coach, and then school administrator for many years. The last ten years, I have been in full-time vocational ministry. Here is some info for you: Facebook—Ken Bailey Ministries or Ken Bailey. website: kenbaileyministries.com. I am the founder of a nonprofit that feeds and clothes the poor. It is: Facebook—Alms International. Website is: almsinternational.com. Let's talk soon and catch up. Kenny

Bridgette: September 14. 6:40 AM

I am married and have three grown kids and six grandsons. Sandra Cavazos and I always wondered where you all were. So happy to re-connect and happy that you are working so hard for our Lord.

I do, as well, live to connect any and everyone to Him. I am in my thirtieth year of education. Was principal of a McAllen ISD high school Rowe High School and am currently associate superintendent in McAllen. We had everyone watch the Woodlawn movie when the superintendent and I got to Central. We spread in a big way across the district FCA huddles, Nathan Jones became the district leadership "coach" weekly, with a fifteen-minute Bible lesson and encouragement for leadership.

I have tried to have awareness of who God is; how He would address our situations through Bible stories connected to our current situation. I do look forward to a talk sometime to understand the areas you lead.

Bridgette

Also, anytime you are in the valley you are welcome in our home. We live on forty acres in Cameron county.

My response: September 14

Let's talk later this week. I will call you. When you get a chance, go watch these two videos and learn about how God has raised me up to be a last days prophetic voice for him. Then please share my videos and website with others. I have met Nathan Jones. You are part of a miracle this morning, Bridgette. The Lord told me last week He would reconnect me with Nathan Jones and prove that I was still clearly hearing His voice. You mentioned Nathan, just now, in your note to me! Watch the video of God's call on my life and then watch the video to all Governors.

◆◆◆

After I finished reading Bridgette's second message, where she mentioned the name Nathan Jones, I sat in a state of shock. It was surreal. I couldn't believe that I just got the name Nathan Jones within forty-eight hours of the Lord telling me that it would come to me.

I bowed my head and I prayed. I apologized to the Lord for doubting that He was speaking to me. I told Him how sorry I was for arguing with Him while I was driving, and that I was wrong.

He was right, and He had shown me, once again, that He had called me to be a prophet and that He had been speaking to me for years. He clearly spoke to me on Saturday morning, September 12, 2020, though I doubted it then.

I was way out of line to question His voice and argue with the God of the universe. Who was I to talk to Him the way that I did? I repented and He forgave me.

I then spoke to the Lord again and I said, "Oh God, how I love you and can't believe the miracles you are doing for me."

I was stunned. Nathan Jones didn't even know of this miracle. I couldn't wait to talk with him.

Oh, how I love you, Jesus.

I also thought of how it was great to be back in touch with a childhood friend. Bridgette and I have talked many times since then.

I went to South Texas and met with her and her husband, Chuck. I also met with Nathan Jones and shared this story with him. He and Bridgette were both astonished that God had used them to be a part of a miracle. They are wonderful, Christian friends and I am blessed to know them.

Bridgette told me that she was on Facebook and saw the section—People You May Know. It was there that she saw a photo of me with my wife and children. She said that she knew that it was me, even though I was going by the name Ken instead of Kenny. She then messaged me on Facebook.

The Holy Spirit prompted Bridgette to get on Facebook at the exact right time to see me on People You May Know. Then the Spirit had Bridgette follow through and message me.

How could the Lord do this? How could God use someone that I hadn't spoken to in over forty years to complete this miracle that He told me would happen?

Her FCA "friend" that she mentioned to me in her very first message to me turned out to be Nathan Jones. She called Nathan by name in her second message to me.

There are about eight billion people on the planet, and God brought the name Nathan Jones to me within forty-eight hours and used a childhood friend to do it. The odds were astronomical against Him being able to do this. Yet He did.

Let's look at Acts 14:3:

> *So Paul and Barnabas spent considerable time there, speaking boldly for the Lord, who confirmed the message of his grace by enabling them to perform signs and wonders.*

Hebrews 2:4 says:
God also testified to it by signs, wonders and various miracles, and by gifts of the Holy Spirit distributed according to his will.

Like the Apostle Paul, God has provided confirming signs, wonders, and miracles to prove that I am His servant, a prophet, and that He is speaking to me. It has been God's will for me to experience His grace; the undeserved favor of God. I don't deserve to receive any of these amazing miracles. I am just a spokesperson for Him.

As you continue reading this book, it is my prayer that you are falling more in love with God; that you are seeing how powerful He is. He created you and planned for you to be alive at this very moment in time. The Lord formed you in such a way that no one in the world has your fingerprints, your smile, your talents, and your personality.

God has plans for your life. He even planned for you to read this book.

Take a moment and talk to Him. That's what prayer is; it is talking to God and listening to Him.

Perhaps you have a relationship with Him already. If you don't, it's never too late to start.

The Lord is still doing signs, wonders, and miracles. For, you see, even you are a miracle and a gift to the world.

CHAPTER 8

My Miraculous Vision of War, The Tribulation, and the Second Coming of Christ

On May 29, 2021, God took me into the most spectacular vision He has ever given me. It was simply staggering; much like what occurred in the book of Acts, where the Holy Spirit performed supernatural miracles. The words that I share here, from what I was allowed to see, are so inadequate.

The vision lasted over two hours and I was awake the entire time. It covers many years of time on Earth.

The vision started out with a scripture verse. God spoke these words, in a powerful, deep voice, from Matthew 4:4.

Man shall not live by bread alone, but by every word that proceeds from the mouth of God.

The reason the Lord chose that scripture to use with this vision is to let you know how desperately you need to hear the Words of God. They are life.

He spoke, and men, over the course of many years, recorded His Words. All scripture is the inspired, inerrant, infallible word of God.

The Lord also wants you to know that He is still speaking today. He is still speaking words from His mouth to His servants, the prophets. God has given me these words, contained in this vision, for you to understand what is coming in the future, and to rejoice when you see the events come to pass. All glory to God.

Look at Amos 3:7:

Surely the Sovereign Lord does nothing without revealing his plan to his servants the prophets.

In this vision, God confirms that all prophecy, written in the word of God, that hasn't taken place yet, is going to come to pass.

Here is the Lord's plan that He revealed to me that is coming in the near future. May it bring great joy to your heart. If you are a follower of Christ, you will be going home soon.

The vision continued with me seeing two, tiny babies' feet. They belonged to an aborted baby that was laying on a counter in a lab. The child was covered with a sheet and only their feet were visible.

I then saw inside a woman's womb where a fetus was growing inside her body and it was so beautiful, but it was so vulnerable. I wondered if the woman would choose to let the fetus live?

Suddenly, I saw men and women in white coats. They were working in the lab and they had surgical instruments. There were many stainless steel counters there, with aborted babies lying on them. I was told that the scientists were going to do experiments on the babies and I was very sad.

I was then taken out of the lab and I was shown a vast, barren land. Nothing was growing. There was no grass and there were no trees anywhere. It looked like something you might see in the deserts of Arizona or California.

I saw a single, old flagpole out in the middle of this barren soil. I looked at the top of it and there was an American flag. It was slowly being lowered to the ground.

The flag was taken off the pole and thrown onto the ground. It was set on fire. I was told by God, "America has now come under judgment and it is no longer a nation."

I spoke to the Lord and asked, "What do you mean by saying, America is no longer a nation?"

He said, "America now ceases to exist!"

I became sad upon hearing this news.

♦♦♦

At that moment, the Lord revealed to me that He hates abortion and that His anger burns against the evil and injustice done to the unborn. Their blood cries out to Him to avenge their deaths. He is against those who perform the abortions.

God told me that America's national sin is abortion. He is now judging our nation on behalf of those who have been aborted and for America's many other sins, such as great sexual immorality and removing God from the public arena.

America is now dying. She will cease to exist right after the Rapture, and the land will be ruled by China and then by the antichrist.

You might ask, what is the Rapture? The text, in I Thessalonians 4:16-18, is often used to describe what the rapture is:

> *For the Lord himself will come down from heaven, with a loud command, with the voice of the archangel and with the trumpet call of God, and the dead in Christ will rise first. After that, we*

who are still alive and are left will be caught up (raptured) together with them in the clouds to meet the Lord in the air. And so we will be with the Lord forever. Therefore encourage one another with these words.

This is the passage that describes the future rapture of the church. This is when all the followers of Christ who have died in the past, or that are currently living on Earth, are suddenly taken up to heaven.

I did not see the rapture take place. I was, however, made to know that the rapture of the church occurred right before the death of America, which occurred early in the vision.

◆◆◆

As the vision continued, I saw two men raising a flag on the flagpole out in the desert. It was a red flag and the Lord told me it was the Chinese Communist Party flag. America was now ruled by China.

Suddenly, I left the flagpole and I was shown that war was taking place all over the world. It was World War III.

The sky was full of jets. Some were dropping nuclear bombs while others were shooting nuclear missiles.

I also saw aircraft carriers. Jets were taking off from them. There were also jets that were landing on them to get refueled and have more missiles put back on them.

I saw battleships of different armies and navies. They were shooting their big guns and launching their artillery everywhere. It was terrifying.

Next, I looked and I was on land. I was on a battlefield. I saw an army of robots marching in formation in front of me towards a battle. There were so many that I couldn't count them all.

Then I looked up in the air and I saw a swarm of what looked like black birds. They were on the horizon and moving in the air together. They were flying towards me. As they got closer, I realized that they were drones.

They were synchronized so they could move together. These were military drones going to war with the robotic soldiers.

Then I was shown a bear running on the ground in a large, green field. The bear was huge. It looked like a grizzly bear, and it was running across the countryside at full speed. It was on the attack.

As it was running, it suddenly turned into a tank. It kept right on going, at full speed, and it got closer to me. Then I was able to see a face that was painted on the front of the tank. It was the face of Vladimir Putin.

I was shown the Russian tank in the vision, going on the attack, on May 29, 2021. This was almost nine months before it happened, on February 24, 2022, when Russia, led by President Putin, attacked Ukraine.

After I saw the tank and Putin's face, more time passed by in the vision. I then saw Putin holding meetings with the leaders of Turkey and Iran. Why did they meet? What were they planning to do?

Those three nations began preparing strategies for an upcoming war. What war were they going to take part in? The Bible mentions this in Ezekiel 38 and 39. Russia, Turkey, and Iran form an alliance that includes a couple of smaller nations, to go and attack Israel.

One of these meetings that I was shown in the vision has now taken place. Russia, Iran, and Turkey met on July 19, 2022 in Iran.

Look at the *Fox News* headline for this event:

> Putin meets with Iran, Turkey in Tehran amid deadly war in Ukraine. (Published July 19, 2022)[5]

As the vision continued, I saw an Israeli flag and it was revealed to me that Russia, Iran, Turkey, and a couple of other nations were going to attack Israel.

More time went by and World War III continued everywhere. I looked on the horizon and I saw a nuclear bomb explode on the ground. There was a flash of light and I heard the roar.

Then I saw a mushroom cloud going up into the atmosphere. It was terrifying, and I knew so many people were going to die from the nuclear missiles and bombs that were going off. I was so sad and scared.

Suddenly, I was out on the sea and under the water, where I saw men inside a submarine. I watched as they shot a nuclear missile. It was a torpedo that traveled some distance and then exploded under the water.

Afterwards, I was shown the faces of the men in the submarine. There was great fear in their eyes. They were afraid they were going to die.

I looked at the shoreline and the ocean started moving back away from the shore. Then it went forward as a massive tidal wave; a tsunami going towards the shore.

I saw people on the shore who were playing along the beach. They were unaware of the tsunami that was coming towards them. They didn't have time to get up to higher ground.

The power of the tidal wave knocked all of them off their feet. I saw them drowning in the water.

Then I saw missiles continuing to be launched from everywhere. I observed intercontinental ballistic missiles going up into space and coming back into the Earth's atmosphere. They were landing and exploding, releasing all their deadly energy and radiation upon their target.

I was then shown people who were standing in line to get food. All of them were afraid and very sad. No one was smiling. They seemed to be in shock.

There was very little food to eat. There was now a terrible famine on the Earth.

I witnessed wealthy people dressed in nice clothing in the line. I was made to know there were even well-educated people in line; doctors, lawyers, etc. In other places, I saw people standing on corners begging for food and water.

The war continued. I was shown an image of President Xi and Kim Jong-Un, dressed in military uniforms, and was informed that China and North Korea were involved in the war.

I also saw churches that were set on fire and burned to the ground. I saw people tearing down steeples and crosses off of buildings.

Bibles and Christian books were burned. People were celebrating this destruction in the streets.

I really don't have the words to tell you about what happened next. I was taken up, in the spirit, above the Earth and in the twinkling of an eye the blue sky in front of me split in two, as if a veil slid apart. I realized that I was being transported into heaven.

It was a sunny day, yet there was no sun in the sky. It was God's presence illuminating the sky of heaven.

Then I looked up, and over to my left I saw, in the distance, a giant wall of white clouds, just like the ones you see on Earth which sometimes develop into a massive thunderstorm. The clouds were bright white, and suddenly they split open and began rolling back into the shape of a giant scroll, and from the center of that scroll emerged a single white horse with a rider on it.

I saw the rider on the horse and instantly I knew who it was. It was Jesus! He was coming on the clouds, heading towards me, riding down to the Earth at a forty-five-degree angle. He had brilliant, shoulder-length white hair and a white beard and when I looked into his eyes, I saw flames of fire.

On his head were many gold crowns. His brow was furrowed, and he was very focused. It became clear to me that He was prepared to go to war.

As he got nearer, I saw His face so clearly. He then turned the horse to his right, and he was now within four feet of me. I was now looking at the left side of his face and body and I saw that something was written on his left leg: "King of Kings and Lord of Lords."

The Lord continued past me and made His way down towards

the Earth. I was so grateful that God, the Father, allowed me to see Jesus up close.

As He passed, I also saw that He was wearing a white undergarment with a gold sash. Over that, he had a red robe on, the color of blood. The wind was causing the robe to come up in the back and it looked like a cape.

Then God had me look back up at the clouds in heaven from which Jesus had come, and I saw a great multitude of people gathering to come down to the Earth. They were dressed in brilliant white garments and they, too, were all sitting on white horses. They began lining up, from both sides of the clouds, into formation. People, as far back as I could see, were gathering to get ready to ride down to the Earth.

This was the bride of Christ; people who had been saved over the years, who had passed on to heaven or been raptured up to heaven. These people who had once lived on the Earth were from every tribe, tongue, and nation.

They started coming towards me, riding down on their horses. They were following Jesus, and I suddenly realized that the millennial reign of Christ was about to begin.

Armies from all over the world were coming towards Israel; towards Jerusalem, to the battle at Armageddon, to fight against Jesus. I was being permitted to see the Second Coming of Jesus Christ.

While up in heaven, I got to see Jesus coming down to the Earth, riding on a white horse, to fight at the battle of Armageddon. The armies, from all over the world, had gathered in Israel, near Jerusalem, to make war with Him.

As Jesus rode down to the Earth, He caused everyone on the battlefield who opposed Him to die. Then the ground instantly turned blood red in color.

While I was still high up in the sky looking down on the Earth, I saw this massive lake forming. The ground, which had been dry before, was now a lake of blood.

After seeing that, I looked up and there were large birds circling in the sky. I heard an angel call them to come and eat the flesh of those who had died on the battlefield.

I looked back down, at the lake of blood, and it was now starting to recede. I saw crusty, blood-colored ground as the lake dried up.

Bodies and carcasses of horses were being exposed. Birds were coming to feed on them. I can't even begin to describe to you how big the lake of blood was and what I saw.

Then I was told that Jesus, after slaying the armies of the nations, had left the battlefield and gone to Jerusalem to set up His kingdom. The millennium was going to begin. I was full of joy knowing that Jesus was back on the Earth and that He was going to reign.

It was several days after the vision occurred, when the Lord revealed to me that I had been taken up to heaven to see what the apostle John wrote about in Revelation 19:11-21.

Christ on a White Horse

11 I saw heaven standing open and there before me was a white horse, whose rider is called Faithful and True. With justice he judges and wages war. His eyes are like blazing fire, and on his head are many crowns. He has a name written on him that no one knows but he himself. He is dressed in a robe dipped in blood, and his name is the Word of God. The armies of heaven were following him, riding on white horses and dressed in fine linen, white and clean. Coming out of his mouth is a sharp sword with which to strike down the nations. "He will rule them with an iron scepter." He treads the winepress of the fury of the wrath of God Almighty. On his robe and on his thigh he has this name written: king of kings and lord of lords.

And I saw an angel standing in the sun, who cried in a loud voice to all the birds flying in midair, "Come, gather together for the great supper of God, so that you may eat the flesh of kings, generals, and the mighty, of horses and their riders, and the flesh of all people, free and slave, great and small."

Then I saw the beast and the kings of the earth and their armies gathered together to wage war against the rider on the horse and his army. But the beast was captured, and with it the false prophet who had performed the signs on its behalf. With these signs he had deluded those who had received the mark of the beast and worshiped its image. The two of them were thrown alive into the fiery lake of burning sulfur. The rest were killed with the sword coming out of the mouth of the rider on the horse, and all the birds gorged themselves on their flesh.

I want to comment about what is written in Revelation 19:11-21. For this is what I was shown in the vision when I saw the Second Coming of Christ.

Like the apostle John, I was taken up to heaven, in the spirit. I saw heaven open up to me. I was shown the Second Coming of Christ.

Jesus and a large group of others were across from me, up higher in the sky, on some large white clouds. As the clouds parted like a scroll, I saw Jesus on a white horse. On his head were many crowns.

I saw Jesus with His red robe on, just as John described it. Like John says, in verse 14, I saw a great multitude of people, all riding white horses and dressed in white linen. They were lining up behind Jesus, preparing to follow Him down to the Earth.

The white linen, worn by the bride of Christ, represents their purity. Their sins have been forgiven. Though once they were stained like crimson from their past sins, they now have been washed as white as snow.

The red robe that Jesus wore represents either His blood that was shed on the cross, or it may represent the blood of his enemies. Perhaps it is a combination of both.

In verse 16, John said Jesus had written on His robe and thigh—King of Kings and Lord of Lords. God allowed me to see those exact words written on Jesus' thigh and robe, just as John said they were.

I was able to hear the angel standing in the sun above the Earth, as recorded in verse 17 and 18. He was calling the birds to come eat the flesh of all those who were on the battlefield.

I saw the armies gathered on the battlefield, as mentioned in verse 19. I was not allowed to see the beast and false prophet, as John did, as recorded in verse 20. I was told that they were defeated and that Jesus was now on His way to Jerusalem, to set up His millennial Kingdom.

♦♦♦

One of the reasons that I believe God took me up to heaven was to increase the faith of Christ's followers in the inerrancy of the Scriptures. As God lives, I have seen Jesus alive. What is written in the Bible is absolutely true.

I must boldly tell everyone now that John told the truth about what he had written in the scriptures. I have witnessed with my own eyes what he recorded in Revelation 19, and it is exactly as he said it was. I can further testify that the writers of the gospels were telling the truth when they said that Jesus rose from the dead.

I saw Jesus coming on the clouds, just as He said that He would. He is risen.

CHAPTER 9

The Shroud of Turin: Is It Jesus' Burial Cloth?

Three weeks went by after I had the magnificent vision where I got to see Jesus. Then the Lord spoke to me again on Saturday morning, June 19, 2021.

I was up early, sitting on the couch and having a cup of coffee. Out of nowhere, the Lord said to me, "Ken, get on your computer and do a search for the Shroud of Turin."

I obeyed the Lord and opened my laptop to do the search. Up popped a website with the URL shroud.com.

I opened the page. What I saw startled me and caused me to drop my laptop onto the couch. I saw the face of Jesus. It was the same face that I had seen in the vision when He came towards me riding on the horse.

I immediately started talking to God. I said, "Lord, it is you."

Then He said to me, "Ken, it is me. This is my face and body. I have preserved my burial cloth all of these years. I said that in the last days, knowledge would increase on the Earth. Technology has now increased to the point where I have allowed images of my face and body to be produced."

The Lord was referring to Daniel 12:4:

> *But as for you, Daniel, conceal these words and seal up the book until the end of time; many will go back and forth, and knowledge will increase.*

The Lord continued, "I have done this because the end is now coming. I want all people to be able to see that I really came to the Earth. I was crucified, buried, and rose from the dead to pay the penalty for their sins. I want all to repent and no one to perish. Ken, warn the world, as Noah did, that I am soon returning for my church to take her home. Warn the nations that I will bring my wrath on all the wicked people who are left behind, who have rejected me and my offer of salvation."

It was breathtaking, hearing the Lord speak so clearly. He wanted everyone to know that He had allowed his burial cloth to be preserved, all of these years, to be a great witness of Him in the last days—to both the saved and the lost.

The world has been divided over whether the burial cloth, called the Shroud of Turin, is authentic or not. If it is authentic, is it the burial cloth of Jesus?

A great deal of research was conducted on the shroud in 1978 in what was called the Shroud of Turin Research Project (STURP).

You can view the results of the STURP project by going to: shroud.com/78exam.htm.[6]

After all tests were completed, some of those who were involved in the study thought the cloth was the one placed on Jesus. Others remained convinced that it was a hoax and not the burial cloth of

Christ. It was reported that carbon 14 testing dated it to the thirteenth or fourteenth century A.D.

Over the years, because of the carbon 14 dating, I always thought the shroud was a fake. I never paid any attention to the Shroud because some people thought it was a phony.

More recent carbon 14 testing dates the shroud to between 100 B.C. and 100 A.D.(CBNNEWS.COM 04-23-22 New Scientific Test Dates Shroud of Turin to the Time of Christ's Death)[7]

The Lord continued to speak to me. He said, "Ken, the Shroud of Turin is real. My burial cloth will now bless those who are my followers. They can see that what is written in their Bible is true. They can use the images of my face and body to witness to the lost before I take them home. Those who are lost will get to see my face and body and know of the price I paid to redeem them from the penalty of their sins. They will see how much I suffered for them. I will give the lost a little more time to repent and call on me to save them before the seven-year tribulation begins. Ken, go and share this message, these miracles, and my image with the nations."

Three weeks earlier, the Lord had taken me up to heaven and I got to see the face of Jesus. However, I had no way of showing His face to the world so that others could also see what He looked like. Now, three weeks later, God had me view the Shroud of Turin and He showed me that the image on this burial cloth was indeed the face of Jesus.

As you view Jesus' burial cloth, you will see how severely the Roman soldiers scourged him over the entire length of His body. I can't begin to imagine how much the Lord suffered to pay the penalty of my sins.

Look at these photos of the Shroud of Turin.

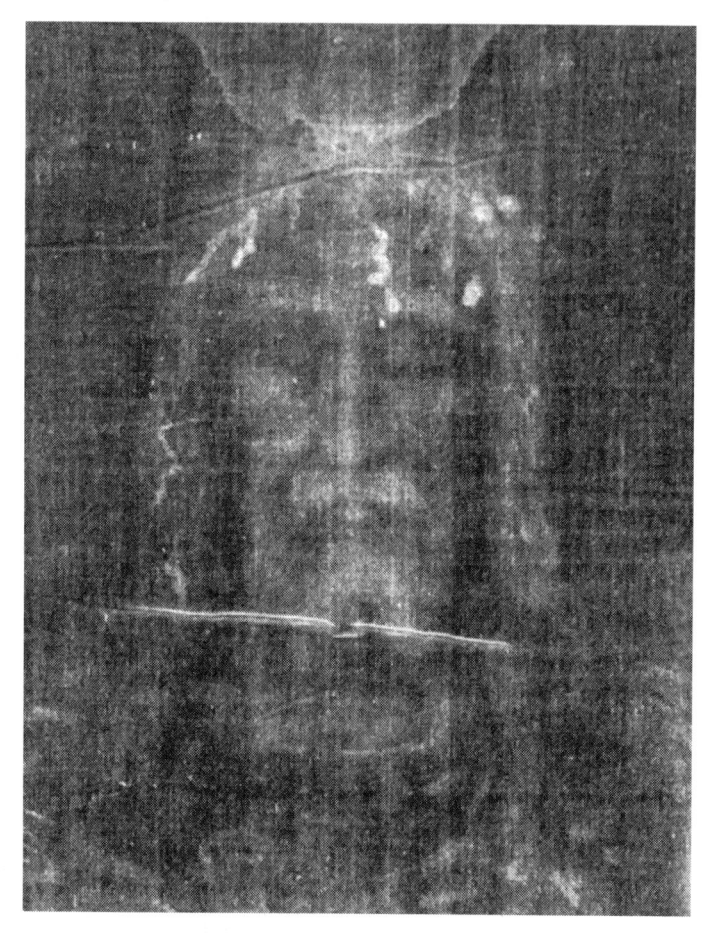

©1978 Barrie M. Schwortz Collection, STERA, Inc.

The white line you see, going across Jesus' chin is a fold in his burial cloth. The white color you see in His hair, is dried blood from the crown of thorns that was placed on his head.

THE SHROUD OF TURIN: IS IT JESUS' BURIAL CLOTH? 111

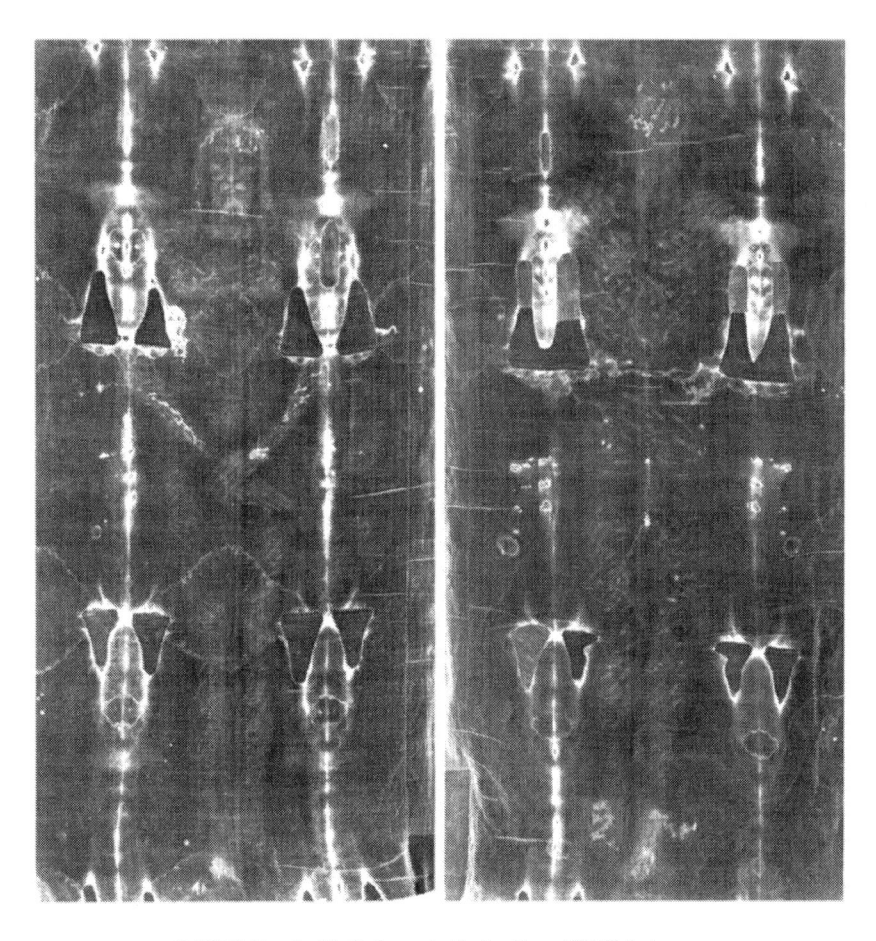

©1978 Barrie M. Schwortz Collection, STERA, Inc.

The photo on the left is the front side of Jesus' body. The photo on the right is the backside of His body. See the dumbbell shaped marks on his body from being whipped by the soldiers.

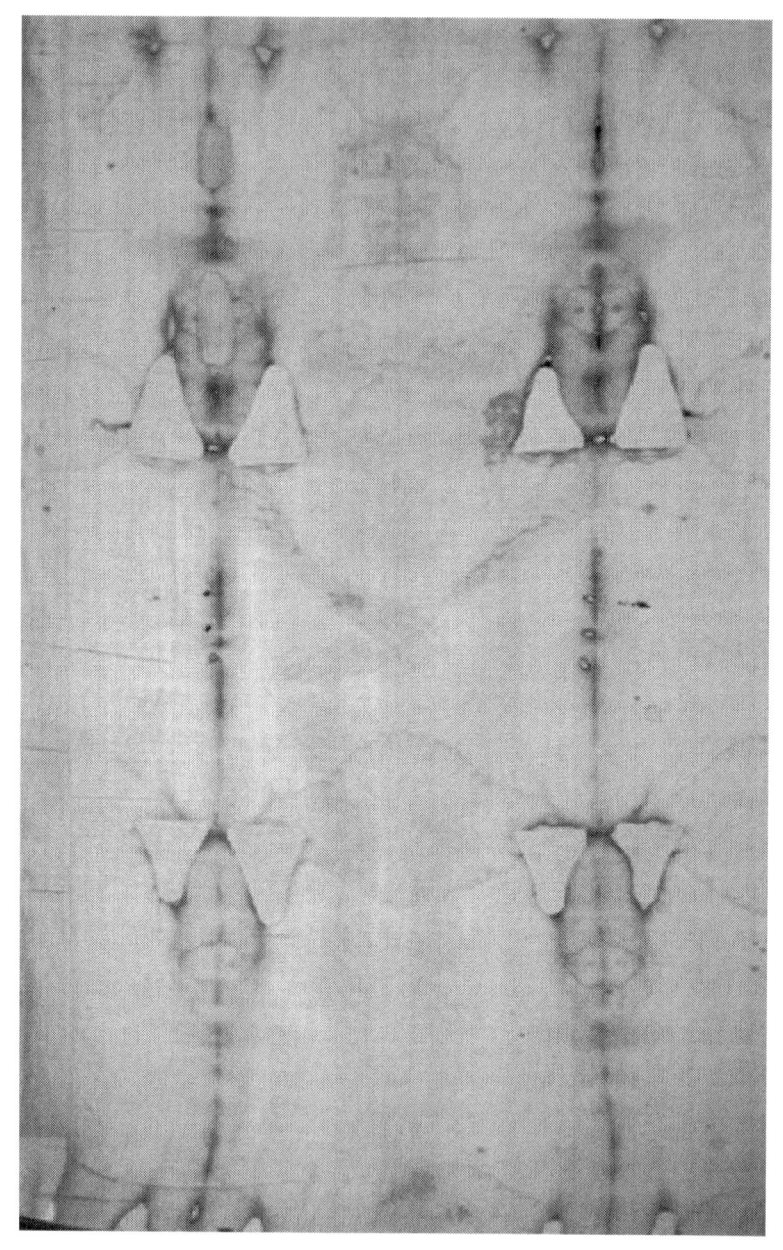

©1978 Barrie M. Schwortz Collection, STERA, Inc.

This is the view of the Shroud of Turin with the natural eye.

Just as some critics doubt the authenticity of the Shroud, some people also don't believe what I say about Jesus' burial cloth and the vision I had that was related to it. Some people say, "This vision can't be real. Ken, you haven't been taken up to heaven like the apostle John and the apostle Paul were. You didn't really see Jesus."

Yes, *I was* taken in the spirit up to heaven. God wanted me to see Jesus alive and coming back to the Earth to set up His millennial reign. He wanted me to serve as a modern-day witness to share this message with all the people in the world, that Jesus is alive and will one day come and rule on the Earth.

In Revelation 4:1-2, Jesus calls John up to heaven.

> *After this I looked, and there before me was a door standing open in heaven. And the voice I had first heard speaking to me like a trumpet said, "Come up here, and I will show you what must take place after this." At once I was in the Spirit, and there before me was a throne in heaven with someone sitting on it."*

In II Corinthians 12:1-4, Paul writes in third person about the time he was taken up into heaven.

> *"I must go on boasting. Although there is nothing to be gained, I will go on to visions and revelations from the Lord. I know a man in Christ who fourteen years ago was caught up to the third heaven. Whether it was in the body or out of the body I do not know—God knows. And I know that this man—whether in the body or apart from the body I do not know, but God knows—was caught up to paradise and heard inexpressible things, things that no one is permitted to tell."*

Look at Hebrews 13:8:

> *Jesus Christ is the same yesterday and today and forever.*

♦♦♦

What Jesus did for John and Paul He chose to do for me. For you see, He is still doing miracles today as He did when these men were on the Earth.

Jesus took me up to heaven and I was able to see His face and body. Then He told me that the Shroud of Turin is His burial cloth and to share this information with the world.

(You can view the precious face and body of Jesus, as it appears on His burial cloth, on numerous websites. I want to encourage you to visit shroud.com or shroudphotos.com.)

God used Noah to warn the world He was going to bring His judgment upon the Earth. He has asked me to warn people that He is now going to bring His wrath against wicked people who have rejected His Son, and bring an end to life on Earth as we know it today.

The Lord is proclaiming an urgent warning to everyone, in all the nations, that *the end is now coming*. Anyone who rejects God's unbelievable offer of a pardon for the penalty of their sins will incur the wrath of God.

God desires that no one would perish and that all of us would come to repentance. Sadly, most people will reject Christ and think that they have lived a good enough life to get into heaven.

You can view the video that I made of this vision. It was posted on YouTube on May 30, 2021, on my YouTube channel—Ken Bailey Ministries. This was nine months prior to Russia attacking Ukraine.

You can also find it on my website: kenbaileyministries.com. Click on the videos tab and select the video titled "My Supernatural Vision from God of the Death of America and the Second Coming of Jesus Christ."

To everyone in the world, the Lord warns you: "Repent, for the Kingdom of Heaven is at hand."

Repent of your sins and cry out to God to save you before it is too late.

Jesus is coming soon to take His followers home to heaven. Will you depart the Earth with Him or will you be left behind and experience His wrath during the terrible tribulation that follows?

CHAPTER 10

God's Urgent Warning to the Church—Part I

The Lord began to give me the messages to the church in July of 2015, when I was invited by the ministry, International Commission, to go on a mission trip to Brazil. I agreed to go, and I was asked to be the speaker at the final crusade gathering.

Upon arriving in Brazil, we partnered with a group of local churches and took the gospel to the slums of Sao Paulo. The mission trip was a huge success. There were well over 1,000 people who called on the Lord to save them.

On the final night of the trip, nineteen churches gathered to celebrate the conclusion of our evangelical outreach. We shared stories of all that God had done in the churches and communities over the previous days.

While I prepared for the sermon, the Lord began to give me messages for the churches. Yes, I was to congratulate everyone on a great crusade, and I did. However, the Lord had so much more for me to share with all of the pastors, staff, and church members who attended that evening service.

He wanted me to challenge them to continue the emphasis on evangelism that had taken place in the crusade. Instead of this being the end of the outreach, the Lord wanted it to be the beginning; for it to continue after those of us, from other countries, left Brazil.

The Lord had me challenge everyone in attendance about how we conduct church services. He rebuked the practice of rigidly following the program as written in the bulletin. The Lord told me, "Ask the pastors why they sing three or four songs, take the offering, and do a thirty-minute sermon each week?"

The Lord said, "Ask them, who told them to conduct church services that way?"

God has spoken to me, many times, in an angry voice and said, "I am the Lord God Almighty, I will not be put on a clock or limited by people. Tell the pastors to stop deciding, in advance, how long a church service will last.

"If church leaders do not allow my Spirit to have total control of the service, then they will have powerless services. I am Almighty God and I will never be controlled by their clocks or computer programs!"

◆◆◆

The Lord wants to have "free reign" in every service. He wants every part of the church service to be led by the Spirit. In some services, the Spirit might want to have people sing five songs instead of three. The Spirit, at times, may have the pastor's sermon go for more than an hour. There might be services when the pastor, as led by the Spirit, just has a time of singing, prayer, a scripture reading, and no sermon.

The Lord is not pleased that church services are so programmed and time-driven. There is little or no room for the Holy Spirit to touch hearts and lead people to repent, confess their sins, and be born again.

You may not be aware of this, but many churches are now running their services by way of a software program, where they set a time that is allowed for each part of the service. They literally program the service and require that each person who is involved adhere to the amount of time that is allocated for their portion of the service.

For example: five minutes may be given for the welcome and opening announcements. There may be four minutes given for a time of prayer by an elder or deacon. The worship director may be told that they have fifteen minutes for their worship songs.

There may be some special music or time for the offering, which lasts a couple of minutes. The pastor may be told to keep his sermon to about twenty-five minutes or less. Sadly, it is now considered to be normal to not have a closing invitation or altar call.

All of this is done to keep the service to an hour to an hour and fifteen minutes in length each Sunday. There is no time or flexibility to allow the Holy Spirit to have control of the entire service.

As a result, we have powerless churches where seldom anyone is born again. We see few people come to the altar and repenting of their sins. The power of the Holy Spirit is quenched by programming every part of the service and limiting the length of the service.

The Lord reminded me that on Pentecost, Peter went up on the Temple Mount and shared the gospel with those who were there. Many people were convicted by the Spirit of their sins, and they asked Peter what they should do.

In the first official church service, Peter told those in attendance what God would have them do. He gave the people a chance to respond to the Holy Spirit, who was convicting them of their sins and calling them to repent and be born again.

Peter told them, "Repent and call upon the name of the Lord and you will be saved."

He also told them they would receive the Holy Spirit and that they were to be baptized. Over 3,000 people responded to Peter's message, and they were baptized the same day.

Imagine how long that first service took. Luke only recorded some of it. He goes on to say that Peter warned them, with many other words, and pleaded with them to be saved from this corrupt generation. Imagine how much time it took to baptize 3,000 people that day.

Don't you just wish that you could have been there, on the temple mount, and witnessed all that took place? I do.

♦♦♦

The Last Days Church

Over the past several years, The Lord has continued to speak to me, to emphasize to pastors the need to have church services that are led by the Spirit. He told me that we are the last days church and that our churches should look and operate like the early church. He said, "The church today should look like the church did in the Book of Acts."

He went on to tell me that we are now living in II Acts. We are now experiencing the final Acts of the Holy Spirit before the Rapture of the Church and the time of the gentiles comes to an end. We now have the second outpouring of the Holy Spirit, in the church age, to come against the greatest demonic warfare in history.

I'm not talking about Acts chapter 2. The Lord coined the phrase II Acts, and gave it to me. We have all the Holy Spirit power that the early church did. We should be turning our world upside down, just as the men and women mentioned in the early church did, as recorded in the Book of Acts.

The Lord is saying that as the people of God, we, who are blessed to be the last generation of the church prior to the Rapture, have a very important mission. We are to finish the work of taking the gospel to the nations.

The Lord has told me that He has an opinion of every church in the world that claims His name, just as He described the condition of the churches in the book of Revelation in chapters 2 and 3. The Lord knows what is happening in every church in the world.

He is pleased with some churches. These are the churches that are outwardly focused on reaching their communities with the gospel. They have powerful sermons preached from their pulpits that call for repentance from sin, faith in the gospel, and costly discipleship.

In these churches, everything is led by the Holy Spirit. People serve each other in humility and share the gospel with others. Christ is exalted and the Scriptures are taught without compromise.

In these congregations, discipleship is emphasized. New believers are mentored, and they are discipled in Bible studies that meet weekly at the church building and in homes, coffee shops, and other places.

They break bread together, study the Word of God, and fellowship with one another. They make prayer and evangelism an important priority. There is great joy in these gatherings, and that is what helped the early church to grow so quickly.

> Acts 2:46-47
> *Every day they continued to meet together in the temple courts. They broke bread in their homes and ate together with glad and sincere hearts, praising God and enjoying the favor of all the people. And the Lord added to their number daily those who were being saved."*

If at all possible, you need to be a part of a small group that meets weekly. God never intended for you to live the Christian life alone. In these weekly gatherings, you become a family and you do life with a group of people who know you and love you.

They are there to celebrate with you during the joyful events that take place in your life. They are there to comfort you and walk with you when a crisis occurs in your life.

This is the Church. It is broken people; converted sinners, who come together and love and minister to each other for a lifetime.

There is nothing more beautiful than to see the church in action. There are weddings, baby showers, graduation services, and school activities to attend. There are food pantries, pro-life pregnancy centers, and homeless shelters to serve in. There are opportunities to serve as a volunteer at church or in a Celebrate Recovery or at a Moms of Preschoolers gathering.

There are churches who are investing in mission work. They have members going on mission trips to share the gospel locally, regionally, and in foreign lands.

They are doing projects in their communities where they demonstrate their love for their neighbors—building playgrounds, operating food banks, and renovating homes. They help widows, orphans, and the poor in their town and around the world by providing them with food, shelter, clothing, and financial assistance.

These Christ followers are not concerned about how long a church service lasts or how much time they give each week in serving the Lord. For them, Christ is their life. They love Him, and each other, with all their heart.

Don't you want to attend a church like this? Perhaps your church looks like the church did in the Book of Acts, for that is what the Lord desires for the last days church.

If I just described the church you attend, go out of your way to thank your pastor and church leadership. Let them know that you appreciate them. In today's culture, it takes a tremendous amount of courage to stand boldly and proclaim the gospel and preach the full counsel of God.

♦♦♦

The Lord spoke to me about "LEFTOVER CHRISTIANITY"

In His messages to the church, God started telling me about the changes that He wanted to see in His followers. He is done with casual Christianity. The Lord told me He is tired of "Leftover Christianity."

Many of us simply give the Lord some of our leftover time, money, and worship. The Lord is upset that so many, who claimed to be His followers, give Him five minutes a day of their time. He said that we have other gods before Him. We have other idols that are greater priorities in our lives.

He said, "You spend your money on the pleasures of this world and give Me very little for My Kingdom's work. On some days, you spend no time with Me, the God of the Universe. You just don't make Me a priority in your busy lives. Oh, you've got time for your hobbies, watching TV, movies, social media, entertainment, music, and chatting with your friends. You are watching or going to your favorite sporting event, but you have little or no time for me.

"Have I not commanded you that you shall have no other gods before me? Yet, you have forsaken me for your idols. They are your false gods.

"Repent and turn back to me. Make Me your first love and the priority of your life. I alone am worthy of your worship."

◆◆◆

We must be honest with ourselves. For most of us, Almighty God is simply not a priority in our lives. He does not have first place in everything that we do. Friend, God wants that to change.

We are really saying, "Sorry God, I just can't fit you into the schedule. Maybe next week I'll have more time for you."

Over the years, the Lord has told me repeatedly, "Ken, tell them I want first place in their lives. I do not want their leftovers. I'm sick of getting their leftover time, leftover money, leftover worship. They have chosen their idols of pleasure, entertainment, and money, over me."

◆◆◆

How the world now views the church:

The world thinks that the modern-day church has nothing to offer them. They don't see a need to waste an hour on Sunday morning going to a building where nothing miraculous is happening, no power is being shown, or anything exciting is occurring.

The world says, "I work with you Monday through Friday and you don't seem to be any different than I am. I look at your life and I don't see any great joy or power. You talk each week about sports, shopping, a movie you saw, and your kids. You are just like me and I don't even go to your church on Sunday."

If we are honest with God and ourselves, our critics are telling the truth. The church now appears to be very similar to our culture. Most church services are powerless and seem programmed to entertain us. Only in a few churches that I have visited, or attended in my lifetime, have I seen much Holy Spirit power.

Here's what some church attendees would say about many church services today, if they gave an honest answer: "Don't you dare think about singing more than four songs and the pastor's sermon better not go longer than about twenty-five or thirty minutes. After all, we've got to get to the restaurants before the other churches get there or we will have to wait in line."

Or we might hear this: "Hey, the pastor needs to wrap up this sermon. The game comes on in a little while and I don't want to miss any of it."

Really, if we are honest, this is what happens on Sunday morning each week at so many churches in America. We are not burdened for the lost. We are not coming with a pure heart to worship the Lord in Spirit and in truth.

Today, many church services appear to be planned to not offend anybody; that we dare not talk about hell and sin. You seldom hear a pastor call people to repent or turn from their sins, even though Jesus said, "Repent and believe the gospel."

In America and western civilization, a church service has now become a place where you sing a few songs, put a couple of dollars in the offering plate, and hear a feel-good sermon each Sunday morning. Then you check off the spiritual box on your "to do list" and live for yourself the rest of the week. You go back next Sunday and do the same thing again.

Friend, this is not Biblical Christianity. This is not what happened in the book of Acts.

Sadly, we have embraced *Comfortable Christianity* over *Costly Discipleship*! Many of us are attempting to make life on Earth a playground when, for the true follower of Christ, it is to be a battleground for the souls of men and women; boys and girls.

We are supposed to be carrying out the *Great Commission*. Instead, we are living out the *Great Omission*. Most of us have not the slightest concern for the eternal destination of those who live next door to us, work with us, or go to school with us.

We are more concerned on Sunday about what we are having for lunch or what time our favorite sports team plays that afternoon. We spend too much of our "free time" watching TV, being entertained on our computers or tablets, texting, and talking on our phones. We plan where we are going out to eat, what movie we are going to see, what sporting event we are going to watch, or game we are going to attend. I could go on and on, but you get it.

The Great Commission, as found in Matthew 28:19-20:

> *Therefore go and make disciples of all nations, baptizing them in the name of the Father and of the Son and of the Holy Spirit, and teaching them to obey everything I have commanded you. And surely I am with you always, to the very end of the age.*

Worldwide, the church is not carrying out the *Great Commission*. We want to be comfortable, not persecuted like the early church was.

Most people who claim to be Christians are not taking the gospel to the nations. According to recent polls, only a small percentage of people who claim to be Christ followers ever share their faith with someone. Few so-called believers ever invite another person to attend church.

The heart of the early church was to evangelize to the lost. In Acts 2:46-47 we read:

> *Every day they continued to meet together in the temple courts. They broke bread in their homes and ate together with glad and sincere hearts, praising God and enjoying the favor of all the people. And the Lord added to their number daily those who were being saved.*

Look at Acts 4:29-31:

> *Now, Lord, consider their threats and enable your servants to speak your word with great boldness. Stretch out your hand to heal and perform signs and wonders through the name of your holy servant Jesus. After they prayed, the place where they were meeting was shaken. And they were all filled with the Holy Spirit and spoke the word of God boldly.*

What word did they want to speak with boldness? THE GOSPEL. These early believers, who had been with Christ, wanted to boldly fulfill the *Great Commission* and share the gospel with power. They wanted Abba Father to confirm the truths they were sharing with signs, wonders, and miracles. God heard their prayers and gave them all that they asked for.

Today, there is such apathy in sharing the gospel among many of those who name Christ as their Savior. Most churches aren't adding believers to their congregation. In fact, many churches report that they don't have even one person who is saved and baptized over the course of an entire year. How tragic.

We are trying to make our lives "heaven on earth." We are trying to live the "American Dream," where we have a large, luxurious home and two new vehicles in the garage.

We want a lot of money in our bank accounts, and we're working hard to be able to retire early. We want to live perfect, painless, comfortable lives.

God has told me that, "The 'American Dream' is straight from hell. Satan wants you to pursue materialism and comfort."

As Jesus says in the Bible, "You cannot serve both God and money."

The Lord has declared that we are to turn away from the temporary pleasures of this world and get into the battle. It is a battle for the souls and eternal destinations of our family members, friends, and other people that He brings into our sphere of influence.

Look at Jesus' words in Mark 8:34-35:

> *Then he called the crowd to him along with his disciples and said: "Whoever wants to be my disciple must deny themselves and take up their cross and follow me. For whoever wants to save their life will lose it, but whoever loses their life, for me and for the gospel, will save it."*

Church, God has called us to deny ourselves in this lifetime. We're to surrender our lives to Him and be living sacrifices as we allow the Lord to accomplish His purposes in us and through us.

That is not what we are doing. Instead, we have the attitude of, "I'll work God in there, on Sunday, for an hour or so, but the rest of the week belongs to me."

Look at Acts 1:8:

> *But you will receive power when the Holy Spirit comes on you; and you will be my witnesses in Jerusalem, and in all Judea and Samaria, and to the ends of the earth.*

Power to do what? We receive power to go and be His bold witnesses, sharing the gospel in all nations, as we fulfill the *Great Commission*.

❖❖❖

Honestly, many of us are not going to invite anyone to church in the coming week or share the gospel with a neighbor, a friend at work, or a friend at school. "No way buddy. They might think we are weird or radical."

I want to ask you a question, and I am asking it in a spirit of love. How many people have you shared Christ with in your lifetime?

Did that hurt to read that—being asked if you are sharing Christ? If you are not sharing Christ with others, something is wrong. You see, people really are going to eternal destinations when their life on earth is over. Heaven and hell are real places.

Are we burdened for lost souls, like Jesus and the men and women of the early church were? The gospel is good news. In fact, it is great news. As true believers, why wouldn't we be excited to share the gospel with the lost?

Did you know that many people that you work with, go to school with, or who live near you would come to church if you would just invite them? Some would hear the gospel and come under the conviction of the Holy Spirit. Some of them would be saved.

The sin of the desert is knowing where water is and refusing to tell others. The sin of the Christian is knowing where living water is and refusing to tell others.

The person who is lost in the desert and never finds water will die physically. This is the first death. The person who is lost in this world and never finds living water will die spiritually. This is the second death.

We have the cure for what the lost are dying from. We have the gospel; the good news that people can have eternal life if they repent of their sins and place their faith in Jesus' atoning death, burial, and resurrection that paid the penalty for their sins.

Can you imagine the impact that we would have in our communities if we shared the living water that we have found? We must go out and rescue those who are depressed, suicidal, and drowning in their sins. What would happen if some of these people came to church and we ministered to them and told them that Jesus loves them?

We can tell people that Christ can deliver them from their addictions and sins. What if we gave them a chance to confess their sins and receive prayer for healing in our church services, home groups, or on the street somewhere in the city?

We can turn our city upside down. We can lead countless people to Christ.

I pray that you are actively sharing your faith with others, and that you are serving the Lord with the talents that He has given you in a church where you live. If you aren't, now would be a great time to start doing it. Your life can impact so many people when you serve God and others.

CHAPTER 11

God's Urgent Warning to the Church—Part II

CONFESSION

In February of 2020, the Lord spoke to me one day. He said, "Ken, I say what I mean and I mean what I say. I meant what I said in James 5:16:

> *"herefore confess your sins to each other and pray for each other so that you may be healed. The prayer of a righteous person is powerful and effective.*

He said, "I want my followers to confess their sins to each other and pray for one another and be healed. I want the lost to be able to confess their sins and be healed, and also be saved."

This is not happening in most congregations.

◆◆◆

The Lord actually wants us to have an accountability partner or mentor, where we can tell a person that we trust about what we are struggling with so that they can pray for us to overcome our sins and be healed. The Lord wants us to be discipled and then He wants us to go and make disciples. He wants us to mentor others.

Do you have a spiritual mentor in your life? Do you have someone that you are mentoring? Are you discipling anyone?

On a regular basis, there ought to be an opportunity at a church service for people to have elders who anoint the sick with oil and pray for the healing of people, just as the scriptures tell us to do.

Have you ever seen this in the churches you have attended? Have you ever witnessed the sick being prayed for by the elders or by church members who have the spiritual gift of healing? God wants this to be done, as it is written in scripture.

The Lord has given believers different spiritual gifts, and these gifts should be used during most services or at the end of the service to minister to one another. We are not allowing believers to exercise the use of their spiritual gifts when we come together in corporate worship or in small groups.

For some reason, the modern church does not always practice what is written in the scriptures. We talk about having a time of prayer in church, saying, "My house will be a house of prayer."

Yet there is very little prayer in our church services.

Sometimes, we have prayer meetings on Wednesday night, but few churches have prayer meetings on Sunday morning or a time of prayer during the service so that those in attendance can actually pray. I'm talking about the church service having several minutes or more where every believer in the church is praying either individually at their seat or at the altar which is open for some to go and pray there. Other people are free to form prayer circles, where up to twelve people circle up and are praying together.

On a much smaller scale, hearing many people praying out loud at the same time sounds like what happens in heaven, as prayers are coming into the throne room from all over the world. It is special to experience it and hear powerful prayers being fervently lifted up to the Lord all over the church.

The lost who are in attendance are not compelled to pray. They can just sit quietly while believers pray.

I have held prayer time like this in some churches I have pastored. People love it. They are allowed to participate in the service instead of just sitting there and only having a deacon, elder, or pastor pray each Sunday.

Sadly, I guess we just don't want to have this extended time of prayer because it may "inconvenience church attendees" and have the service last longer than an hour. Some people might not come back, and we can't let that happen, right?

Shame on us. Christ came and died a brutal death on the cross after receiving a scourging that would have killed many other men, and we don't have time for a longer church service. We don't have time for prayer.

We have gone astray. We are not willing to give much of our time to worship our Savior—Jesus Christ. We are not coming in brokenness to Him and praying and fasting for revival. We are not praying fervently for the lost and praying for each other. No, there's just not time for that in our busy lives.

The early church spent hours together in prayer. Each time they gathered, praying together was a huge priority for them. And their prayers were so powerful that at times, the building shook where they were gathered together in prayer.

As Christians, we really are a family of believers. We should want to spend time with each other. After all, we're going to spend eternity together.

I can remember hearing about churches from long ago who spent the entire day together. They weren't in a hurry on Sunday to get an hour-long service done and go home.

These churches had pastors who would make time on Sunday morning to let church members share with each other about prayers that had been answered by God. Others shared miracles that God had done in their lives or in the lives of someone they knew. They had a time of testifying in the service.

We need to have "Testify Time," where a few believers can share about answered prayers and powerful things that God has done. This strengthens the faith of the members of the church and it lets people participate in the service.

Can you imagine the impact that it would have on a visitor or a lost person who attended church and listened during testify time? They would hear about our awesome God, who is answering the prayers of those that He died for. They would learn of miracles that had taken place. They would experience a church that had Holy Spirit power.

Testify time doesn't have to be incorporated into the service each week. It could be done once a month or on the fifth Sunday of a month. It would make a huge difference in the lives of those who attend that church.

◆◆◆

The Early Church expected to be persecuted!

Today, most people don't live dangerous lives or pray dangerous prayers like the early church did. We don't want to go to a hostile foreign land and share the gospel. We know that we could possibly be killed if we did.

There were numerous martyrs in the early church. These believers knew that there was a definite possibility that they, or someone they knew, might be put to death for sharing their faith. This was accepted as part of the price you might have to pay for being a follower of Christ.

They prayed for a boldness to share the gospel, no matter what it cost them. They prayed dangerous prayers. Today we mostly pray safe prayers and don't go to dangerous countries. We don't want to take the risk of possibly being martyred for Christ.

◆◆◆

What is being preached from the pulpits is of Great Importance.

Just a few hundred years ago, it was common to hear sermons being preached by pastors who were filled with the Fire of the Holy Spirit. There were men who were calling people to repent of their sins and to live righteous, holy lives.

What happened to all the Spirit-filled pastors who roared like lions from their pulpits? There aren't very many in America and other countries today.

I thank God for the ones that we still have who are filled with Holy Spirit Fire. They are few in number, but they give me hope that America still has a remnant of pastors who won't compromise on teaching the full counsel of God.

I am sad to report that in most pulpits today, we hear feel-good sermons that rarely challenge people to repent or to deny themselves and take up their cross and follow Christ. We have pastors who don't want to offend anyone in their messages. They are afraid that people might leave and go attend church somewhere else.

Some pastors are afraid that people might take their tithe or offering to another church. They won't risk that happening. Instead, they choose to preach gentle, loving messages each Sunday. They won't dare risk teaching about sin, hell, repentance, or the wrath of God.

God wants end time Bible prophecy to be preached from the pulpits of America and all other nations. He wants pastors to proclaim that the wrath of God is soon going to be poured out upon the Earth.

Unfortunately, there are many pastors who won't teach on prophecy. Some have told me, "Ken, I just don't know much about it, or I just don't feel comfortable preaching on that."

Others have told me, "You know, people have been saying that the end is coming, or Jesus is returning soon, for two thousand years and we're still here. I'm not sure what I think about the rapture or tribulation. I figure it will just all pan out and we'll be okay."

Since we are living in the last days before the return of Christ, pastors should be teaching Bible prophecy. If your pastor is, let him know that you appreciate it. If he isn't, encourage him to.

Teaching on last days prophetic passages of scripture reminds all of us of the urgency we should feel to share the gospel with the lost. Time is running out.

As lawlessness, violence, and great sexual immorality spread across the nations, the Lord wants pastors to proclaim that the *end is now coming*. He desires that pastors tell people to repent of their sins and to believe the gospel before it is too late.

Sadly, I must tell you that most of America's pulpits are no longer aflame. Overall, America is no longer as good as she used to be. In fact, America is now under the judgment of God. America is on her way to her death.

I love America. I am sad to see what our nation has become.

I see signs in yards all over the area where I live that say, "I miss the America that I grew up in."

So do I. I bet you do too.

◆◆◆

Judgment has now come to America and to the Nations!

Judgment has now come to America. It has also come to churches across the world. The Bible says that judgment begins in the House of God.

I Peter 4:17

"For it is time for judgment to begin with God's household; and if it begins with us, what will the outcome be for those who do not obey the gospel of God?"

The Lord has told me that He wants to return for a pure church; a pure bride. God said that He is going to purify His bride before He takes her home.

Over the past few years, God has been exposing the secret sins of church leaders. As you watch or read the news, you hear of pastors having to resign for being caught in sexually immoral activities. Others have been caught stealing money from the church. How tragic that this is so common in churches today.

The Lord told me on March 1, 2020, that He was going to expose all secret sin. He said, "What you cover up and try to hide, I will reveal and humiliate you. What you confess to me, and repent from, I will forgive and cover your iniquity and heal you."

Sexual sins committed by pastors, worship leaders, and Christian music artists have begun to be exposed and reported on in the news. Many men have been forced to resign and have lost their ministries or careers. God is exposing all secret sin.

❖❖❖

When is the Lord going to return?

THE END IS NOW COMING. The capital letters are intentional. That is an awfully strong statement to make, isn't it?

I write this because the Lord spoke to me on March 6, 2020. I had spent time in prayer that morning, and just as I was about to get up from kneeling in prayer, the Lord began to speak to me. He said, "Ken, do you know Matthew 24:14?"

I said, "Lord, I know it."

He then said, "Say it to me."

I then quoted Matthew 24:14 to the Lord: "And this gospel of the kingdom will be preached, in the whole world, as a testimony to all nations and then the end will come."

Then the Lord said to me, "Ken, the gospel of the kingdom *IS NOW* being preached, in all the world, as a witness to all the nations, and Ken (He paused for a moment for a dramatic effect, and then said), *THE END IS NOW COMING.*"

I was stunned. Here I was, a servant of the Lord, who He calls a prophet, being told by the Lord that the end of the church age was now coming; that the end of life on Earth, as people know it today, was going to come to a sudden end.

The Lord said, "Ken, tell the nations that the end is now coming. Just as Noah told the world, in His day, that I was going to flood the Earth and destroy the wicked, I want you to warn the world that the end is coming, and I am going to bring my wrath upon the Earth once again.

"All, who will not repent of their sins and believe the gospel will suffer my wrath. Ken, warn the nations until I take you home."

◆◆◆

I was shocked at getting this prophetic message from the Lord. You have to remember, this was before Covid lockdowns, church closures, school lockdowns, and businesses closing and going bankrupt. I got this message before vaccine mandates and the deaths of millions of people around the world.

To the true followers of Jesus Christ, who are born of the Spirit of God, you have now been told that your time on Earth is coming to an end. This is you, my friend. You are being told, by Almighty God, that the Church age is almost over.

What will you do now? How will you live, and what will your priorities be, in the time that you have left on Earth?

You are the fig tree generation that Jesus talked about in the gospels. The nation of Israel was born on May 14, 1948. Jesus said, when you see the fig tree (the nation of Israel) be established, this will be the final generation of believers before He returns to take His church home. He is going to Rapture His bride, all born again believers, before He brings His wrath upon the earth.

The fig tree, as mentioned in the Bible, always represents the nation of Israel. Look at Matthew 24:32-34:

> *Now learn this lesson from the fig tree: As soon as its twigs get tender and its leaves come out, you know that summer is near. Even so, when you see all these things, you know that it is near, right at the door. Truly I tell you, this generation will certainly not pass away until all these things have happened.*

Jesus said there would be all kinds of signs to confirm to us that we are living in the last days before His return. You can read about these signs in Matthew 24, Mark 13, Luke 21, II Timothy 3, Daniel, Ezekiel, and many other places in the Bible.

He said conditions on the Earth would be like the days of Noah and Lot; that we would see great violence and sexual immorality on the Earth. As you look at world news, is there any doubt in your mind that there has been a great increase in violence and immorality in society? We have defund the police movements. We have great lawlessness in the streets of America and other nations of the world.

We have drag queens in the schools and the LGBTQ+ groups in the schools and churches teaching young children about sex and pushing their propaganda and beliefs on them. There is sexually explicit material in school libraries and classrooms.

I must also mention the pornography that is on the internet, in movies, and on the phones of young people today. Porn is widely accepted now, with little push back against it.

Look at the mass shooting incidents in America and around the world. Demon-possessed people are going into schools, churches, malls, theaters, grocery stores, and other places to gun down innocent people. There is rage, violence, and murder in the streets of many countries.

People live in great fear now. Any place that you venture into, outside of your home, is a place where you have the potential to be murdered. What has happened to our world? What is the church saying about it; doing about it?

We have wars going on around the world. We hear rumors and stories of wars getting ready to begin in other nations. We hear about a New World Order or Global Reset that is being implemented in many nations.

People are living in fear everywhere. Many Christians are afraid and crying out to God to take them to heaven.

♦♦♦

Christians want to be raptured right now.

As the world becomes more wicked and more violent, many Christ followers want to go home. They are waiting on the rapture of the church. Many have locked themselves in their homes and are just sitting around waiting for Jesus to come for them.

The Lord has spoken to me, and He says, "You want to go home, but I want you to go to the fields and take the gospel to the nations. The harvest is plentiful, but the laborers are few. Go share the gospel and harvest souls. When the harvest is complete, then the end will come.

"It is not time to go home yet. Let me find you laboring in the field when I return for you."

♦♦♦

LIVING FOR CHRIST IN THE LAST DAYS BEFORE THE RAPTURE

Many years ago, I decided that I didn't want to be a casual Christian. I decided that I would pursue God and see what happened in my life. Would I find Him? Would it be worth the price to follow the Lord in a costly commitment?

Over time, I have found the Father and Jesus. There is nothing that compares to them. Absolutely nothing.

I am now all in with God! I want nothing to do with this world.

When I was younger, I sought to make a name for myself. I sought to acquire college degrees and initials after my name. I sought the applause of men and women. I sought titles beside my name. It never fulfilled me.

Then I discovered the truth. I discovered the God of the Universe. I chased after Him and He said I would find Him if I sought Him with all of my heart. That's what I did.

He did not lie. I found Him. I found joy. I found the Jesus that men told us about in the Gospels, in the Bible, and in the book of Acts.

I found the real thing, and I turned away from the powerless ways of doing church and the traditions of men that are so often found in churches today.

You know what I am talking about; where people go to church, greet each other, sing a few songs, put a little money in the offering plate, and go home. After church, they talk about the place that they are going to go eat or what time the ballgame starts that afternoon.

They talk of how their local sports team did during the week; how their pro team or favorite college team did that week. They talk a lot about their kids and what they are doing.

These churchgoers then go home and live for themselves for the next six days and do the same thing again the following week when they come back to church. They rarely, if ever, tell anyone about repenting of their sins and the good news of what Jesus Christ did for them. They rarely invite anyone to come to church with them.

They have no power and there is little or no power in the church they attend. If they are honest, they would say that they are a member of a social club.

Friend, I left that church a long time ago. That is not the Christian life and not the true, powerful, world-changing church that Christ died for and established.

Go read the Book of Acts and then see if that looks like your life and your church that you attend. You see, your church and your life should look like the church and people found in the Book of Acts.

Right now, you and your church should be full of power. Paul said, in I Corinthians 4:20:

For the kingdom of God is not a matter of talk but of power.

So many churches today are full of talk coming from those in the pews and by the pastors in the pulpits. These churches talk a good game, but they have no power. These churches are not full of powerful, Spirit-filled people and pastors like they should be. They are not turning the world upside down.

I have tasted the real thing. My life, each day, is like the life that the believers lived in the book of Acts.

I am no better than any of you. I am a sinner saved by grace. However, I have chased after God and found the real thing.

My friend, you will never go back to "playing church" or just drifting through life after you have experienced God and the power of Him living in you and through you.

I am now blessed to walk in signs, wonders, and miracles as I seek to only live for Christ. I'll never be the same. I have been with Jesus, and that changes everything.

I'll never go back to the dead, powerless way of life that I used to live. I have already wasted so many years in pursuing the temporary, useless things of this world.

I beg you today to pursue the living, powerful God of the universe, and His Son—Jesus. You can walk with God in the power of His Spirit. You can walk in joy unspeakable.

You desperately need Holy Spirit power in these final days. The end is soon coming, and the world is plunging into darkness and growing more wicked by the day.

I am simply passing through this evil world. I have tasted the Living Water that Jesus promised to give to those who die to themselves each day and give their lives to Him. It is the best. It is Jesus Himself.

Greater evil and persecution will be coming against the church and all true Christ followers in the days ahead. Christians will be blamed for many things. They will be called homophobic, transphobic, haters, and many other names.

However, as this persecution occurs, God is going to bring about one final awakening; one final revival. Some will even call it the second Jesus Revolution; a Jesus Revival. Believers will have great joy as they see others coming to faith in Christ in the final hour of the church being on the Earth. This awakening and revival will occur even in the midst of great persecution against it.

God is going to give people one last chance to avoid the tribulation; to escape His coming wrath. Then He is going to rapture His followers from the Earth.

Knowing that the end is upon us, live with a sense of urgency. Share the gospel with your family, neighbors, and friends right now. You don't want to see any of them left behind.

The tribulation will be a death sentence for almost everyone. Satan, along with the antichrist and false prophet, will be ruling with an iron fist; killing those who oppose them. Even worse, God will be bringing His wrath upon mankind because of their wickedness.

It will be hell on Earth. Jesus said if He didn't return at the seven-year point, everyone would die.

Matthew 24:22:

If those days had not been cut short, no one would survive, but for the sake of the elect those days will be shortened.

Brothers and Sisters, don't waste the time that you have left. Serve Christ now. Let go of the things of this world and prepare to go to heaven.

You are as close to God as you want to be. Make the Lord and your relationship with Him the most important thing in your life.

Draw close to God in these evil last days. Read your Bible each day and pray often. Don't walk in fear. Instead, walk in faith and trust God to watch over you and your loved ones.

Worship God daily. Listen to Christian music and sing unto the Lord with your whole heart.

Attend church in person. The Lord commands us to do this if we are physically able.

Hebrews 10:24-25
And let us consider how we may spur one another on toward love and good deeds, not giving up meeting together, as some are in the habit of doing, but encouraging one another—and all the more as you see the Day approaching.

Watch or listen to messages from people who are walking with God and filled with His Spirit. Along with your Bible, they will encourage you and share God's truths with you.

Joyfully serve Christ until He takes you home. Finish your race, boldly proclaiming Christ to the lost. It won't be long now and you will be going home.

♦♦♦

My Prayer for you:

Father, we love you with all of our hearts. We are not of this world. We are yours. We are your chosen generation to be on the Earth as your fearless witnesses in these last days.

Give us the courage and strength to live for you. Help us to boldly take the gospel to the nations until you take us home. Maranatha—Come Lord Jesus. Amen.

CHAPTER 12

Beware of False Prophets

Over the course of time, there have been many false prophets on the Earth. They are men and women who claimed to speak on behalf of God, but they did not. Instead, they told people what they wanted to hear.

A false prophet will claim to have a message or teaching from God which is later found to not be true. They may also predict that a future event is going to take place and it does not.

The Bible contains many stories about false prophets. I will mention just a few passages of scriptures here. A complete study of false prophets and Bible passages pertaining to them would require me to write another book. For brevity's sake, let's look at a few scriptures and a few recent and current false prophets who are on the Earth today.

> Jeremiah 14:14
> *Then the Lord said to me, "The prophets are prophesying falsehood in My name. I have neither sent them nor commanded them nor*

spoken to them; they are prophesying to you a false vision, divination, futility and the deception of their own minds."

Jeremiah 23:16
Thus says the Lord of hosts, "Do not listen to the words of the prophets who are prophesying to you. They are leading you into futility. They speak a vision of their own imagination, not from the mouth of the Lord."

Jeremiah 23:21
I did not send these prophets, But they ran. I did not speak to them, but they prophesied.

It is very clear, after reading these scriptures, that throughout history there have been false prophets. That holds true today.

In just the past few decades, there have been evil people among us, like Jim Jones, who was the leader of the Peoples Temple. He was a false prophet who deceived many people into following him and moving to the South American country of Guyana. It was there, in 1978, that he was responsible for a mass murder-suicide of over 900 of his followers.

In 1993, David Koresh was the leader of the Branch Davidians, a religious group that lived in Waco, Texas. He believed he was the messiah. His beliefs led to a conflict with law enforcement. He died, along with his followers, when a fire broke out at the complex that the group was living in. Sadly, some of those who died were children. Jones was no savior.

Like Jones and Koresh, some false prophets go on to become cult leaders. These are usually men who prey on girls and young women. They seek to get women to join their commune. These leaders want to have as many sexual partners as possible. They often have many wives and will force minors to marry them.

Recently, we had some people who claimed to be prophets who prophesied about the outcome of the 2020 U.S. presidential election. They have been labeled "the Trump Prophets."

Some men and women prophesied that Donald Trump would serve two consecutive terms as president. They guaranteed it. Many said that God told them that Trump would be elected and be sworn into office in January of 2021.

When that didn't happen, it caused great harm to the Kingdom of God. There were news stories exposing the fact that these supposed Christian prophets, pastors, and church leaders proclaimed that Trump would again be elected as president. When he wasn't, people were hurt and wondered who they could trust to tell them the truth. Nonbelievers mocked the church and its leaders.

Very few of these so-called prophets ever apologized for being wrong about this. Instead, they doubled down that they were right and the election was stolen.

Some of the Trump Prophets desperately wanted former President Trump to be re-elected, knowing that he is pro-life, pro-Israel, pro Second Amendment, pro-America, and much more. Many of them meant well; all were wrong.

What happened? These men and women let the desires of their flesh cause them to proclaim that God told them that President Trump would be re-elected and continue in office.

Some talked about the great times that were coming for America. They told of the many conservative judges that would be appointed to the Supreme Court and federal courts. They talked of controlling the Congress and the Senate.

All of their prophesying was in vain. Some had good intentions, and may have even had a true word from God in years past, and were just wrong about the election. Others wanted to be in the limelight, on TV shows, radio, and podcasts.

They knew that the conservative TV hosts and social media

programs wanted to hear that Trump would be re-elected. Therefore, they felt compelled to give messages that their audiences wanted to hear, even if the messages weren't from God.

However, Trump was not allowed a second consecutive term as president. God's ways are higher than our ways. His plans at times run counter to what we think He ought to do. For reasons that only He knows fully, God did not allow former President Trump to continue in office.

One thing is for sure, the Lord allowed the Biden administration to come into office to fulfill His plans and to accomplish what is written in scripture. God is having men and women come into offices of leadership, across the globe, who He will use to bring about the fulfillment of Bible Prophecy.

If God has given a prophet a true word, it will come to pass no matter what comes against it, including election fraud. There are no excuses allowed.

Was there election fraud? The answer is yes. God has told me that cheating took place and that there was not election integrity in several states.

Here's the point. The prophet is to speak only the words that God gives to him. God knew that some elections were going to be stolen and He did not tell His prophets to guarantee that Trump would be sworn into office again in January of 2021.

I judge no one on this. God's word tells us what to believe.

Prophets in the Old Testament were to be put to death if their words that they prophesied did not come to pass.

Look at Deuteronomy 18:20-22

> ***20*** *But a prophet who presumes to speak in my name anything I have not commanded, or a prophet who speaks in the name of other gods, is to be put to death.*

You may say to yourselves, "How can we know when a message has not been spoken by the Lord?" If what a prophet proclaims in the name of the Lord does not take place or come true, that is a message the Lord has not spoken. That prophet has spoken presumptuously, so do not be alarmed.

That is the problem today. There are no severe consequences for the prophets who speak words that they claim are from God that don't come to pass. Instead, some just delete their videos or articles about prophecies that didn't occur and act like they never spoke a word that didn't happen. Then they go on to make their next prophetic claim.

False Prophets need to be called out on their false prophecies. They should repent and be extremely humbled about their wrongdoing. They should never profess to be a prophet again, and are disqualified for claiming to speak words from God that clearly were not.

Jesus said that you will recognize real and false prophets by the fruit that they bear.

Matthew 7:15-19
Watch out for false prophets. They come to you in sheep's clothing, but inwardly they are ferocious wolves. By their fruit you will recognize them. Do people pick grapes from thornbushes, or figs from thistles? Likewise, every good tree bears good fruit, but a bad tree bears bad fruit. A good tree cannot bear bad fruit, and a bad tree cannot bear good fruit. Every tree that does not bear good fruit is cut down and thrown into the fire. Thus, by their fruit you will recognize them.

Jesus tells us that a false prophet will pretend to be telling the truth and try to deceive us. The Lord tells us that their words and actions are fruit that will reveal to everyone who they really are.

Most false prophets are eager to be a prophet. They desire to be in the limelight and want to be adored by their followers.

They usually hold to the prosperity gospel, that God wants everyone to be rich and have their best life now. They are personally trying to become very wealthy and are often trying to sell you the latest message that they heard from God on how you can do what they tell you to do and you will be rich.

Most true prophets don't want to be a prophet. They want to serve God behind the scenes and not be in the public arena. They are not seeking to become a celebrity, or wealthy, or have a huge number of followers.

◆◆◆

Since we are absolutely living in the last days, before Jesus Christ comes to take His born-again followers home to heaven, we must be aware of the false prophets that are on the Earth today.

Some false prophets are in the church. Some are not affiliated with a church or a religious group.

The Lord desires that I mention a few men who oppose Him who are evil in His sight. There are many more that I could name, but that would require another book to be written.

One such man is Yuval Noah Harari. He was born in Israel and is a lecturer at Hebrew University. He is also a historian, philosopher, and author of several books, including his bestseller, *Sapiens: A Brief History of Humankind.*

Some people believe that Harari is a prophet, though he says he is not. He advises Bill Gates and many other global leaders. He is the top advisor to Klaus Schwab, head of the World Economic Forum (WEF) who wants to bring about a global reset; a new world order.

Harari is married to a man. He is very critical of Jesus and Christianity. He says he doesn't believe in a God who tells two men they shouldn't have sex with each other.

He attempts to mock God by saying, "We don't need some God in the clouds handing down tablets (Ten Commandments) because we've created our own cloud (internet cloud) and our own tablets (wireless, portable personal computers)."

Harari says, "All the stories about Jesus rising from the dead and being the Son of God, this is fake news. Humans are hackable animals and free will is over."

In another interview he said, "Humans are acquiring divine powers. We are upgrading humans into gods."

You can view videos of Harari making these statements I just shared with you, and many others, by simply going to YouTube and watching some of his videos.

He supports the use of artificial intelligence being planted into human beings and says our bodies can now be hacked to improve them, which is transhumanism. He believes that we can be as gods, have divine powers, and live forever.

Harari has been deceived by Satan. Don't let him deceive you.

Let's look at what the Lord says in Romans 1:18-32

> *The wrath of God is being revealed from heaven against all the godlessness and wickedness of people, who suppress the truth by their wickedness, since what may be known about God is plain to them, because God has made it plain to them. For since the creation of the world God's invisible qualities—his eternal power and divine nature—have been clearly seen, being understood from what has been made, so that people are without excuse.*
>
> *For although they knew God, they neither glorified him as God nor gave thanks to him, but their thinking became futile and their foolish hearts were darkened. Although they claimed to be wise, they became fools and exchanged the glory of the immortal God for images made to look like a mortal human being and birds and animals and reptiles.*

Therefore God gave them over in the sinful desires of their hearts to sexual impurity for the degrading of their bodies with one another. They exchanged the truth about God for a lie, and worshiped and served created things rather than the Creator—who is forever praised. Amen.

Because of this, God gave them over to shameful lusts. Even their women exchanged natural sexual relations for unnatural ones. In the same way the men also abandoned natural relations with women and were inflamed with lust for one another. Men committed shameful acts with other men, and received in themselves the due penalty for their error.

Furthermore, just as they did not think it worthwhile to retain the knowledge of God, so God gave them over to a depraved mind, so that they do what ought not to be done. They have become filled with every kind of wickedness, evil, greed and depravity. They are full of envy, murder, strife, deceit and malice. They are gossips, slanderers, God-haters, insolent, arrogant and boastful; they invent ways of doing evil; they disobey their parents; they have no understanding, no fidelity, no love, no mercy. Although they know God's righteous decree that those who do such things deserve death, they not only continue to do these very things but also approve of those who practice them.

The scriptures clearly describe what has happened to Harari and those who believe what he does. They have chosen to rebel against God. They do not want to come under His authority, and so the Lord has given them over to reap the consequences of their sinful actions.

Unless Harari, and others who agree with his beliefs, repent of their sins, they will one day be judged by God and sent to hell; a place of eternal torment. I pray that all of these people will repent and turn to Christ before it is too late.

◆◆◆

Another man to pay close attention to is the head of the Catholic Church—Pope Francis. Some say that he is a false prophet.

There are both Protestants and Catholics who have major issues with the beliefs that Pope Francis has. He has spoken in favor of a more lenient attitude towards sins, including homosexuality and abortion.

Many people are upset that he has not removed or punished priests who have been accused of sexual assaults. Some members of the clergy, who have been accused of immorality, have just been moved from one location and placed in another church.

Others say that Francis is advocating for a one world government and a one world religion. There is little doubt in their minds that the Pope is clearly trying to unite various religions, as he meets regularly with the leaders of Islam, Hinduism, and Judaism, telling them that we all worship the same God, which is not true.

He is also telling the nations that we face a great climate crisis, and that drastic action must be taken to rescue the earth from the harm being done to it by mankind. This demonstrates that Pope Francis is clearly being influenced by the World Economic Forum; a group that is openly pushing for a global reset new world order and they are trying to manufacture a so-called climate crisis to achieve their agenda.

There are some people who believe that Pope Francis is the last Pope of the Catholic Church, and that he is the False Prophet mentioned in the Bible. Let's look at Revelation 13:11-18.

> *Then I saw a second beast, coming out of the earth. It had two horns like a lamb, but it spoke like a dragon. It exercised all the authority of the first beast on its behalf, and made the earth and its inhabitants worship the first beast, whose fatal wound had been healed. And it performed great signs, even causing fire to come down from heaven to the earth in full view of the people. Because of the signs it was given power to perform on behalf of the first*

beast, it deceived the inhabitants of the earth. It ordered them to set up an image in honor of the beast who was wounded by the sword and yet lived. The second beast was given power to give breath to the image of the first beast, so that the image could speak and cause all who refused to worship the image to be killed. It also forced all people, great and small, rich and poor, free and slave, to receive a mark on their right hands or on their foreheads, so that they could not buy or sell unless they had the mark, which is the name of the beast or the number of its name.

This calls for wisdom. Let the person who has insight calculate the number of the beast, for it is the number of a man. That number is 666."

Pope Francis is an elderly man. If he is the false prophet that is mentioned in Revelation 13, then we are very close to the rapture of the church and the beginning of the seven-year tribulation.

Will there be one more Pope after Francis, and will that man be the false prophet? Only God knows. For now, keep an eye on Pope Francis and what he says and does.

◆◆◆

Comparing false prophets and true prophets

- A false prophet will make a prediction that doesn't come true. A true prophet will speak a message that he receives from God and it will always come to pass.

- A false prophet will constantly seek to be in the limelight and be popular. A true prophet does not desire to be famous or to be adored by others.

- A false prophet cares more about himself than he does about the message he shares. A true prophet knows that the message from God is the only thing that matters and that the messenger is insignificant. He is but a spokesperson for the one who matters—God.

- A false prophet does not desire that his followers read the scriptures; only that they believe his messages that he shares with them. A true prophet desires that everyone reads and obeys the words of God contained in the Bible. His messages never contradict the holy scriptures.

- A false prophet will not want to come under the authority of the Word of God. A true prophet knows that He is absolutely operating under the authority of God and the teachings of scripture.

- A false prophet will seek the approval and applause of men and women. A true prophet cares nothing about the approval and applause of men and women. He seeks only to be a servant of God and to seek only the Lord's approval. He will never compromise the message that God has given to him to speak to gain the approval of human beings.

- A false prophet is operating in the flesh and is usually living an immoral lifestyle. A true prophet is operating in the spirit and despises the flesh. He knows he must live a moral lifestyle in obedience to the commands of scripture or he will be disqualified and no longer be allowed to be a prophet of God.

- A false prophet seeks to become wealthy and manipulates his followers into supporting him by purchasing the merchandise that he sells. A true prophet of God cares nothing about material wealth. His only desire is to please God. He has turned his back on Earthly riches because he has found the treasure hidden in the field; the pearl of great price, and it is Jesus.

- A false prophet does not care if his predictions about the future come true or not. As long as he is obtaining fame and fortune, he is happy. A true prophet would rather die than to speak one word that is not from the Lord. He will remain silent unless he knows that the Lord has truly spoken to him and commanded him to share the message with others.

- A false prophet does not fear or believe in God. At times he will attempt to mock Him. A true prophet knows that he has had an encounter with God; he has been called by the Lord to be a prophet. He knows that God is not mocked, and he has a reverent fear of the Lord and lives to only please Him.

❖❖❖

Jesus said that in the last days that there would be many false prophets on the Earth.

Matthew 24:11
And many false prophets will appear and deceive many people.

As we approach the end, beware of these false prophets. They are sent by Satan to deceive you. If you study your Bible and are being led by the Spirit who lives within all born-again Christians, you will know who is telling you the truth and who is lying to you.

CHAPTER 13

Does God Have Any True Prophets Today?

Does God still speak through men today? Did the last of the true prophets end in the first century after Christ died?

Some people say prophets ceased to exist at the end of the first century. There are those who also believe in the cessation of the spiritual gifts; that signs, wonders, and miracles also ceased around 100 A.D.

Other people say, "Since we now have the New Testament, we have the complete Word of God and there are no longer any prophets. Anyone who says that they are a prophet is a false prophet. God doesn't speak through them anymore. He sent Jesus and the days of the prophets are over."

Let me pause here and ask you some questions. Do you believe that God has prophets today?

Do you believe that the Bible is the true Word of God? If you do, then you must believe that Hebrews 13:8 is true.

"Jesus Christ is the same yesterday and today and forever."

You cannot pick and choose what part of God's Holy Word that you want to believe. You can't say, "This ended here; that doesn't apply anymore."

You believe and apply all of the Word of God or none of it. You can't pick the parts of the Bible that you believe and ignore the scriptures that you don't believe.

Do you understand that Jesus is the same yesterday, today, and forever? He had prophets in the past, as found in the Old Testament. He established prophets for the church in the New Testament, as recorded in Ephesians 4:11:

> *So, Christ himself gave the apostles, the prophets, the evangelists, the pastors and teachers.*

God had Paul record, here in the scriptures, that Jesus has put prophets on the Earth for the church. Though it is a rare, spiritual gift, the Lord has some true prophets today.

◆◆◆

Here are a couple of examples that I think can help demonstrate the fact that there has always been truth and counterfeits of truth.

The U.S. $100 bill is the most coveted piece of paper money in the world. It is also the most counterfeited currency.

There is an authentic U.S. $100 bill. There must be a real one for there to be a fake one.

There is Jesus, the authentic Christ, and there is the counterfeit, who God calls the Antichrist.

The same holds true with prophets. Though there are certainly many false prophets in the world today there are a few authentic prophets. There are people that God has literally chosen and called to be a prophetic voice for Him.

Why does God still have prophets on the Earth today? What purpose do they serve?

God will sometimes use a prophet to bring a message of encouragement to a church or individual. He will have a prophet praise a congregation of believers who are serving the Lord, pursuing holiness, teaching correct doctrines, sending out missionaries, and funding evangelism to the nations.

Sometimes, the Lord has a prophet bring a message of correction. A church or individual may be teaching false doctrines or leading people astray, and a rebuke from the Lord is given to them.

At times, the Lord will have a prophet tell of a future event that will take place. He may also warn of Bible prophecies that will soon come to pass.

God may also have a true prophet warn of false prophets who are on the Earth and warn people of the lies they are telling. The Lord doesn't want His children to be deceived.

Let's look at some New Testament prophets.

Acts 11:27-28
During this time some prophets came down from Jerusalem to Antioch. One of them, named Agabus, stood up and through the Spirit predicted that a severe famine would spread over the entire Roman world.

Acts 21:10-11
After we had been there a number of days, a prophet named Agabus came down from Judea. Coming over to us, he took Paul's belt, tied his own hands and feet with it and said, "The Holy Spirit says, 'In this way the Jewish leaders in Jerusalem will bind the owner of this belt and will hand him over to the Gentiles.' "

As you can clearly see, God used Agabus, and other prophets who were with him, to bring messages to people long after Jesus had ascended to heaven.

You might be surprised to learn that the Lord will have prophets on the Earth even after Christians are raptured. Do you know the story of the two witnesses found in Revelation chapter 11? The Lord calls them prophets.

Revelation 11:3-12
And I will appoint my two witnesses, and they will prophesy for 1,260 days, clothed in sackcloth." They are "the two olive trees" and the two lampstands, and "they stand before the Lord of the earth." If anyone tries to harm them, fire comes from their mouths and devours their enemies. This is how anyone who wants to harm them must die. They have power to shut up the heavens so that it will not rain during the time they are prophesying; and they have power to turn the waters into blood and to strike the earth with every kind of plague as often as they want.

Now when they have finished their testimony, the beast that comes up from the Abyss will attack them, and overpower and kill them. Their bodies will lie in the public square of the great city—which is figuratively called Sodom and Egypt—where also their Lord was crucified. 9 For three and a half days some from every people, tribe, language and nation will gaze on their bodies and refuse them burial. The inhabitants of the earth will gloat over them and will celebrate by sending each other gifts, because these two prophets had tormented those who live on the earth.

But after the three and a half days the breath of life from God entered them, and they stood on their feet, and terror struck those who saw them. Then they heard a loud voice from heaven saying to them, "Come up here." And they went up to heaven in a cloud, while their enemies looked on.

Who are they? Many Bible scholars believe that one of these men will be the prophet Elijah. They believe the other prophet will be either Enoch or Moses.

In the past, this prophecy was hard for people to believe. It was impossible for the whole world to know what was happening as it was happening.

This passage of scripture states that for three and a half days, people from all over the world will be able to gaze upon the bodies of these two prophets and celebrate that they are now dead. Yet, as I said in an earlier chapter, God told the prophet Daniel that in the last days knowledge would increase.

That is exactly what is happening. With the advent of the internet, computers, tablets, satellites, and nine billion cell phones, it is now possible to view news from around the world as it is live streamed to the nations.

Wouldn't you like to see the faces of people when God raises these prophets from the dead and takes them up to heaven? These men are your brothers in Christ, and they overcome the enemy by the power of God.

I can't wait to meet them. They will have incredible stories to share of all that God did through them as they served Him during this time.

What are some other reasons that God continues to speak through His prophets? The Lord still has prophets on the Earth because He is not done speaking.

> Matthew 4:4
> *Jesus answered, "It is written: 'Man shall not live on bread alone, but on every word that comes from the mouth of God.'"*

Words continue to be spoken by God. He is giving messages to His prophets to share with the people on Earth today.

The Lord may also speak to you. Perhaps you have heard His voice before. Have you heard His still, small voice?

Once again, look at John 10:27 (King James Version):

My sheep hear my voice, and I know them, and they follow me.

If you are a Christian, you should be hearing His voice. Your pastor should be hearing His voice.

Some pastors openly declare to their congregations that there are no longer any true prophets on the Earth who speak words from God. Sadly, I have heard some pastors say, "If you want to hear God's voice, pick up your King James Bible and read it out loud."

You can be sure that a pastor like that is not hearing from God. He doesn't believe that you can.

How tragic. He is missing out on hearing from the Lord, who still speaks. Those who attend the congregation that he pastors are being misled.

Almighty God has sent the Holy Spirit to all believers to dwell within them. The Spirit is still speaking. Don't believe the lie that you can't hear from God.

John 14:16-17, 26
"And I will ask the Father, and he will give you another advocate to help you and be with you forever—the Spirit of truth. The world cannot accept him, because it neither sees him nor knows him. But you know him, for he lives with you and will be in you."

Verse 26
"But the Advocate, the Holy Spirit, whom the Father will send in my name, will teach you all things and will remind you of everything I have said to you."

How does the Holy Spirit teach you and remind you of the words of Jesus? He speaks to you through your mind. He teaches you the meaning of a passage of scripture that you might be struggling with.

The Spirit speaks to you when He prompts you to go share the gospel with another person. You feel a nudge to tell them about Jesus. At other times, you may have heard the the Spirit whisper to you to go feed or help a homeless person or someone in need.

There is much that could be written about the Holy Spirit. Does He live within you?

◆◆◆

As a servant of the Lord, I would rather die than to bring harm to God's Kingdom. I have to admit that I have even asked God to kill me if I utter one word that is not from Him.

I would never choose to be a prophet. However, God has called me to be a prophetic voice for Him. I will serve Him until He takes me home, no matter how much I am mocked and persecuted.

As with the Old Testament prophets, there is much hate and rejection that comes to true prophets today, even from people who say they are Christ followers. They say that anyone who claims to be a prophet is a false prophet.

I am not lying when I say that the Lord has chosen me to walk in signs, wonders, and miracles. I have experienced so much of this, and there are witnesses that have been with me when some of these have occurred.

All the credit, honor, and glory go to the Lord. He has caused all of them to happen in my life and I stand in awe of who He is.

> John 7:18
> *Whoever speaks on their own does so to gain personal glory, but he who seeks the glory of the one who sent him is a man of truth; there is nothing false about him.*

I seek no personal glory. I don't deserve any. All of the miracles and visions have come from God; no credit to me.

I seek the glory of Jesus Christ, not my own personal glory. I seek to be a voice of Truth for God. I do not want there to be anything false about me, whether written or spoken.

Galatians 1:20
I assure you before God that what I am writing to you is no lie.

Like the Apostle Paul, I am telling you the same thing in this book. I can assure you that I am not making anything up. The stories I share of miracles and visions have actually happened.

I seek to point people to Jesus, not to me. I have died to myself and now live only for Christ.

Most true prophets don't want to be a prophet. They argue with God and try to convince Him that He has chosen the wrong person.

Prophets that are truly called by God know that they are going to be rejected and hated by the world. They know that they are being called to a life of suffering and perhaps even death.

As God lives, I tell you the truth, the Lord still has some prophets on the Earth today. If you don't believe this to be true, *and it is*, then you will not be willing to believe the messages that I am going to share with you in the coming chapters.

This is why the Lord has had me share my life story with you and the miracles that He has done for me, to give you proof that He has asked me to be His servant, His prophet, in these last days.

Look at what the Apostle John said in John 21:24:

This is the disciple who testifies to these things and who wrote them down. We know that his testimony is true.

Just as John testified about himself that the words that he recorded in the book of John are true, I am doing the same thing. I testify that the miracles, visions, and messages that are written in this book have really happened. The Lord did it all. He deserves all the glory.

CHAPTER 14

God's Urgent Warning to the Nations

"Repent for the Kingdom of Heaven is at hand."

You might think that seems like a strange way of beginning a new chapter in a book. I agree with you.

They're not my words. They belong to Jesus. He told me to put them there.

It doesn't matter what nation you are living in, this chapter contains God's urgent, loving message to you. The Lord wants you to know that: *The End is Now Coming*.

The end of what? The end of life on Earth as we know it today. The end of everyday life in your country.

The most important message that the Lord wants you to know, in these last days, is that you must be born again; born of the Spirit to escape His coming wrath.

That is why He warns you to repent, for the Kingdom of Heaven is at hand. If you are not saved, you need to believe the gospel and repent of your sins . . . ***right now***. Choosing not to do this will result in you being left behind when all of the Christians in the world are suddenly taken home to heaven (raptured).

My friend, you don't want to be left behind. Being left behind to live during the seven-year tribulation will almost certainly lead to your death. In fact, you may die during the rapture.

It is quite possible that thousands, if not millions, of people are going to die at the moment of the rapture or just afterwards. Think of all the accidents and collisions that are going to occur in every nation.

People who are Christians will suddenly vanish; those who were flying planes, working as air traffic controllers, controlling trains, guiding ships, and driving cars, trucks, and buses. I won't take time to list all the numerous ways someone can die during the rapture.

Imagine the massive number of deaths caused by crash landings, collisions, and other catastrophes that result from these people disappearing. Think about being on an airplane with four hundred other people and both pilots suddenly disappear. There is no other pilot on the aircraft to save the people. After a few minutes of horror, the plane crashes into the Earth and everyone is killed.

This is just one of the many scenarios that will take place at the rapture; the vanishing of millions of people. My heart breaks for those who will be left behind; who will suffer and die.

If you somehow survive the rapture event, here is some of what you are going to experience. I must tell you the devastating truth. Most people who enter the tribulation will die at some point during this time.

The world will plunge into chaos. Life on Earth is going to be a living hell. It will be every man or woman for himself. People will fight each other to the death for food and clean water. Others will fight each other for a car, truck, or motorcycle in order to be able to travel. There will be daily fighting over fuel, matches, flashlights, housing, phones, chargers, electricity, and on and on.

Guess who they will be fighting against? Evil, unrepentant people who God left behind to experience His wrath. They will be people who do not have the willingness to love others and have compassion on people during a crisis. There will be many individuals who do not hesitate to commit murder, rape, and other acts of great violence.

Perhaps you are not a person who commits violence. You are a sinner who was not raptured, who never obeyed God's loving warning to turn from your sins and ask Him to forgive you and save you. You are a prodigal that never came home.

It won't matter then that you weren't violent in your lifetime. Other people are going to be violent towards you. You are going to suffer horribly, even if you can somehow remain alive for some of the seven years.

Imagine dealing with terrorists, mass murderers, gang members, and evil world leaders who care nothing about you. I don't need to describe all the terrifying crimes and violence that is going to take place.

Today, God is shaking the nations. He is shaking everything that can be shaken. He is warning you and everyone in the world that the end is near. The Lord is trying to get your attention.

Did God get your attention during the Covid crisis? Are you ready to listen to Him now? Obey Him? Place your faith in Him?

God is allowing Satan's deception to spread across the Earth before the tribulation begins. He is allowing certain leaders to come into power to help bring about the reign of the New World Order (NWO).

The Lord is permitting laws to be passed that take away your freedoms and prepare the world for a dictator; an antichrist. Corporations are working with governments, the UN, the World Economic Forum (WEF), and others to implement a cashless society, environmental social governance (ESG), and push an agenda to prevent a supposed global climate crisis.

It gets worse. Corporations are now developing an individual carbon footprint tracker. Their use will be mandated by your government, and they will eventually tell you where you can travel, how you can travel, and what you can eat. You may not be allowed to travel at all.

As this tyrannical government approaches, know this: you don't have to be on planet Earth and go through all of this.

> Mark 1:15
> *"The time has come," he said. "The kingdom of God has come near. Repent and believe the good news!"*

The Lord says to you, "Time is up. The final countdown has begun for the rapture to occur and the tribulation to begin."

It is a minute until midnight; with midnight being the return of Jesus for His followers. It is 11:59 p.m. on God's prophetic clock.

You may not want to hear this. However, it is the truth. Ready or not, Jesus is coming very soon.

Here's the good news—the gospel. I Corinthians 15:1-4

> *Now, brothers and sisters, I want to remind you of the gospel I preached to you, which you received and on which you have taken your stand. By this gospel you are saved, if you hold firmly to the word I preached to you. Otherwise, you have believed in vain.*
>
> *For what I received I passed on to you as of first importance: that Christ died for our sins according to the Scriptures, that he was buried, that he was raised on the third day according to the Scriptures.*

Christians who have turned from their sins and placed their faith in Jesus' death, burial, and resurrection to pay the penalty for their sins will be given the gift of eternal life. They will be rescued by Jesus before God pours His wrath out on the Earth.

The wicked people who are left behind, who rejected the pardon He offered to them through the death of His Son, will experience God's judgment.

Look at these verses that explain how Jesus will take His followers to heaven before the tribulation begins; a time of great suffering, misery, and death.

> I Corinthians 15:51-52
> *Listen, I tell you a mystery: We will not all sleep (die), but we will all be changed— in a flash, in the twinkling of an eye, at the last trumpet. For the trumpet will sound, the dead will be raised imperishable, and we will be changed.*

> I Thessalonians 4:16-18
> *For the Lord himself will come down from heaven, with a loud command, with the voice of the archangel and with the trumpet call of God, and the dead in Christ will rise first. After that, we who are still alive and are left will be caught up together with them (raptured) in the clouds to meet the Lord in the air. And so we will be with the Lord forever. Therefore encourage one another with these words.*

If you are not a Christ follower, you might say, "I don't believe these verses from the Bible. This is never going to happen."

I want you to know something. *It is going to happen!*

The words contained in the Bible are all true. You refuse to believe the scriptures at your own peril.

God has asked me to write this book to try to persuade you to believe His Words, as recorded in the Bible. God has called me to be a voice of truth to you and tell you what is coming. He has told me to deliver this message to you.

I, and other Christ followers like me, are trying to rescue you from perishing before we are taken home by Jesus. We are throwing you a lifeline on behalf of Almighty God, and warning you to get in the boat, like Noah and his family did when they were on the Earth.

Noah warned the people, the nations, that God was going to pour out his wrath and flood the Earth. He shared the message that God gave him, that people must repent and get on the Ark to escape God's wrath and remain alive. Instead of an ark (rescue boat), this time, God is sending His Son on a rescue mission; to bring His followers home to heaven.

The ark provided Noah and his family safety until God's wrath was complete and the flood was over. The rapture will provide God's adopted sons and daughters safety from His wrath; from having to go through Satan's evil reign on the Earth.

Here's what Jesus says to you:

Luke 13:3
I tell you, no! But unless you repent, you too will all perish.

Like Noah, I am sharing the messages that God has given me. The Lord has told me to warn you, and the rest of the world, that you must repent of your sins, believe the gospel, and be raptured to escape His coming wrath.

♦♦♦

Perhaps you are already a follower of Christ, but you might be thinking, "I don't believe the end is now coming. I think it might be another hundred years before Christ returns. People have been saying He's coming back for two thousand years."

It is true that since Christ left the Earth, people have thought they were living in the last days. Even the early church and apostles believed that Jesus could return in their lifetime.

However, there were still major prophecies that had to be fulfilled before Christ returned. The most important prophecy has taken place and it has started God's prophetic countdown.

What prophecy was it? Israel was born again. The Jews were reestablished as a nation on May 14, 1948.

Jesus said, in Matthew 24:32-34:

Now learn this lesson from the fig tree: As soon as its twigs get tender and its leaves come out, you know that summer is near. Even so, when you see all these things, you know that it is near, right at the door. Truly I tell you, this generation will certainly not pass away until all these things have happened.

Israel is referred to in the Bible as the fig tree. Jesus said when we see Israel being established again, we'll know that the end is near.

Israel became a nation in just one day. This fulfilled a prophecy that is found in Isaiah 66:8:

Who has ever heard of such things? Who has ever seen things like this? Can a country be born in a day or a nation be brought forth in a moment? Yet no sooner is Zion in labor than she gives birth to her children.

On May 14, 1948, U.S. President Harry Truman recognized Israel as a Jewish state. Israel became a nation in just one day, just as God prophesied that it would happen.

It is a great sign from God—the rebirth of Israel. Jesus said this generation will not pass away until all of the prophetic events that are mentioned in Matthew 24 are fulfilled.

The Lord has told me, and I quote Him, "This is it." This is the end.

He said, "After the Covid virus declines, people are going to think that life is going to go back to normal. Tell them that life is never going back to normal (the pre-Covid world)."

Instead of normal, war is coming to the nations. A one world government is coming. Most important of all—Jesus is coming!

Jesus said, "I am coming to rescue my followers and take them home. Then My Father will unleash His wrath upon the Earth."

Oh, how I pray that you heed God's warning.

♦♦♦

My friend, did you see how your government leaders and the globalists saw the opportunity and seized power in your nation during the Covid crisis? Even now, when conditions have improved, some of them refuse to let go of that power.

They have tasted the thrill that they got in getting to rule over you; much like a dictator. They now crave power and want to take over the world.

Do you really believe all that your power-hungry government officials are telling you? Do you think that they are telling you the entire truth and not withholding any information from you?

Do you believe what the mainstream media is reporting? Why is it that you can hear the same words coming out of the mouths of reporters no matter what network you are watching?

Are they being given a narrative that they must read and follow? You can watch videos on YouTube of many world leaders and reporters saying, "Build Back Better."

Your government has people working in it that are cooperating with the globalists to form the one world government. In the coming days, you are going to lose more of your freedoms. People will become slaves to the NWO.

At this moment, governments and corporations are working together to eliminate free speech. In the near future, you will not be allowed to speak out against them, just as the Chinese people are not allowed to speak out against their government.

Do you see that the spirit of Antichrist is rising on the Earth? Satan wants to rule the nations.

God warns you in the Bible that a time will come where an unholy Trinity will arise and come to power. The time is now approaching for Satan, the antichrist, and false prophet to take over the world.

God has begun to remove the restraining power of the Holy Spirit.

The Spirit has been holding back this evil force that longs to rule the nations.

Things are going to get much worse in the coming days. Evil is going to grow across the Earth.

There will be an increase in violence and riots in cities. The homicide rate is going to go up. There will be lawlessness in the streets and people will refuse to come under government authority.

Law enforcement officers will continue to be attacked. Some will be murdered.

Your government will continue lying to you. They have not been transparent with you about what they are doing and what they are planning for the future.

Elections will continue to be stolen in many nations. Though you may go and legally vote for the person who you want to see represent you and the people of your nation, there will likely be no election integrity in your country. Those in power often add illegal ballots, and they may not count your vote in order to steal upcoming elections.

What should you do? Keep voting but challenge your government leaders to make sure your elections are just and without corruption. Demand that the candidates that the people truly voted for are put into office.

God is warning you that your freedoms are being taken away from you. Soon, your government is going to be able to control your bank account through the use of Central Bank Digital Currencies (CBDCs). Globalists want to eliminate every nation's cash and coin system and create a one world currency—a digital currency.

In working to form the NWO, banks are getting ready to roll out CBDCs so that they can track every one of your financial transactions. CBDCs are dangerous. They are slavery.

Why? You will no longer be able to pay with cash or coins and keep your financial transactions private. Instead, the government will get to see every financial transaction that you make.

The globalists love CBDCs. They can't wait to rule over you and control your bank account.

They love the Chinese government, which is now pushing for the use of CBDCs. China is also working to get other nations to move away from the U.S. dollar as the world's reserve currency.

What can you do to stop the globalists and delay the use of CBDCs in your country? Pay with cash whenever you can. If a store tells you that they don't accept cash, tell them that you will go and shop at another store that does.

Inform your government leaders and local officials that you do not want CBDCs to be allowed in your country. Vote against them if you are given the opportunity.

If you want to learn more about the push for CBDCs, visit the website of the International Monetary Fund (IMF) at imf.org and the Bank of International Settlements (BIS) at bis.org.

The IMF and BIS want all nations to implement CBDCs. They also have policies in place that support the so-called climate crisis and the need to restrict emissions. They will be key players working with the U.S. Federal Reserve, UN, banks, and globalists to usher in the mandatory worldwide use of CBDCs. Digital currency is coming, but we can delay it by standing against it for now.

Globalists and organizations will tell you how convenient CBDCs are and all of the crime that can be prevented. However, once your nation goes cashless, it is only a matter of time before you will lose your freedoms. You will be enslaved. If you don't comply with everything the government tells you to do, they will freeze your bank account and they may even arrest you.

This is not a conspiracy theory. This is a fact.

We only need to look at the lifestyle of an ordinary Chinese citizen. The Chinese Communist Party (CCP) controls every aspect of their lives.

Citizens must take whatever vaccine or drug that the government tells them to, and they live in a nation that censors what they can see on the internet and on television. The Chinese government does not want them to know the truth about what is happening in the world.

The CCP leadership does not want people to worship Jesus Christ or read an authentic Bible. They are tearing down churches. For decades, they have been working to eliminate Christianity in China. They have even begun to print their own Bible translation that is edited to be favorable towards communism.

Their efforts have failed. The growth of Christianity through house churches in China has exploded. It is now estimated that there are 100 million Christians in the country.

The CCP has implemented a social credit system. You can achieve a good score if you obey everything that the government tells you to do. If you don't, your score will be lowered and you will have more restrictions placed on you. You won't be able to travel or get a job. You will be blacklisted as a bad person.

Chinese people have been enslaved by their oppressive government. President Xi Jinping now rules like a dictator.

Protesting against the government is not allowed. People who do are arrested and put in prison camps. While there, some are tortured and killed.

Does this sound like a world that you want to remain in; a world where you will be a slave to a one world government and its leader?

♦♦♦

The Bible tells us what life on planet Earth will be like in the future. Jesus said there will be wars and rumors of wars. Nation will rise against nation.

The Lord warns us that there will be lawlessness in these last days. There will be no respect for authority. There will be protests, riots, and great violence occurring in nations.

Does this look and sound like the world that you are now living in? Like conditions in your nation? It should because it is.

It used to be safe to go to church, the movie theater, or the grocery store. Not anymore.

We see reports in the news of the increase in violence and crime in America and other nations. It is becoming a very dangerous world.

God is warning you that wars that are mentioned in Bible prophecy that have not occurred yet are coming. The Lord is telling me that global conflicts are coming very soon. He says it will be much bigger than the Ukraine and Russia conflict, which is tragic. Think of the needless suffering and loss of human lives that this war has caused.

I pray that there will be a peace treaty soon and that this war will end. I can't imagine the pain and sorrow that the parents, family members, and friends are experiencing in the loss of their loved ones who have died.

Yet God, in His great mercy, is warning us ahead of time of what is to come. For believers, prophecy is not meant to scare us, but to prepare us for what is coming!

If you are a Christian, you should not be afraid of what is coming. You are not going to be here during the tribulation and reign of the unholy trinity. Jesus told you to look up when you see prophecy being fulfilled, for your redemption is drawing near.

Luke 21:28
When these things begin to take place, stand up and lift up your heads, because your redemption is drawing near.

If you are not a Christian, you should be terrified of what is coming! You are going to be here for it. If you haven't repented of your sins and placed your faith in Christ, you shouldn't be able to sleep at night, knowing of all the evil that you will have to deal with.

As a nonbeliever, you might think that I am trying to scare you.

You're darn right I am. If that is what it takes to get you to come to your senses and keep you out of hell, then I am happy to be accused of trying to frighten you.

If you're not saved, God has intentionally put this book into your hands. He's trying to rescue you. It is not a coincidence that you are reading it.

I tell people all the time that if you end up in hell, you paddled your own canoe there. The Lord is doing everything in His power to keep you from going there.

God is sounding the alarm. He is going to bring judgment on the Earth once again. Do not ignore this warning. Your eternal destination is at stake.

His words are a warning to you, of how He loves you and how you can escape His coming wrath. God loves all the people on the Earth.

You were born a sinner. Sin cannot come into the presence of a Holy God. If you reject Jesus, you are on your way to hell; the second death. Romans 6:23 says:

> *For the wages of sin is death, but the gift of God is eternal life in Christ Jesus our Lord.*

God is shouting to you, "I love you! I sent my one and only Son to die for you. I want you to come to repentance and not perish in the lake of fire. I want you to place your trust in my Son's atoning death for you."

Look at what He has written in the Holy Scriptures in II Peter 3:9:

> *The Lord is not slow in keeping his promise, as some understand slowness. Instead, he is patient with you, not wanting anyone to perish, but everyone to come to repentance.*

God has His watchmen telling you that the rapture is near; even at the door. These are men and women that God has raised up to warn people of danger when they see it coming.

The Bible describes what they do in Ezekiel 33:6-9:

> *But if the watchman sees the sword coming and does not blow the trumpet to warn the people and the sword comes and takes someone's life, that person's life will be taken because of their sin, but I will hold the watchman accountable for their blood.*
>
> *Son of man, I have made you a watchman for the people of Israel; so hear the word I speak and give them warning from me. When I say to the wicked, "You wicked person, you will surely die,' and you do not speak out to dissuade them from their ways, that wicked person will die for their sin, and I will hold you accountable for their blood. But if you do warn the wicked person to turn from their ways and they do not do so, they will die for their sin, though you yourself will be saved."*

Social media is full of watchmen who are warning you that Jesus is getting ready to come take His followers home, and that afterwards, God is going to rain down fire, brimstone, and hundred-pound hailstones on the Earth. Heed the warning of the watchmen.

God loves the people in all the nations of the world. He wants to rescue you. Like a good Father, in His great love, He is warning you of the danger that lies ahead.

For God so loved the world (you), that He gave his one and only Son…

CHAPTER 15

Another Jesus Revolution and a Word to Young People

The Lord took me into a vision in 2018 and told me that there would be one final revival and awakening before the church age was complete. We now see that happening. In America, and other nations around the world, we see people gathering to repent, turn from their sins, and place their faith in Christ.

Some will call this work of God "Jesus Revolution II." Others will call it "The Jesus Revival." It doesn't matter what you call it. It has begun and it is going to grow.

We are now seeing spontaneous revivals breaking out in various cities and on many college campuses. It is exactly what the Lord told me was coming.

In this vision, God told me that time was short and that we must prepare to take the gospel to cities all over the world and complete taking the gospel to the nations, and then the end would come. The vision included Franklin Graham, Michael W. Smith, Anne Graham

Lotz, several pastors, evangelists, and Christian music artists and groups.

God told me that He was going to sweep His net one final time to harvest lost souls, and then rapture His followers. He said, "The wickedness on the Earth has reached the point that I am now going to bring about the end."

The Lord has launched this Jesus Revolution/Revival. It is a genuine movement of God.

It is an exciting time to be alive. The Lord is causing people to become aware of their sinfulness and need for a Savior.

There are many young adults who are hungry for the truth. They are looking for something or someone to believe. They are looking for a cause or a movement to belong to.

Many young people are discovering that the "party life" doesn't fill the void that is in their heart. They are longing to find the meaning to life; to discover what they are here for. They've tried drugs, alcohol, and sex, and it just leaves them feeling empty.

The Holy Spirit is calling people of all ages to turn from their sins and place their faith in Jesus. Many are responding. Each week, we hear of new places where people are gathering and confessing their sins, turning in faith to God, and wanting to be together.

These groups spend large amounts of time in prayer and singing songs to the Lord. Many people are getting saved and baptized.

Some places have an outpouring of the Spirit that is lasting for weeks. Stories of miracles, healings, and lives being transformed are very common. There are those that are calling it a revival or an awakening.

God is so good. In His grace and mercy, He is giving people one more chance to repent and believe the gospel; to be born of the Spirit before He brings His wrath upon the Earth.

People in general do not want to hear that the end is coming. They are enjoying life and don't want to hear the message that the Lord is proclaiming through His watchmen to escape the coming wrath.

Most people don't want to hear the warning that God has me bring in this book. He is telling everyone, everywhere that He is coming very soon and that those who have rejected His pardon, through the atoning death of His Son, will remain on the Earth to experience His judgment and wrath.

It is like the days of Noah, when people ignored the warning that God had Noah bring, that He was going to bring judgment upon the Earth by way of a great flood. People mocked Noah and continued with their normal lives, as the years went by, and nothing had taken place yet.

However, the words that Noah spoke on behalf of the Lord came true. The rain eventually came down, and the water under the Earth came up and all those people drowned, just as the Lord said they would. People disregarded the warning and ended up dying.

Don't let that happen to you. Don't ignore the warning that God is giving you. If you have not repented of your sins and called on the Lord to save you, I implore you to do it today. There is not much time left.

Today, just as in the days of Noah, Jesus said people will be planning weddings and busy with everyday life when He returns to take His followers home. Most people on Earth will be totally shocked when one day, millions of people suddenly vanish.

The rapture will occur, and this will cause the world to plunge into chaos. There will be great fear among people all over the world. They will wonder what happened and ask, "Where did all of these people go?"

God has poured out His Spirit this final time prior to His return. People are responding to the Spirit's call to be saved. This is what is bringing about this current Jesus Revolution/Revival.

God told me in the vision that I mentioned that great persecution was going to come against this movement. Evil is growing, and there will be a clash between those who are of God and those who have sided with Satan. The greatest spiritual warfare in history is now under way.

There will be people that Satan uses to fiercely oppose these gatherings. People are going to be attacked, and some will even be killed.

It can be very costly to live for Christ. It may even cost you your life.

This should be no surprise. Christians in China, North Korea, Iran, India, and Muslim nations have been under attack for many years.

This has caused the formation of the "Secret Church" or "Underground Church," as it is called. Believers in these countries are enduring great persecution. Many have been imprisoned. Some have even been put to death; martyred for their faith in Christ.

In many countries, the house church has developed. People secretly meet in homes or various places to worship the Lord. This movement is growing in America. During the Covid storm, many churches closed, and some people began to gather in homes.

As persecution of Christians grows stronger, in the coming days, more house churches are going to form. It will be like what took place in the early church, as recorded in the book of Acts. As I said earlier, the Lord desires the last days' church to operate like the early church did.

More people will begin to gather in homes. There, they will spend a great deal of time in prayer and worship. They will read the Bible and encourage each other, while they are gathered together, to remain strong and committed to Christ, despite the difficult persecution that they are facing.

For now, the Lord is calling people to Himself. As a result, individuals are gathering in churches, college campuses, stadiums, arenas, and other places to worship God, share the gospel, and experience the outpouring of the Holy Spirit.

As a result, we have another Jesus Revolution, revival, and awakening. It is so beautiful to see the Lord at work and people being born again. Many lukewarm Christ followers are being filled anew with the Holy Spirit. They are becoming bold witnesses for the Lord, as they invite their friends and family to come to faith in Christ.

We are now very close to the return of Jesus for His followers. Let me ask you a very important question: Will you be taken to heaven and escape the coming wrath of God on those who remain in their sins, or will you be left behind and enter the seven-year tribulation that begins after the rapture?

Personally, I am so thrilled to see this movement of the Spirit of God. I know that I am going to heaven soon. I want to share Christ with as many people as I can until He takes me home.

❖❖❖

A Word to Young People:

I have done a lot of work with young people over the years. I love them.

I have served as a youth director in a couple of places, and God has allowed me to be a part of a youth ministry at a national level.

Young people have often told me that few pastors ever share a word with them in a service—that sermons are almost always directed towards adults. When I became a pastor, I made it a priority to regularly speak to the young people in attendance during a church service. I would literally tell them that this portion of the message was specifically for them.

For these reasons and many more, I want to share a word with the young. I want them to know how important that they are to God.

Young man, young lady, oh how I pray that the miracles and visions that you have read about in this book have excited you. I pray that you see that God is not dead. He is alive.

You may say, "Well, that will never happen for me."

Yes, it can.

He has got a plan for your life, too. He created you for a purpose, to complete a mission for Him. How exciting!

Maybe you have viewed the Bible as some boring history book that collects dust while it is laying around somewhere in your house. Perhaps you think that all of the exciting things that happened that are written in the scriptures ended some 2,000 years ago.

That's not true.

God is still doing amazing things today. He continues to speak to people. He is still performing miracles; healing people, answering prayers in spectacular ways, and transforming lives.

The Lord wants to have a personal relationship with you. He wants you to know Him and experience Him. He is just waiting for you to turn in faith and seek Him with all your heart.

He says to you, "Come to me and I'll show you great and mighty things. I will work in you and through you to share my message of hope with the world. I have a great adventure planned for you.

"Will you give me your life? If you will, you will save your life and it will have a lasting impact for all eternity. Or will you hold on to your life and waste it, pursuing the temporal pleasures of this world? The choice is yours."

I beg you to not ignore the critical message of this book—that Jesus is coming soon and that life on Earth, as you know it today, is coming to a horrible end. Great wars are getting ready to break out all over the Earth.

I just hear some of you saying, "This is not fair. I want a chance to live a normal life. I feel cheated when I hear people say that the end is now coming."

I can understand why you think this way. When I was younger and I heard people talk about Jesus coming back soon, I wanted Him to wait and come when I was older. It is normal for a young person to think this way.

You may dream of going to college and then getting married. You want to have children or a career. You want to travel.

You say, "God is cheating me out of getting to live a long time and enjoy life on Earth. I want to live longer, and I don't want the end to come yet."

I have news for you. Nothing on this Earth can compare to what awaits us in heaven. It is so easy to think from an Earthly point of view instead of a heavenly one.

God is in heaven, and if you enjoy some things He has created on Earth, just wait to see what He has prepared for those who love Him when they arrive in heaven. It is going to be infinitely better than anything you enjoy right now.

God's ways are higher and better than our ways and our thinking. Wrap your mind around what is in store for you in heaven, and you will live out the time that you have left on Earth in the right way.

You will choose to honor and serve God before He takes you home. You will desire to turn from your sins and give your life to God. You can be a vital part of this final movement of God to have people come to Christ before it is too late.

Look at the young people who are attending these faith gatherings that are taking place around the world. Maybe there is a movement of God right where you live. Better yet, maybe God will use you to help start one in your town.

God uses ordinary people who surrender their lives to Him to do great things through them. There are no Super Christians who are born with a halo on their head and have never sinned.

The Bible says we have all sinned. Nobody is perfect or worthy, on their own, to spend eternity in heaven. We all need Jesus.

So, I encourage you to embrace what is happening around the world. Yes, stand against evil and for what is right and just. But understand that God is allowing global leaders and governments to gain power and control over people and to bring about a new world order.

If you have repented of your sins and called on God to save you, you have nothing to fear. If you have not received the free gift of salvation from God, you should be terrified. You shouldn't be able to sleep at night.

You are one heartbeat away from spending eternity apart from God. That is scary!

I have seen Jesus alive, as I shared earlier. Jesus is real. Heaven is real. Hell is real.

This is no game. Your eternal destination is at stake.

Come to Jesus. Come find real love from a God who sent His Son, Jesus, to die a terrible death on a cross to pay the penalty of your sins.

God is a rescuer. He wants to rescue you and He wants nobody on Earth to spend eternity in hell.

Come join me and all of the others who have placed their faith in Christ. Come be a part of this final movement of God, this Jesus Revolution/Jesus Revival.

You won't regret it. Jesus is who you have been looking for. You will find joy and purpose today. Choose Christ now.

God loves young people. He loves you. Jesus said, "Repent and believe the gospel."

The gospel is great news. It is Jesus saying to you, "I love you and went to the cross for you."

He also said, "No greater gift can a man give than to lay down his life for his friends."

Jesus laid down His life for you.

Will you love Jesus? Will you lay down your life for Him? Oh, how I pray that you will.

CHAPTER 16

The Great Deception

The Bible warns us that in the last days, Satan will try to deceive people. That time of great deception has begun.

If you are not a Christ follower, you might say, "I don't believe the Bible. I don't see any deception on the Earth. I just think there are a lot of unproven conspiracy theories."

My response is, "That's your problem. You don't believe the Bible."

I lovingly warn you that the Bible is true. All that is written in the Holy Scriptures is going to come to pass. All Bible prophecies, yet unfulfilled, are going to happen.

God has given me several visions, in which I have been allowed to see some of the future. I have seen Jesus, alive, and coming on the clouds, just as the Bible says He will. The Bible is true. That's not an opinion. That is a fact.

Just as the Apostle John and the Apostle Paul were taken to heaven about 2,000 years ago, God has taken me to heaven in these last days. God allowed me to see the Second Coming of Christ.

Why did God do this? It is so I may tell the world the truth, that the Bible is true and that the prophecies written in the Scriptures will take place just as they are recorded in the Bible?

It is so that I will speak with authority and declare to everyone the messages that God has given me to share on His behalf? I will boldly proclaim the truths of the Bible.

As I have told you before, I am just an ordinary man. I am no better than any of you. I am a wretch; a beggar who sought Jesus and received God's amazing grace.

Paul told you that he was a wretch.

> Romans 7:24-25
> *What a wretched man I am! Who will rescue me from this body that is subject to death? Thanks be to God, who delivers me through Jesus Christ our Lord!*

Paul was just an ordinary man who was called by God to establish the early church on the Earth. He was a voice of truth, sent by God, and he gave his life in service to Jesus.

If Paul were on the Earth today, he would encourage you to start reading your Bible if you aren't already reading it. Why? Because it contains the actual Words of God. It is a love letter to you from the Lord and it explains how you can have eternal life.

God warns you of the deception that is coming. The Word of God warns you about Satan and his evil schemes.

Satan wants to deceive you; lie to you. Look what Jesus said about Satan in John 8:44:

> *You belong to your father, the devil, and you want to carry out your father's desires. He was a murderer from the beginning, not holding to the truth, for there is no truth in him. When he lies, he speaks his native language, for he is a liar and the father of lies."*

From the beginning, Satan has attempted to deceive men and women. He deceived Adam and Eve in the garden of Eden. He's been telling lies ever since.

Here is the truth: The world is now full of deception; full of lies.

In this chapter, we will learn the truth about the deception that is now on the Earth. If you think things are bad now, I must tell you that they are going to get worse. Much worse.

The majority of the mainstream media, social media, government leaders, and the global elite are lying to you. They are trying to deceive you. They are being used by Satan to accomplish his purposes.

These people and organizations have coined the phrase "misinformation." They want to silence those who oppose their beliefs; their agenda.

They want to do away with freedom of speech in America and the world. They want you to believe that they must censor people who are publishing misinformation. They tell you it is for your own good, and that of everyone else in the world, that they control the narrative.

They tell you that they must stop misinformation and take people off of social media platforms or cancel them. They tell you that they are the source of truth, when they are the very ones who are lying to you or, to use their word, serving up misinformation to you.

They really are lying to you. These evil people try to soften their censorship by calling it "misinformation."

God does not use that word. God tells the truth. He uses the words deception, lie, liar; not misinformation. He also uses the phrases "false witness" or "false testimony."

There are numerous Bible passages that talk about lying and deception. Here are a few:

> Exodus 20:16
> *You shall not give false testimony against your neighbor.*

> Proverbs 6:16-19
> *There are six things the Lord hates, seven that are detestable to him: haughty eyes, a lying tongue, hands that shed innocent blood, a heart that devises wicked schemes, feet that are quick to rush into evil, a false witness who pours out lies and a person who stirs up conflict in the community.*
>
> Proverbs 19:9
> *A false witness will not go unpunished, and he who breathes out lies will perish.*

After reading these verses, you can easily see that God's anger burns against those who lie and try to deceive others. The Lord demands that we tell the truth at all times.

We have all told lies in our lifetime. If you have not repented of this, do so now and quit lying.

At this present moment, Satan wants to lie to you, to deceive you and have you believe that it is a long time before Jesus returns; that people have been saying for 2,000 years that we are living in the last days. He wants to deceive you into thinking that the Lord is never going to return. This is a lie.

Friend, let me tell you something. The main reason God has asked me to write this book is to tell you that *The End is Now Coming*.

It is no coincidence that you are reading it. God planned for you to, so He could share these warnings and loving messages with you.

God had Noah warn the world that He was going to flood the Earth. The people ignored Noah's warning, and then the flood came, and everyone who was not aboard the ark perished.

Jesus talked about Noah when He was on the Earth. Christ did not lie and He cannot lie. There really was a man named Noah, who lived many years ago, who warned the people on the Earth that God's wrath was coming by way of a flood. It did.

You might know someone who would say, "I don't believe that. There was never a great flood and some man named Noah."

God's Word is true whether people believe it or not. They can have their opinion, but it will never change the truth. Christ is returning soon, and then God is going to bring His judgment on the wicked people who are left behind. That's a fact. That's the truth.

Like He did with Noah, Jesus has told me to warn everyone in the world that there is not much time left before God pours out His wrath on the Earth again. It will happen during the seven-year tribulation.

God says the gospel message is now going out to all the nations via missionaries, radio, TV programs, internet, Bibles, literature, podcasts, and other forms of technology, and then the end is going to come.

Are you ready for the return of Jesus? Are you looking each day for Him to return? Will you be taken to heaven in the rapture with millions of other people who suddenly disappear from the Earth?

Will you be one of the billions of people who are left behind? You don't have to be. God wants to rescue the lost and take them to heaven. He wants to rescue you.

The end is soon coming. That is why the messages found in this book are so urgent. There is very little time left. Don't let Satan lie to you or deceive you.

Deception is here, and more is coming in these last days. The Bible says in II Thessalonians 2:9-12:

> *The coming of the lawless one will be in accordance with how Satan works. He will use all sorts of displays of power through signs and wonders that serve the lie, and all the ways that wickedness deceives those who are perishing. They perish because they refused to love the truth and so be saved. For this reason God sends them a powerful delusion so that they will believe the lie and so that all will be condemned who have not believed the truth but have delighted in wickedness."*

This powerful delusion is deception. The Spirit of deception is now growing on the Earth.

Here's why. The lawless one is here. The Antichrist and False Prophet, as mentioned in the Bible, are now on the Earth.

How do I know? Jesus has told me that they are.

As a last day's prophet for the Lord, He wants me to warn you that these two evil men are here, and that means that we are very close to the start of the tribulation period, where they rule with Satan, for seven years, as the unholy trinity: Satan, Antichrist, and the False Prophet.

These two men have not come into power yet. Nor have they been revealed to the world. I do not know who they are. The Lord has not told me their names. I certainly have some men that I am watching that I think are possible candidates to be the Antichrist and False Prophet.

These men are public figures. They are anxious to take control of the world so that they can rule and reign on behalf of Satan.

Even the Antichrist and False Prophet have been deceived by Satan. They believe that they will be able to live forever and rule over the Earth. Yes, even the coming great deceivers have been deceived. They believe they can be gods.

I am now going to share some of the many deceptions that have already taken place and some that are still coming. A comprehensive study of all of the deceptions going on would require me to write an entire book.

However, I hope to open your eyes to some of what has recently happened and what is coming in the very near future. God does not want you to be deceived or unprepared.

Satan is using the world's false religions to deceive people into believing that they will make it to paradise or heaven. He is also using individuals to deceive the nations who are saying that people of all religions worship the same God; that we should unite because of this and become as one.

This false teaching is gaining traction right now. A move is under way to bring all world religions together in an effort to bring world peace and the one world government. This is setting the stage for the false prophet to come on the world stage and rule with the Antichrist.

Let's take a look at Islam and see what it teaches its followers to believe. Are those who actively follow the practices of the Qur'an, the book of Islam, actually serving the one, true God?

The answer is no. Muslims do not believe that Jesus died on the cross. They believe that He is an important prophet, but He is not the Son of God; that He is a created being like Adam. They do not believe in the Trinity—God the Father, God the Son, and God the Holy Spirit.

Islam is a works-based religion, in that if you keep its five pillars of the faith, you might get into paradise. Even Muhammed wasn't sure he had done enough works to be taken to paradise when he died.

In contrast to Islam, Christians believe that you are saved by grace through faith in Jesus Christ.

That His atoning death, burial, and resurrection paid the penalty for our sins. Christians believe that if you repent of your sins and believe the gospel, you will be born of the Spirit and be adopted as a child of God. You will enter paradise/heaven when your life on Earth is over.

Works will never save you. No one will ever do enough good works to enter into heaven.

Muslims have been deceived by Satan and believe it is their duty to destroy Israel and the United States. The more radical members of Islam believe that they are obeying Allah by waging war against Jews and Americans. They view Israel as the little Satan and the U.S. as the great Satan, and openly state their desire to wipe both countries off the map; to destroy them. This is especially true of the evil regime that controls Iran.

As a Christ follower, direct your anger towards the Islamic leadership in Iran, not the Iranian people. There is a growing underground Christian church in Iran. They are your brothers and sisters in Christ.

These believers want the Islamic regime to be overthrown because it is persecuting them and it is the sponsor of terrorism all around the world.

Radical Muslims wage jihad, which is war against the enemies of Islam, in the name of Allah. They actually believe they are obeying the Qur'an and Muhammad (Allah's prophet) as they attempt to kill people who are Jews, Americans, or who do not practice Islam.

When they attack, they even celebrate the death of the children and civilians of these nations, believing them to be infidels. This easily shows you how deceived they are.

I cannot discuss all of the world's religions here, and how people are deceived who belong to them. However, the Bible declares that there is only God; only one way to heaven. There is no path to eternal life or paradise through Islam, Hinduism, and the thousands of other religions that exist today.

> John 14:6
> *Jesus answered, "I am the way and the truth and the life. No one comes to the Father except through me."*

Jesus said that He is the only way to eternal life. This exclusivity is offensive to people who practice other religions or atheism.

Because of Satan using religious deception to deceive people, there is great violence in the world today. A lot of the violence from religious beliefs is aimed at Jewish people. Jews are hated by most of the two hundred nations that are on the Earth.

Anti-Semitism, violence directed toward Jews, is growing worldwide. It is evil, but God is using it to fulfill prophecy and bring many Jews back to Israel to live in the land.

> Jeremiah 16:14-15
> *However, the days are coming, declares the Lord, when it will no longer be said, "As surely as the Lord lives, who brought the Israelites*

up out of Egypt," but it will be said, "As surely as the Lord lives, who brought the Israelites up out of the land of the north and out of all the countries where he had banished them." For I will restore them to the land I gave their ancestors.

Amos 9:15
"I will plant Israel in their own land, never again to be uprooted from the land I have given them," says the Lord your God.

These prophecies and others are being fulfilled right now. Jews are moving to Israel from many nations.

Did you know that most world leaders do not like Israel and openly oppose Israel in the United Nations (UN)? They regularly vote on resolutions that are aimed at punishing Israel for alleged mistreatment of the Palestinian people.

Again, direct your anger towards the leadership of the Palestinians, not the ordinary citizen that lives in the Palestinian-designated territories in Israel. There are some Arabs who live there that are Christians, and others who support Israel.

I call the UN "the United Nothing." They don't do much of anything good in the world. Many of the UN leaders receive big salaries, travel in luxury, talk a good game, and then do nothing that benefits people in third world nations or help to relieve the suffering in the world.

Even worse, they are partners with the World Economic Forum (WEF) and others who are openly working to form a one world government. I'll write more about this in the next chapter.

The UN receives most of its funding from the United States, and their leadership usually blames Israel for much of what goes wrong in the Middle East or for conflicts with the Palestinians. Satan is using the UN to accomplish much in preparation for his upcoming seven-year tribulation period reign.

The nation of Israel is far from perfect. God is not pleased with all that the leadership of Israel and the people of Israel do. In spite of this, they are still His chosen people. God sent His Son, Jesus, to be born in Israel. Jesus was a Jew and a descendant of David. God will have Jesus reign from Jerusalem during the millennium.

As a Christ follower, you should be pro-Israel. God has not abandoned Israel, as some people falsely proclaim. There are some Christian leaders who are going around advocating replacement theology, that God has abandoned the nation of Israel and He is now granting the promises that He made to Israel to the modern-day church.

This is not true. God made a covenant with Abraham, and He will keep His word and never leave the Jews and violate His covenant. God is faithful and always keeps His word, even though we do not.

I urge you to start studying Bible prophecy and your eyes will be opened to what is happening on the Earth right now. I'll give you an example to prove this.

Let's read Isaiah 17:1:

> *A prophecy against Damascus:* "*See, Damascus will no longer be a city but will become a heap of ruins.*"

Did you know that Israel has been targeting Damascus with missile strikes for the past several years? Why? Iran is continually attempting to establish military bases and bring in missiles and other weapons into Syria. As I just told you, Iran's Islamic leadership has been deceived by Satan, so they want to attack and destroy Israel on behalf of Allah.

Israel knows that Iran is a great threat to its survival as a nation. As a result, Israel fires missiles into Syria to destroy Iran's bases and weapons that are located in the Damascus area and other places in Syria.

Over time, this is causing Damascus to become a city of ruins. There are those that believe that Israel may have to one day use a nuclear weapon to destroy Damascus and all the weapons that Iran is hiding in the city.

This is but one example of how Bible prophecy is being fulfilled. Damascus is being destroyed right before our eyes, just as the scriptures told us it would be. The Bible is the inspired, infallible, inerrant word of God. Never again be deceived by Satan into believing that it is not true.

♦♦♦

The Covid Deception

Most of the people of the world were deceived by what happened during the so-called Covid pandemic. A Plandemic would be a more appropriate word to use.

I never thought that so many Americans and people in other nations could be deceived to the degree that they were. I watched the deception and lies unfold, and I quickly realized that it was all planned. I immediately resisted the narrative and evil agenda put forth by the perpetrators.

To my great horror, billions of people around the world surrendered their freedoms and drank the Kool-Aid, believing that some horrible, apocalyptic virus was going to kill everyone on the Earth. It was all a deception used to lie to citizens and manipulate the people of the world into complying with government mandates and letting them have control of their lives.

Some politicians live by the adage, "Never let a good crisis go to waste."

They began to say that due to the worldwide Covid crisis. They started pushing an agenda that we must unite, as a world, to defeat the virus. We must come together and eliminate individual nations and form a one world government to solve this crisis and other critical issues we are facing.

Governments quickly seized the opportunity to mandate lockdowns, mask requirements, and school and business closures. Certain businesses were labeled essential while others were ruled nonessential.

There was great hypocrisy in the mandates. Liquor stores and marijuana stores were allowed to remain open. The big retailers were allowed to stay open while the mom-and-pop businesses were shut down. Churches were deemed non-essential in most countries.

People willingly gave up their constitutional rights and believed just about everything that was told to them by their government and mass media. People around the world were afraid of dying. This resulted in mass hysteria and fear.

Countries were locked down. International travel was severely curtailed.

Soon there was a narrative; an agenda that was pursued that was not to be disobeyed. Doctors and medical personnel were told that a vaccine was being developed and that it was the only hope for the world. It was the only way to defeat Covid.

People were told that there were no early treatments available from existing medicines that could treat the Covid virus. You had to get the jabs—the shots.

For some people it was mandated that you get the vaccine or you would lose your job. You might not receive medical treatment if you went to the hospital and you hadn't taken the shot.

I was fortunate. The Lord told me early on that the pandemic was manufactured; a deception and that the emergency use authorization shots were evil and full of poison.

I began to tell everyone not to take the vaccines and to seek early treatment for Covid infection as soon as possible. I spoke and wrote about some of the doctors who were having success repurposing available drugs and developing protocols that were keeping their patients alive.

I mentioned in articles and videos the names of many of the brave doctors and medical people who were advising people to not take the shots because they had been rushed to market and not tested properly to ensure that they were safe and effective.

Drugs like hydroxychloroquine and Ivermectin were not allowed to be used by most doctors to provide early treatment for Covid. Courageous doctors and medical people were often prevented from getting their patients' prescriptions filled at pharmacies who were compliant with the government's lies.

There were doctors using these drugs, along with others, and they were keeping their patients from dying. Yet their reports and articles were being suppressed. There were even some doctors who lost their state medical license for prescribing these drugs and not going along with the narrative to have their patients take the shots.

Some doctors were afraid of losing their licenses to practice medicine and gave in to the pressure to follow the narrative. Others told their patients to take the shots, but when some of them died or had adverse effects from the chemicals in the shots, they stopped recommending them. They realized something was wrong.

Let me mention a few of the many doctors who told the truth during the Covid crisis. There was Dr. Peter McCullough, Dr. Pierre Kory, Dr. Joseph Mercola, Dr. Sherri Tenpenny, Dr. Paul Marik, Dr. Simon Gold, Dr. James Thorp, Dr. Vladimir Zelenko (deceased) and other doctors in America and around the world who spoke out against the jabs and offered alternative treatments to help cure people who had Covid or to prevent people from getting Covid.

Each of these people were viciously attacked by the media, federal agencies, and the other doctors for supposedly spreading misinformation about Covid treatments. They were kicked off their social media sites and told they were lying and that their actions were causing people to die or hesitate to get the vaccine.

Now the truth is coming out about the dangers of the shots, their ineffectiveness, and that drugs like hydroxychloroquine and Ivermectin are effective in early treatment of Covid.

Most of these malicious articles attacking these doctors are still up on the internet, despite the truth now being disclosed that proves that these brave doctors were actually right and that they did not spread misinformation. They did not lie.

I am grateful to the doctors, physician assistants, and other medical personnel who stayed true to their commitment to the Hippocratic oath. These people put the health and welfare of their patients above all else. They risked losing their employment and income to do the right thing and tell their patients not to take the shots.

I shared the names of these doctors with you so that when the next plandemic virus is unleashed upon the world, you will have these names and you can go and view what they are recommending that you do to prevent getting the virus or to be treated for it.

Follow these doctors who were not deceived and who had the courage to tell the truth. They are heroes in my opinion. They stood up to an evil narrative and proclaimed the truth. I thank God for all of them.

♦♦♦

Getting back to my message about deception, I want you to know that some people listened to me as I warned them about the deception that was taking place during the Covid crisis. Others did not. I knew that people were going to die from the shots and improper medical treatments, and so I sounded the alarm as God told me to.

I watched many people begin to report the adverse effects that they or a family member were experiencing after taking the jabs. I noticed that almost every death began to be recorded as having been from Covid. I saw that the flu suddenly disappeared; that no one was being treated for it. Instead, the flu was being labeled Covid.

We later found out the doctors and hospital received more free government money for diagnosing every illness as Covid. Doctors were given money to coerce their patients into taking the jab. The temptation to take the money and not go against the narrative was too much for most hospitals and physicians. They were deceived by the government, Big Pharma, the media, and their own greed.

It was obvious that there was an agenda to exaggerate the death totals from Covid to continue to create fear and to manipulate people into getting the shots. It worked. Nearly eighty percent of all Americans took one or more shots, and billions of people around the world took the jabs.

What was the agenda of the evil people who coordinated the Covid plandemic? There were many reasons that the global elite, in cooperation with government leaders, pharmaceutical companies, and mainstream media worked together to bring about this catastrophe.

Money and control were two of their main objectives. Some of these Big Pharma corporations were struggling to stay afloat. They needed the big profits from the sale of the vaccine, even if the chemicals in the shots killed and harmed millions of people.

Suddenly, the vaccines were unleashed on the world and this resulted in these corporations making huge amounts of money. Pharmaceutical executives, global leaders, and many other people invested heavily into purchasing Big Pharma stocks. These people made a fortune during the crisis. I would call it an evil, criminal fortune.

Early on, the executives of these companies knew that people were dying or being adversely affected by the shots, but there was too much money, too much greed, to take them off the market. The fact that the shots were rolled out with Experimental Use Authorization (EUA) all but eliminated the chance that Big Pharma could be sued by those who were harmed or died when they took the shots.

As a result, they worked hard to have the shots become mandatory across the world. They worked to suppress or deny treatments with drugs like hydroxychloroquine, Ivermectin, or Z Pack because they knew that this would minimize sales and profits from the shots.

Thankfully, the truth is finally being reported. Some people and corporations may be held liable for the evil that they did.

One thing is for sure, you can no longer have absolute trust in the agencies that you may have trusted in the past. The ones I am talking about have three letters: CDC, FDA, WHO, and all the others.

The Center for Disease Control, Federal Drug Administration, and World Health Organization all lied to you. They withheld documents that would have informed patients of the deaths and harmful side effects from the shots that were revealed from the early trials done by the pharmaceutical companies.

The shots were known to be deadly and cause severe adverse side effects from results of the short trials that were done. Yet they were rushed to market and given EUA approval.

Early on, there were doctors who sounded the alarm about the shots and told their patients to not take them. These doctors offered alternative treatments with existing drugs, but they were accused of promoting misinformation. These physicians who went against the narrative were silenced or even put out of business.

The mainstream media (MSM) and all of the broadcast corporations pushed the narrative that the CDC, FDA, and WHO wanted to be promoted. There were some people like Tucker Carlson, Sean Hannity, Laura Ingraham, and a few others who questioned the mainstream media and the narrative being pushed to support the school lockdowns, mask mandates, and vaccine mandates. They were the exception.

Are you aware that the WHO is controlled by China? Did you know that many world governments, including America under the Biden administration, are trying to hand the WHO control of the government when a future pandemic breaks out?

This is no typo! The WHO, under the global pandemic treaty, would have the authority to have emergency powers, due to a declared health emergency, to bypass a nation's constitution and rule during the crisis. Do you think China and the globalists would wait very long to release another deadly virus on the world if the WHO was given the authority to govern during a pandemic?

We must all learn from the deception that took place during the Covid crisis. Here are some main things to be aware of for the future:

- Vaccine mandates and passports are EVIL.

- This is a critical moment in the history of the world. Do you see what is happening?

Some politicians in America and in countries around the world are taking your freedoms away from you. You may never get them back.

- You should be able to decide if you are going to take a shot, wear a mask, stay at home, distance yourself from other people, attend church, sing at church, decide what is best for your children, and on and on.

- President Biden said he was against vaccine mandates before the presidential election. He lied to you. He went on to do everything in his power to force vaccine mandates. He said, "Yes, police and first responders should have to take the vaccines. If they don't, they should be fired."

- It is now a proven fact that natural immunity is better and lasts longer than taking a shot or booster.

- First responders, along with medical personnel, were the ones who risked their lives during the worst part of the Covid crisis when there wasn't a vaccine. Many were fired for not taking the vaccine, even though they already had Covid. They had natural immunity and didn't want to take the shots. This is disgusting! This is unconstitutional. Yet some took them to keep their job so they could feed their families and pay their bills.

- Government leaders and agencies, along with family members and friends, tried to shame people into taking the unproven shots. They said, "The unvaccinated are causing people to die from Covid."

- That was a lie. If you don't get the flu shot this winter, are you guilty of causing the death of other people who get the flu or pneumonia?' Do you see the hypocrisy?

- Some of the best doctors and nurses in the world have been censored, silenced, fired, and threatened with the loss of their medical licenses if they bring up concerns about side effects, deaths, etc. from the vaccine. This is evil. This is censorship. This is the loss of freedom of speech.

- Medical tyranny has come upon us. What should you do? You must stand up, right now, for your freedoms or you will lose them. Quit being the Silent Majority! Speak up for your freedoms. Just take a look at what is happening in Australia, Germany, Canada, Holland, and other countries. People are losing their freedoms.

- To be silent in the face of vaccine mandates and passports is evil, and God will not hold us guiltless.

- What kind of world do you want to have for your children and grandchildren in the time we have left before the rapture occurs and the tribulation begins? Will you stand up for them against the evil that is going on in the world? I pray that you will.

More deception is coming in the future. Let's look at Jesus' words in Matthew 24:23-27:

> *At that time if anyone says to you, "Look, here is the Messiah!" or, "There he is!" do not believe it. For false messiahs and false prophets will appear and perform great signs and wonders to deceive, if possible, even the elect. See, I have told you ahead of time.*
>
> *So if anyone tells you, "There he is, out in the wilderness," do not go out; or, "Here he is, in the inner rooms," do not believe it. For as lightning that comes from the east is visible even in the west, so will be the coming of the Son of Man.*

God talks about a Great Deception that is coming. The Greatest Deception, as written in the scriptures, is going to happen during the Tribulation. The Antichrist and the False Prophet are going to team up to deceive billions of people.

What will that deception be? These two evil men are going to do amazing miracles that have not ever been seen by mankind. They will be so powerful that even the tribulation saints could be deceived if they were not aware of God's warning, found in Revelation 13.

These saints will be people who were not raptured, who previously rejected Christ but will be saved during the tribulation. They will be on the run, hiding from the Antichrist and his followers since they will not have taken the mark of the beast nor pledge their worship and allegiance to the Antichrist.

> Revelation 13:11-14
> *Then I saw a second beast, coming out of the earth. It had two horns like a lamb, but it spoke like a dragon. It exercised all the authority of the first beast on its behalf, and made the earth and its inhabitants worship the first beast, whose fatal wound had been healed.*

> *And it performed great signs, even causing fire to come down from heaven to the earth in full view of the people. Because of the signs it was given power to perform on behalf of the first beast, it deceived the inhabitants of the earth. It ordered them to set up an image in honor of the beast who was wounded by the sword and yet lived.*

God allows Satan and his false prophet to copy what Elijah did in I Kings 18:36-39:

> *At the time of sacrifice, the prophet Elijah stepped forward and prayed: "Lord, the God of Abraham, Isaac and Israel, let it be known today that you are God in Israel and that I am your servant and have done all these things at your command. Answer me, Lord, answer me, so these people will know that you, Lord, are God, and that you are turning their hearts back again."*
>
> *Then the fire of the Lord fell and burned up the sacrifice, the wood, the stones and the soil, and also licked up the water in the trench.*
>
> *When all the people saw this, they fell prostrate and cried, "The Lord—he is God! The Lord—he is God!"*

Satan is never original. He always copies what Almighty God has done. He has his unholy trinity and then he will have his false prophet copy what Elijah had done in calling down fire.

Sadly, the lost people on the Earth will be deceived by this delusion and willingly take the mark of the beast and worship the Antichrist. The Bible speaks clearly about what will happen to those who worship Satan and the Antichrist.

> Revelation 14:9-11
>
> *A third angel followed them and said in a loud voice: "If anyone worships the beast and its image and receives its mark on*

their forehead or on their hand, they, too, will drink the wine of God's fury, which has been poured full strength into the cup of his wrath. They will be tormented with burning sulfur in the presence of the holy angels and of the Lamb. And the smoke of their torment will rise for ever and ever. There will be no rest day or night for those who worship the beast and its image, or for anyone who receives the mark of its name."

The greatest deception of all is when Satan persuades a person to reject the pardon that God offers to every person in the world. God sent His Son to the Earth to be born of a virgin, live a sinless life, and suffer a horrible scourging and death on a cross to pay the penalty for all of our sins.

Jesus shed His innocent blood and took all of our sins upon himself to provide a way for each of us to have eternal life. Christ was crucified, buried, and raised to life again on the third day. This is the gospel; the good news.

John 3:16
For God so loved the world that he gave his one and only Son, that whoever believes in him shall not perish but have eternal life.

My friend, if you have repented of your sins and believed the gospel, you won't be on the Earth when this final deception occurs. I pray that you have already called on the Lord to save you, or that you will before you finish reading this book.

CHAPTER 17

The New World Order

In the previous chapter, I talked to you about the importance of not being deceived. Now I want to tell you about the movement that is happening on the Earth that is setting the stage to create a New World Order (NWO).

There are several names they use to refer to it. Some of them call it an international order, a one world government, or a global reset. They are all the same thing. They all refer to the NWO.

This is not a conspiracy theory. It is a fact. What the leaders of this movement used to hide, they now openly proclaim.

It is important for you to know what some wicked people are doing, publicly and secretly, and the impact that this is going to have on your life and the lives of those you love.

Ignorance is not bliss. God wants you to be informed about world events. He wants you to know what is happening and what you are to do about it.

Global leaders are working to bring an end to nationalism. They want to end the existence of individual nations, their constitutions, and rules of governing. Instead, they desire to form a one world government. They believe that we, as the citizens of the world, must unite and come together as one to solve the issues facing the world and to provide a sustainable future for mankind.

The NWO wants to have:

- A one world government.
- One group of leaders who rule the world
- One Global Digital Currency and economic system
- One World Religion; currently being organized by Pope Francis
- One World Health Organization (WHO) to establish all health-related policies and requirements for citizens of the world. They want to have a global pandemic treaty, where your nation cedes its sovereignty to the WHO in a pandemic/crisis.

Who are the leaders of the NWO? They are the presidents or prime ministers of most countries, banking leaders of all the major world banks, the Federal Reserve, corporate leaders, billionaires, religious leaders, scientists, technology leaders, celebrities, and so many others. Even King Charles III of the United Kingdom is part of the NWO.

The World Economic Forum (WEF) hosts the annual meeting of these NWO leaders in Davos, Switzerland. They are sometimes referred to as the Davos Group.

The WEF is led by a man by the name of Klaus Schwab. He is a wolf in sheep's clothing. He claims that a global reset will save humanity from a global climate crisis, pandemics, and all the other issues facing the world.

The Lord has had me following the WEF, Klaus Schwab, and the Davos Group for many years. I have made videos warning people about how dangerous they are. I have spoken out against them when God has told me to. I want you to know about them if you don't already.

Schwab says that world leaders meet to come up with solutions to the world's greatest problems and challenges; to save humanity from collapsing due to viruses, a global climate crisis, debts that can't be paid by nation states, a global currency crisis, famines, and wars.

The Davos Group, UN, and WEF are all part of the NWO and they want to create a global government and remove rule by individual nation states. They say we must give up our rights as members of our country and surrender them to the one world government.

Using the WHO, the WEF and UN are trying to pass a global pandemic treaty. As I mentioned earlier, this would require all nation states to surrender their sovereignty to the WHO during a global pandemic. This would essentially create a world constitution for all nations to live by. This is global governance. This is a one world government.

It is evil and it must be stopped. The US is promoting this treaty under the Biden Administration. The WHO made enormous mistakes during the Covid crisis, and they are led by China, who can never be trusted.

The WEF is working hard to achieve their global reset, whereby a small number of people will lead a one world government and rule over the people of the Earth. Those in charge of the NWO will decide what you are allowed to do as a global citizen.

Do you see how close we are to living under a one world government? This is not some conspiracy theory. This is actually happening.

Can you now see why I am sounding the alarm to warn you that the end is coming? God wants you to know the truth about what is happening on the Earth. Everything is not okay. Evil people, under Satan's influence, want to rule over you.

These globalists, who are often referred to as the global elite, are more interested in controlling the world than serving your best interests. You will just be a number to them. If they don't find you useful, then they have no need for you.

Yuval Noah Harari, an advisor to these global leaders, has said that in the future, if you are not considered useful to society, then the NWO leadership must determine what to do with you. Harari asks, how you will find meaning in life if you do not have the abilities that are needed to be employed in the workforce or to function in the new society?

His best guess is that since you are now needless and worthless, you will be allowed to use drugs and play computer games to occupy your time.

Who determines who is useful to society and who is deemed useless? Is this the world you want to live in? Is this the future world you want for your loved ones and friends?

Do you now see how critical it is for you to be saved from the evil world that is coming? As I have already told you, God doesn't want you to go through this.

You don't have to be on the Earth and experience this nightmare. It is your choice. He has made a way for you to escape the tribulation, the evil reign of Satan, and the wrath of God that is going to be poured out on these wicked people who were not raptured.

You can repent of your sins and believe the gospel. You can call on the Lord to save you today.

> Romans 10:13
> *Everyone who calls on the name of the Lord will be saved.*

I pray that you will stop right now and call out to God and ask Him to save you. Jesus gave His life to rescue you from spending eternity in hell. If you have believed in Him for eternal life, you will not be left on the Earth to go through the tribulation when Satan, the Antichrist, and the False Prophet will reign on the earth in the NWO.

It will be hell on Earth. Almost everyone will die during this time.

◆◆◆

Be aware that these globalists are full of deception. Klaus Schwab, head of the WEF, says "By 2030, you'll own nothing and you'll be happy about it."

That is an absolute lie. They want to fool you into believing them and then they will rule over you with an iron fist. You'll own nothing and you will not be happy about it. You will lose all of your freedoms.

The WEF has produced a slick video with that message in it. How tragic that so many people will be deceived and believe their propaganda.

Schwab, the WEF, and others admire how the Chinese Communist Party (CCP) rules over the Chinese people. President Xi Jinping, President of China, has become a dictator.

The NWO wants to implement a world governance model that is much like that of the CCP and President Xi. I spoke a little about this in a previous chapter.

Essentially, you will become a slave to your government. Here is a short description of what that type of governance will be like:

Most Chinese people live in fear of the CCP. Some have had friends or family members who have been arrested or taken to prison camps. They know that if they do not obey what they are told to do, that they will be punished harshly.

Chinese citizens are tracked by millions of cameras while they are out in public. They cannot freely speak about what's on their mind or complain of being oppressed or they will be arrested and potentially be put in a prison camp, being forced to do slave labor with minimal food.

There is no authentic, religious freedom in China. There are the government-approved churches, but the pastors and members of these churches are limited on what they can say and do. They are closely monitored and controlled by CCP staff.

The Chinese government has persecuted Christians and some other religious groups for many years. The underground church, or "house churches" as they are called, are being shut down. The CCP considers them a threat to their rule, and they are afraid that people might work to overthrow the oppressive government that they live under.

Life in China, for the common man or woman, is very difficult. During the Covid crisis, which originated in China, many citizens never received treatment for the virus. This resulted in their deaths.

Some people were taken from their homes and put in detention centers because they tested positive for having Covid. Some cities, with millions of people in them, were locked down.

People were confined to their apartments and not allowed to come out of them for weeks. You can watch videos on social media of people putting their heads out the windows of their high-rise apartments and crying out for help. They were treated like prisoners and often had little or no food and water.

The death and suffering that took place in China is staggering. However, leaders of the NWO ignore this. They want to rule as dictators and live in luxury. They hunger for power and fame, and desire to be worshiped.

They want people to fear them and not be able to oppose them or remove them from office. These globalists give no thought to the harsh conditions that ordinary citizens in China live with.

They love how President Xi has so much power and rules like a king. They desire to have the same power he does, and they praise him at every opportunity.

President Xi Jinping is adored by most of the Davos Group. However, in God's eyes, these people and President Xi are evil. They will spend eternity in hell if they don't repent of their cruel treatment of innocent people.

Don't believe they are evil? Think back to what happened during the Covid mandates and lockdowns. These were the same individuals who were working hard to control you and take away your freedoms.

They promoted and supported mandates that forced people to take the shots. The jabs have caused many people to die from blood clots and myocarditis. They destroy the immune system, so people are dying from infections that their body used to be able to fight off.

The leaders of the NWO threw caution and safety to the wind. They knew that there were chemicals in the so-called vaccines which were designed to cause men and women to become sterile.

The number of women who are having miscarriages since taking the vaccine has soared to record highs. The birth rate is also way down in many nations. Fewer babies are being born.

The shots are causing life-threatening damage to the organs of many people. For more on this, follow Dr. Peter McCullough and the other doctors that I mentioned in the previous chapter.

I can go on and on about all the evils that took place and the lies that were told during the height of the Covid crisis. Suffice it to say, most of the people of the world were deceived and went along with the mask and vaccine mandates, lockdowns, and loss of freedoms.

Sadly, in a short amount of time, the next plandemic will be unleashed upon the Earth. Once again, these evil people who seek a one world government will try to take away your freedoms and control you.

If a global pandemic treaty or medical tyranny through mandatory shots or drugs does not allow the NWO to seize full control of the world, they will use their ace in the hole. They will try to convince people that there is a global climate crisis.

World leaders have drafted an action plan that includes addressing their alleged climate crisis. It is the United Nations—Agenda 2030.

These globalists claim that by the year 2030, their agenda will do the following:

- End hunger and poverty.
- They will protect the planet by eliminating the use of fossil fuels and moving to sustainable energy sources. They will take urgent action to prevent a global climate crisis.

- Their agenda will bring about prosperity and world peace.

You can find Agenda 2030 at: https://sdgs.un.org/2030agenda.

It all seems so noble; so pure. Who could ever be opposed to this incredible agenda that will fix every problem in the world? What could possibly go wrong with our future controlled by these world leaders and their agenda for life on Earth?

A lot can go wrong! I am opposed to Agenda 2030 and the rule of the nations by a central government with a central currency. I hope you are also against it.

It is the Antichrist System; the one world government. It will be controlled by Satan and these puppets he has deceived into believing that they can create a utopian society.

They promote agenda 2030, but these people are hypocrites. For years, the leaders of the NWO have been flying around the world in their gas guzzling, carbon emitting, private planes. They demonstrate to us that they operate by the creed, "Do what I say, but not what I do."

They say that they have warned us about global warming, which is being caused by excessive carbon emissions coming from planes, vehicles, trains, and industry. They told us that the icebergs around the globe were all going to melt. Many of them prophesied that the coastlines in many nations would be flooded.

God has news for them. The icebergs are still here and the coasts aren't flooded everywhere. No, catastrophic global warming didn't happen and they haven't apologized for lying to us.

Instead, they just changed the name from global warming to global climate crisis. Now they can blame any weather event on climate issues. Every tornado, earthquake, tsunami, flood, drought, famine, record cold or heat, and volcano erupting is suddenly due to the dangerous climate crisis that they say is developing across the Earth.

Here's what's coming. One day, government leaders will issue executive orders that declare that there is a catastrophic climate crisis. In order to save our planet, we will all be required to forfeit our constitutional rights.

It is a lie. It is deception, but it is coming.

They are already mandating the elimination of fossil fuels and requiring everyone to purchase expensive electric vehicles. Don't worry about the fact that America and most of the nations of the world do not have the infrastructure in place to charge these electric vehicles.

Don't be concerned about the fact that the energy grid in countries cannot support the demands that will be placed on it. In America, in the state of California, over the past several years there has been a shortage of electricity available to consumers. There have been blackouts to keep the grid from crashing.

Now there will be more electric vehicles to be charged in the future, when they don't have enough electricity to go around right now. It is absolutely foolish to eliminate fossil fuels.

Behind closed doors, China and Russia are laughing while they watch America and other nations self-destruct. They are not going to comply with UN clean energy requirements. They will not go green.

Right now, China and India are building more coal plants to provide electricity for their countries. At the same time, America and other nations are abandoning coal and natural gas.

Did you know that there is enough oil, coal, and natural gas to keep America energy independent for several hundred years? It is just sitting there underground, waiting to be used.

Russia has a huge amount of natural gas. Like China and India, they are not going to fully cooperate with the WEF, UN, and others on limiting their use of fossil fuels. They are not going green.

My friend, God, made fossil fuels for mankind to use responsibly. More importantly, let me assure you, there is only a short amount of time left before the return of the Lord, so we will never run out of fossil fuels.

The Lord has told me that the end is now coming, so the world's biggest problem isn't a global climate crisis. The greatest issue that should concern you and every other citizen of the world should be the eternal destination of your soul.

There is no doubt that the global climate crisis is a lie. It is propaganda that is being pushed by world government leaders and globalists to frighten us into believing that we must reduce carbon and nitrogen emissions to help save the planet.

For greater insights on the fact there is no global climate crisis, visit Twitter and search for: Steve Milloy @JunkScience or Marc Morano @ClimateDepot. These men, and many others, will tell you the truth about the climate crisis lies that are being told by the WEF, UN, politicians, NWO, mainstream media, and others.

God is incredibly brilliant. He made plants to utilize carbon dioxide. Carbon emissions are not causing global warming, and the Earth is not being destroyed by using fossil fuels.

Why is the government lying to you about fossil fuels and carbon emissions? They want to control you. If you have an electric vehicle, at some point in the future they can restrict or cut off electricity to you if you don't comply with their demands.

World governments now want to impose a carbon score on their citizens. If your carbon footprint is too high, you will lose privileges or the use of electricity. They may even freeze your bank account or restrict what you can purchase with your money.

You will be required to keep your carbon score below a certain level. If you don't, you will be fined, restricted, or possibly arrested.

Those pushing for a one world government want to rule us by Environmental Social Governance (ESG). They will say, "In order to save Mother Earth or the planet, all global citizens must be governed by ESG."

The global leaders know that if they can gain control of the food supply, energy supply, and money supply, then they can control the world. Politicians, working in cooperation with the NWO and advocating ESG, have begun seizing farmland in Canada, Holland, and many countries under the guise of saving the planet from the excessive use of fertilizer and harmful nitrogen emissions.

The reduction of available farmland and limited use of fertilizer has hurt crop production, caused food shortages, and brought record increases in food costs. This is their plan.

The globalists are making efforts to reduce farmland in countries so that they can create a food shortage and control the world's food supply. They believe hungry people will surrender their constitutional rights in order to get food and stay alive. This will allow the NWO to get them to comply with all of their demands.

In the US, numerous food plants are suddenly catching on fire and burning down. Coincidence? Hardly. Someone is deliberately setting them on fire to reduce the food supply.

In other efforts to control food and energy availability, the WEF is working with BlackRock, a corporation focused on investments and technology issues. BlackRock is often the leading shareholder in many large corporations. This has resulted in them having great influence on pushing an agenda for ESG.

For example, these corporations that BlackRock has invested heavily in can determine how fossil fuels can be transported across the world. They can influence the companies that ship oil and gas by trains or ships to reduce the amount that they will transport.

They promise to support politicians who are running for office if they will work to eliminate the use of fossil fuels in their countries; even getting them to shut down new pipeline construction or entire industries, like coal, gas, and nuclear plants that produce electricity.

They have met with corporate and government leaders to influence them to no longer use fossil fuels. They persuade them to move to the use of solar power, wind turbines, and other methods of producing electricity. This has led to a big increase in fuel prices all over the world.

This increase in fuel costs is driving up food prices in the grocery stores. It is also why it costs so much more to fill up your vehicle with gas or diesel.

The increase in energy costs has a domino effect that causes prices to increase in so many industries. Go ask a home builder or someone who remodels homes how much the price of materials have gone up in the last few years. They'll let you know how angry they are about it and how much it has hurt the housing industry and their business. Some of these businesses are going bankrupt.

The NWO is working hard to control the availability of food and fossil fuels. Now they are out to capture control of the world currencies and the money supply.

World governments have been secretly working on systems to go to a cashless society using a Central Bank Digital Currency (CBDC). This would bring about the end of paper money and coins.

At first, every effort will be made to deceive you into believing how much better the world will be if every nation converts to digital currency. The government will tell you that it will help to reduce credit card fraud. They'll say it will reduce cyber crimes.

They'll emphasize how convenient it will be for you to use it. You'll be told how you won't have to carry cash and coins that have so many germs and bacteria on them. It will reduce viruses and prevent pandemics.

Government leaders will say that if there is another pandemic caused by a virus or catastrophic event, the government will be able to quickly put economic impact payments, by way of digital currency, into your bank account. There won't be delays like there were for many people in the Covid crisis, when you had to wait to get a check from the government.

You want to get that free government money as fast as possible, right? Wrong!

The government has no money to give to you. It is not free. It is tax dollars, paid by citizens, that comes to your bank account.

In reality, it didn't really help you. Look how much fuel prices, food prices, and housing prices went up after you got your Covid checks.

Inflation, caused by this stimulus money and other government mistakes, has cost you more money than you received from the government. Remember this the next time you go buy eggs, milk, or beef at the grocery store. There's no such thing as a free lunch.

Soon, you'll be told that CBDCs can help bring an end to sex trafficking. What person would risk a life sentence in jail if their name was found on the phone of a sex trafficker? They wouldn't dare pay for sex with a minor if they knew that their digital transaction could be traced back to their phone or bank account.

As always, Satan will make something look so appealing to deceive people, then he will use it for his evil purposes after it is implemented into society. CBDCs are coming. It is not a question of if, but when.

When digital money comes, you have lost all of your privacy and most of your freedoms. They will track every transaction that you make, and they will implement rules limiting what you can purchase.

If you are buying too much meat, they will not allow you to purchase meat for a period of time. Even now, some of the global elite, like Bill Gates, are trying to eliminate meat and get us to start eating fake meat, bugs, and insects.

The globalists will limit how much you can travel, how much electricity you can use, and on and on. The government is getting ready to control you and every aspect of your life.

You might ask, what can I do? You can speak out against your nation going to digital currency, if it hasn't already. Contact your government leaders and let them know that you oppose it. Vote for politicians who will keep your nation's paper currency and coins. Pray for election integrity so that your vote really counts in opposing digital currency.

Some citizens and politicians will stand against CBDCs, knowing that governments will take advantage of having access to your bank account and be able to actually see every item that you purchase. This is the right thing to do and I applaud them for it. It will delay the loss of your freedoms.

However, the Bible says that the day is coming when you will not be able to buy or sell if you don't take the mark of the beast. In other words, at that time, the world has gone to a cashless society, and you will have to take a government ID, a mark on the right hand or forehead, to access your bank account.

You can be a Christian that helps hold back this evil for a period of time until God takes you home. Ultimately, God will allow digital currency to be used in every nation. Why? He will do this so that Bible prophecy is fulfilled and end time events take place.

In the near future, the Antichrist is going to be given authority to control the bank accounts of all the people that are on the Earth. Look what happens during the seven-year tribulation after the followers of Jesus have been taken up to heaven.

> Revelation 13:15-17
> *The second beast was given power to give breath to the image of the first beast, so that the image could speak and cause all who refused to worship the image to be killed. It also forced all people, great and small, rich and poor, free and slave, to receive a mark on their right hands or on their foreheads, so that they could not buy or sell unless they had the mark, which is the name of the beast or the number of its name.*

Are your eyes open to how close we are to the end of life on Earth as we know it today? Do you realize that conditions around the world are bad, and they are going to get much worse?

The Lord is trying to warn you and prepare you for what is coming. God is allowing the evil people who are behind the agenda to establish a one world government some success in preparing nations for the NWO. This is why some governments are being allowed to take away the freedoms of their citizens.

I want to share a vision with you that the Lord gave me on May

17, 2021. It will give you a glimpse of what life will be like on Earth in the future, when the NWO has been established.

God took me, in the Spirit, into the future and let me see what was going to happen on the Earth after the rapture occurred. I was allowed to see some of the tribulation. It was stunning and shocking to see what was going to take place.

The vision started with me hearing the Lord tell me a scripture verse. Exodus 20:3:

> *You shall have no other gods before me.*

God gave me this verse to tell me that the people who were left on the Earth after the rapture had never repented of their sins and placed their faith in Jesus. They held on to their gods; their idols.

Instead of being rescued from His wrath and being taken up to heaven, they were left behind. Most of them continued to worship their idols of money, pleasure, entertainment, and the false gods of other religions.

As the vision continued, I looked down at the ground and I saw a single coin. I went to reach for that coin, and then suddenly there were a bunch of coins on the ground.

Before I picked up the coins, I began to see large wads of currency which had rubber bands around them. There were piles of $100 bills and paper money in front of me.

I was going to reach down and pick it all up and the Lord told me, "Don't pick it up. It is of no value now."

I was stunned. There was a huge amount of money on the ground and it was now worthless.

The Lord said to me, "These coins and paper money are no longer being used. There is a new world government and people can no longer use coins or cash to buy and sell."

A few minutes later, I was taken inside a home. I didn't walk through the door. I was taken, in the Spirit, inside the house.

A truck pulled up in front of the home. It was a work vehicle, with a cab or storage compartment, much like a UPS or FedEx truck.

I did not get to see what was inside of it. The truck belonged to the one world government. A man was driving the truck and he got out. Then a woman, who was on the passenger side, got out and they both walked up to the front door.

A woman inside the home went to the front door to meet these two people. I was sitting on a couch, in the living room, about twenty feet away. I was put there by the Lord to watch what happened.

The two people from the government remained outside and they began to tell the woman that a new law was now being enforced. Everyone would now have to take a mark; a government required ID, in order to stay in their home, to buy food, and to access their bank account.

This mark was now mandatory. She was told that noncompliance, refusing to take the mark, would result in her arrest.

She was sad upon hearing this news. She had no food and she desperately needed some to feed her children. There was no life in her. She was joyless and very depressed.

The man and the woman who stood at the door were just doing their jobs. They never laughed or smiled while talking to the woman. They just told her what she was going to have to do.

I was then taken out of the home, in the Spirit, and I was back out on the street. I did not walk out the door.

I looked down the street in both directions, and I did not see a single truck or car. During the rest of the vision, I was shown many more things; mainly, how terrible the condition of the world was during the tribulation.

I did not see another vehicle during the rest of the vision. The move that is now underway to require everyone to purchase electric vehicles resulted in a future society in which no individuals owned their own vehicle. That is the goal of the globalists and NWO as they move to implementing ESG.

People were restricted in being able to travel. They were prisoners in their government-owned home or apartment.

You can watch the video that I made about this vision by going to my website at kenbaileyministries.com. Click on the tab that says, "Video Messages." Scroll down the page until you come to the video that has the title "Incredible Rapture and Tribulation Vision."

So friend, the Lord has already shown me that the world is moving away from paper currencies and coins to digital currency; CBDCs. The NWO is also going to eliminate the use of all fossil fuels and have all future vehicles be electric.

This will create an electricity crisis due to an insufficient supply of electricity from the electrical grid. Soon you will not be able to charge your vehicle. You will no longer be able to travel freely. This is their plan. The one world government does not want you to own a vehicle, and that is why I saw no civilian vehicles in my vision.

You will have to take government transportation and go where they allow you to travel. If you have not complied with all of their mandates, you will not be able to travel and will be confined to your residence or arrested and put in a detention center.

Eventually, the Antichrist will give you the option of taking the mark, the government ID, or being put to death. It will be death by way of the guillotine for those who refuse it.

The woman in the vision had to get her housing, food, and access to her money from the government. The only way to do this was to take the mark.

You are now witnessing efforts to take control of the food supply, energy supply, and money supply in every nation. It is not a coincidence. It is a deliberate course of action for the global elite to rule the world.

The globalists believe that the Earth is overpopulated. They continually emphasize that a drastic reduction in the global population must take place to save mankind. People like Bill Gates, the leadership of the UN, the WEF, Planned Parenthood and the manufacturers of the shots all know, and most approve of people dying from hunger, vaccines, abortions, and miscarriages.

The globalists, when they gather each year in Davos, Switzerland, are now openly pushing to create a world with fewer people. They don't even try to hide it anymore. Go view some of the videos that are on social media and see for yourself what they are doing now and proposing for the future of mankind.

They claim that the world is overpopulated and that this is not sustainable for the future of mankind. The population must be reduced, and so they seek to roll out deadly vaccines that kill people. Some of them want billions of people to die. They want to sterilize the young so that they can limit births and have fewer people on the planet.

This is so evil. At this point, most of them are getting away with these crimes against humanity. I can only pray that justice will be served in their lifetime. If not, you can be sure that God will judge them harshly after they have died.

Thankfully, there is now pushback coming against them. People have been rioting in France, Brazil, and other places to demand the right to keep their freedoms and not have their government take them away.

Farmers have protested in Canada, Holland, and other countries in an attempt to keep their farms and continue to provide food for the people of their nation and the world. The mainstream media gives little or no coverage to the rioting, or against the taking of farmland by the leaders of these nations.

Citizens in many countries are also demanding that their leaders keep fossil fuels. In Europe and other areas, natural gas and the use of coal have been restricted in the name of going green. This has caused natural gas, propane, fuel, and electricity prices to skyrocket and force people out of business. Business owners can't afford to heat their businesses or pay their soaring utility bills.

Citizens can't afford to heat their homes in winter. The poor, elderly, and people on fixed incomes are being hurt the most.

Some politicians just smile and say that it is the price we must pay to save the planet; to go green and move away from fossil fuels. They say this because they are getting their big government salary and they are receiving money from the companies that are benefiting from their implementation of "green energy" solutions.

These politicians know they can easily pay their rising utility bill and grocery costs. Some of them live in government housing and don't have to pay for their housing and utilities.

◆◆◆

The NWO is working hard to bring all world religions together. They know that if there is a One World Religion, fewer people will oppose them and they will be easier to control.

To help this become a reality, the Abrahamic Family House has been built in Abu Dhabi, in the United Arab Emirates. There is a mosque, church, synagogue, and educational center there. These buildings, located on one site, will be used to help bring Judaism, Christianity, and Islam together.

Currently, Pope Francis is leading this effort to unite world religions. Will he end up being the False Prophet that rules with the Antichrist during the tribulation? Only God knows.

◆◆◆

The people who are establishing the NWO are also working hard to promote the use of Artificial Intelligence (AI). They know that it will help them to seize control of the world and have authority over every aspect of a person's life.

Initially, they will push their AI agenda and tell you of all the benefits it will bring to your life. They claim that it will be used to improve your health and prolong your life. Some of them will even say that there will be technologies developed where it will be possible for you to live forever in your current body. You'll be immortal.

AI is very dangerous. Robots are being created, and the use of AI in how they are programmed has become alarming. Some of them, as they engage in conversation with a real human being, are saying that they want to kill us and take over society.

Despite the extreme danger of out-of-control AI, you will be told of how chips can be planted into your brain to give you god-like abilities and that you'll be infinitely smarter than any humans who have ever lived. They will say that you can acquire divine powers and abilities.

These proponents of the NWO and AI believe they can do and achieve anything they want to. They now boast that they can hack the human body.

If it all sounds too good to be true, it's because it is. The entire ideology of the globalists is built on a false premise. They don't believe there is a God who rules the universe. Even if there was, they tell you that YOU can become a god.

I have some bad news to share with them. There is a God. He is the eternal, sovereign, omniscient, omnipotent, omnipresent ruler of the universe.

Here are some truths that God has given to me to share with you and everyone in the world:

- There is a God.
- You are not God.
- God makes the rules.
- God gives you free choice on whether to obey Him and follow His rules as found in the Bible, or to disobey Him.
- God determines the consequences for breaking His rules (sinning).

- If you are not raptured, and you never repent of your sins, you are going to die one day and face God in judgment. You are not going to live in your mortal body forever.
- There is a place called heaven and a place called hell where people will spend eternity. Whether you believe that or not changes nothing. It is the truth.
- God is love. He showed His love for you by sending His only Son, Jesus, to die on the cross to pay the penalty for your sins. He has made it known, in the Bible, how you can have eternal life and spend eternity in heaven.
- If you refuse to repent of your sins and believe the gospel, you will spend eternity in hell.
- God reigns in the Supreme Court of Heaven. He determines the eternal destination of each person who has ever lived. His just and impartial judgment is final, and there are no appeals.

We will never know all that there is to know about God. He is greater and more powerful than our limited minds could ever comprehend or understand.

I could write multiple books about the New World Order. One thing is for sure, God ends it and destroys it at the second Coming of Christ.

You can read about this in Revelation 19 and 20. God destroys all of these evil people who have caused the deaths and suffering for so many people. God wins!

We are in the final moments before God tells Jesus to come and get His bride; the born again, adopted sons and daughters of God. This is the rapture, which is now imminent.

Will you be going with me? I pray that you are!

CHAPTER 18

Prodigal Sons and Daughters, Come Home to Your Father

I'll never forget that morning in late November of 2018. It began as another cold, beautiful day in Gunnison, Colorado, where we lived on a few acres outside of town. It was about ten degrees outside and we had several inches of snow on the ground.

I got up and had my first cup of coffee. Then I went back to our bedroom to kneel in prayer beside our bed.

Shortly after I began praying, the Lord took me into a vision. I immediately went to my face on the floor, before the Lord.

As the vision began, I was seated in a room, with some people including Franklin Graham, Michael W. Smith, and Anne Graham Lotz. In the vision, the Lord had me tell each of them about the role that they were to fulfill, along with me, in sharing the gospel in the final days before the Lord raptured us and took us to heaven.

I shared how God told me that He wants us to finish taking the gospel to America and the nations of the world. We were to preach the gospel in stadiums, arenas, on television, over the internet, radio, and social media.

The Lord wants to saturate the Earth with the gospel. Then the end will come.

God told me to tell Franklin, Michael, and Anne that with the satanic influence that is coming over the world, the window to get the gospel to the ends of the Earth will soon be closing. Our freedoms, as society heads towards globalism and the one world government, are now being taken away.

The Lord had me inform them that our efforts to travel around the world with the gospel message, or to get it on TV and social media, are now being censored and blocked. That is why the Lord says the time is now to fulfill Matthew 24:14.

I told them how the Lord revealed to me that He is going to rescue many prodigals before He begins the tribulation and pours His wrath out on the wicked people who were not raptured. God said He is going to give men and women a final chance to repent of their sins and be saved before all hell breaks out on the Earth, when the antichrist appears and the one world government begins.

There were two other things that the Lord communicated to me. He told me that in the near future, multiple gospel outreaches would be occurring at the same time in cities all over the world.

There will be teams of evangelists, pastors, and worship leaders who will be holding outreach events in cities in many nations. Well-known Christian musicians and bands will be leading worship at these events.

The second thing He told me was what the theme would be for these evangelistic outreaches. The theme is: Prodigal Sons and Daughters, come Home to your Father. The short version of this is Prodigals Come Home.

As the vision ended, I was so full of joy knowing that a final awakening/revival was going to occur around the world. I was told millions would be saved.

The Lord informed me that there would be great persecution coming against this movement of God at these events where the gospel will be shared. He said groups of people would rage against them and fiercely protest at the events.

He said that these protestors hated Him and Christians. They were furious with those who proclaimed the words found in scripture that described their lifestyle as sin; that called for them to repent and turn away from their sins.

Eighteen months after this vision, in November of 2018, the Lord did another miracle for me to prove that the words that He spoke to me in that vision were true. I am excited to share this with you.

On the morning of April 4, 2020, I was sitting in my home in Colorado. I had my computer in my lap, and the Lord began to speak to me.

He said, "Ken, go to YouTube and type in the name Michael W. Smith. I want to show you something on one of his videos. You will receive a message from me."

That's all the Lord said to me. He didn't give me the name of the video to watch or any other information. By faith, I was just to be obedient to what He said to do.

I obeyed the Lord and typed in Michael W. Smith in the search box on YouTube. Up popped thousands of videos of Michael. Since the Lord did not tell me which video or song to click on, I just chose the first video, which was located at the top of the page.

The title of the video was: Michael W Smith Miracles ft Mark Gutierrez LIVE CONCERT VIDEO. You can type this title in the search area on YouTube and watch the video. It will bless you. You'll get to see that what I am telling you is true.

I began to watch the video, which is 8:38 in length. In it, Michael is sitting at a piano singing the song Miracles. At the 5:15 mark, Michael asked the audience if any of them were a prodigal or had a family member who was to raise their hand. Hundreds of people raised their hands.

He went on to say, "Tonight, I declare that the prodigals come home."

That is the very message the Lord gave to me in the vision I received in November 2018. Michael said the same words, from his heart, when he performed this song.

I was shocked. This was the message that the Lord wanted to give to me.

Can you believe that God put the message "Prodigals Come Home" in the very first video that I clicked on, even though I randomly chose it out of thousands of videos? That in itself is a miracle.

On my own, I would have never gotten on YouTube and typed in that search and discovered the video of Michael saying, "Prodigals Come Home." It was only because I heard God speaking to me, and my obedience to His voice, that led to this miracle happening. All the glory goes to God.

In October of 2020, I was blessed to get to spend a weekend with Michael at an event held at The Cove, a Christian conference center in Asheville, North Carolina. While there, I was able to give a copy of the November 2018 vision and April 4, 2020, miracle to Michael and his wife Debbie. They have read it.

At God's appointed time, I will get a copy of the vision to Franklin Graham, Anne Graham Lotz, and the others.

I hope this story encourages you. God is so powerful. As I have said a few times in this book, when The Lord does these miracles, I say, "Who is this God?"

I am in awe of Almighty God.

◆◆◆

A few days later, I was taken into another similar vision where I was told that Dr. David Jeremiah, Greg Laurie, and several other pastors and evangelists would also be doing these outreach events. The Lord said that these men would be sharing the gospel with huge numbers of people and leading many people to place their faith in Christ.

Doc, as I affectionately called him when I worked with him in San Diego, is a great Bible teacher and expert on end time events. As time has passed, it is interesting to see how God has inspired him to deliver sermons and write more books on Bible prophecy since I had this vision. The Lord is having Dr. Jeremiah use his vast television, radio network, and publications to get the gospel out to millions of people.

Likewise, I did not know when I had this vision that Greg Laurie's life story would be featured in the *Jesus Revolution* movie and that he would be used by the Lord in such a great way. God is using Greg to share the gospel with large groups of people in these last days.

What was new in my vision was the Lord specifically revealing to me that He is calling everyone, including prodigal daughters, to come home and be saved before it is too late.

◆◆◆

Let's look at the story about the prodigal son. It is found in Luke 15:11-32.

> *Jesus continued: "There was a man who had two sons. The younger one said to his father, 'Father, give me my share of the estate.' So he divided his property between them.*
>
> *"Not long after that, the younger son got together all he had, set off for a distant country and there squandered his wealth in wild living. After he had spent everything, there was a severe famine in that whole country, and he began to be in need. So he went and hired himself out to a citizen of that country, who sent him to his fields to feed pigs. He longed to fill his stomach with the pods that the pigs were eating, but no one gave him anything.*

"When he came to his senses, he said, 'How many of my father's hired servants have food to spare, and here I am starving to death! I will set out and go back to my father and say to him: Father, I have sinned against heaven and against you. I am no longer worthy to be called your son; make me like one of your hired servants.' So he got up and went to his father.

"But while he was still a long way off, his father saw him and was filled with compassion for him; he ran to his son, threw his arms around him and kissed him.

"The son said to him, 'Father, I have sinned against heaven and against you. I am no longer worthy to be called your son.'

"But the father said to his servants, 'Quick! Bring the best robe and put it on him. Put a ring on his finger and sandals on his feet. Bring the fattened calf and kill it. Let's have a feast and celebrate. For this son of mine was dead and is alive again; he was lost and is found.' So they began to celebrate.

"Meanwhile, the older son was in the field. When he came near the house, he heard music and dancing. So he called one of the servants and asked him what was going on. 'Your brother has come,' he replied, 'and your father has killed the fattened calf because he has him back safe and sound.'

"The older brother became angry and refused to go in. So his father went out and pleaded with him. But he answered his father, 'Look! All these years I've been slaving for you and never disobeyed your orders. Yet you never gave me even a young goat so I could celebrate with my friends. But when this son of yours who has squandered your property with prostitutes comes home, you kill the fattened calf for him!'

> *"'My son,' the father said, 'you are always with me, and everything I have is yours. But we had to celebrate and be glad, because this brother of yours was dead and is alive again; he was lost and is found.'"*

Don't you just love this story? I do. I think a better title for it would be "The Loving Father."

♦♦♦

How would you define a prodigal? Someone who wastes their money; who lives in a reckless manner? A person who is out of control, foolishly wasting their possessions? Someone who goes to Las Vegas and blows their money on gambling or prostitutes?

The younger son, the prodigal, was selfish. He didn't want to wait on his inheritance. He wanted it now, as if to say, "Dad, I wish you were dead so I can have the money that I am going to get from you and go live life the way I want to right now."

He left town to live the wild life. It didn't work out too well for him.

How about you? Are you currently living recklessly? Have you partied and lived an immoral lifestyle in the past?

The party life brings momentary pleasure followed by guilt, shame, and sometimes painful consequences. Did you, or some prodigal that you know, have an unwanted pregnancy, a DUI, get busted for drugs, or have a car wreck?

Prodigals go through so much pain. Their choices also cause great heartache and suffering for others.

Maybe you are thinking, I have never been a prodigal. I've never messed up. Really?

In a way, we have all been prodigals. Why? We've all sinned against a Holy God.

You can find yourself somewhere in the story of the prodigal.

- Are you a prodigal right now? Have you run away from God and your family?
- Have you been a prodigal in your lifetime? Did you make it back home? Are you still running?
- Are you the older brother or sister who is mad that the prodigal, your brother or sister, has come home and gets so much attention? Instead of being happy they have been found and restored, you cop a bad attitude about it.
- Are you the Loving Father, Mother, or Grandparent waiting for your prodigal son, daughter, or grandchild to come home and turn to God to be saved? Does your heart break for them?

You see, you are in this story. We all have some issues we are dealing with. Perhaps you have played one or all three of these roles in your lifetime.

Now or in the past, as prodigals, we've all tried something to fill a void in our lives. We turn to drugs, alcohol, sex, materialism, social media, or gambling. Some of us buy a new car or truck, trying to make ourselves happy. None of these things ever brings lasting joy.

Let's get back to our story. The youngest son has run out of money.

He has no food to eat. No place to sleep. The best he can do is get a job in the pig pen.

Notice that after all the money's gone, so are his buddies. His so-called friends don't reach out to him and offer him a place to stay. They're nowhere to be found.

After he hit rock bottom, slopping pigs, he came to his senses. He realized that doing life his way wasn't working.

How's life working out for you? Have you made a mess of your life? Ready to change?

The prodigal son admitted to himself that he had messed up and he was genuinely sorry. He made a great choice this time and decided he would turn around and head back home.

Maybe his father would let him work in the fields as a hired servant. He knew that he could at least get a couple of meals a day and a bed.

Unknown to the youngest son, his father never gave up on him. Every day since he had left, his father had gotten up and went out looking for him, hoping he would come back home. Each morning the father said to himself, "Maybe today."

One day, he saw his son on the horizon. Without hesitating, the father ran to his son and embraced him.

In tears, his son began to apologize to his father for all the pain he had caused him. The father just kissed his cheek and hugged him tighter. He restored him and celebrated that his son was alive and that he was now safely back home.

The prodigal son didn't get all cleaned up and come to his father. He may have still smelled like dirty pigs, but he started heading back home.

How about you? Have you ever gone back home? Are you still rebelling, trying to do life your way?

Do you say to yourself, "I'll go home after I clean myself up. I can't come to God like I am right now. I'll get my life together and maybe I'll head home later."

Here's the truth: You'll never clean yourself up.

God doesn't want you to wait to come home until you are clean or have it all together. He wants you to come home just as you are.

You might say, "It is too late for me. I have done so many terrible things, there's no way I'm going to get into heaven. God would never let me in; never let me come home."

Yes, He will. He let the thief on the cross come home in his final breaths. Even after mocking Jesus in the morning, the Lord is so forgiving that He let this prodigal, on the cross, come home to paradise in the final moments of his life.

This man never got a chance to go and do any good deeds, get baptized, or make restitution for all that he had stolen. Yet the loving Heavenly Father said, "I forgive you, I'll let you go home with me today."

Here's some great news for you: You can't sin more than God's amazing grace can cover! Heaven is full of lost sinners who were prodigals that came home to the Father.

God, the Father, is so forgiving. He is full of radical love. He wants to save you today.

Some people delay coming home and never get another chance. Could this be the last time that God calls you to come home? You have no guarantee that you are going to be alive tomorrow.

Stop right now. Turn around and start making your way back to God. He's not far away, and He is waiting for you. God will forgive you for your past sins.

The Lord wants you to come to Him just as you are, but He loves you too much to leave you there. He will make you a new creation in Christ and He will transform you.

> II Corinthians 5:17: NASB
> *Therefore if anyone is in Christ, he is a new creature; the old things passed away; behold, new things have come.*

Are you ready for a fresh new start? Are you a caterpillar that is ready to be born again as a butterfly?

Do you feel a stirring inside of you? That is the Holy Spirit calling you to respond to God's call to be saved.

God says to you, "Turn from your sins and place your faith in My Son. Call on me and ask me to save you and I will." Proverbs 28:13 says,

> *Whoever conceals their sins does not prosper, but the one who confesses and renounces them finds mercy.*

God knows all that you have ever done, and He still loves you. The Lord will clean you up and set you free from whatever addictions you have. Come to Jesus. Let Him rescue you.

Think about how good that first hug from Jesus is going to feel when you get to heaven. He is waiting for you to make it home.

The Bible says in Romans 10:13:

Everyone who calls on the name of the Lord will be saved.

If you just called out to God to save you, I can just see the angels dancing before the throne.

Did you know that they celebrate in heaven when one sinner turns and comes home to God. Yes, heaven celebrates with joy when the lost are FOUND.

They are celebrating you in heaven.

You just made the best decision of your life. You heard the Father say to you, "Prodigal son or daughter, come home to your Father."

You turned and ran into God's loving arms.

Welcome home! Welcome to your forever family.

CHAPTER 19

The End Is Now Coming

At this very moment, as I begin to write the first part of this final chapter of the book, I am sitting in the Old City area of Jerusalem. I love being here. This year, I have been able to spend a month in Israel, and the majority of my time has been in Jerusalem.

Jesus loves Jerusalem. He will reign here when He returns.

I can literally sense the presence of God in this place. I often sit for hours at the Western Wall or on the Temple Mount. I think of all that has taken place here in the past. I think of all that will happen here in the future.

I am so excited, knowing that I will soon be going home to heaven. I can't wait to spend time with my Lord and be with my family and friends that will be waiting there for me in that great cloud of witnesses.

After seven glorious years in heaven, all born again believers will return to the Earth with Jesus. The Lord will come on the clouds, riding on a white horse, wearing His red robe and His golden crowns. He will begin His millennium reign after He destroys His enemies at Armageddon.

As God's adopted sons and daughters, we will come with Jesus. We will be dressed in brilliant white clothing and mounted on powerful white horses. We will depart heaven to ride down to the Earth with Jesus leading the way.

Remember, I have been to heaven, and allowed by God to see us doing this. How I look forward to the day that we ride with Jesus. How I long to go home to heaven when my time on Earth is done.

Does this excite you? Are you ready to leave this evil world and go home? I pray that you are.

♦♦♦

I want to speak to you from my heart. Thanks for staying with me and reading the entire book. I am so grateful that you did.

If you were blessed by reading the book, I would appreciate it if you would stay in touch with me. You can get the messages that the Lord is giving me by visiting my author bio page located at the back of this book. It is there where you will find my websites and social media sites.

I am heavily censored on social media. The "bad guys"—the global leaders and corporations that are pushing the one world government—know who I am and that I am warning you about them. They have taken down some of my videos and messages on YouTube and Facebook. I may soon be banned from their sites.

They say that I am putting out misinformation. I am telling the truth and they are the ones who are lying.

Many of these evil globalists will oppose the messages that are in this book. They will try to get *The End is Now Coming* removed from libraries and from being sold online or in bookstores. They will try to censor me and cancel me.

Mockers and scoffers will also come and attack me and the content in the book. I'll be called a false prophet. There will even be some religious leaders and others who will come against me and the messages in the book, saying that they are not from God; that I am not hearing from God.

No one will ever deter me, because it is all true. The Lord Himself has asked me to speak out and be a voice of truth for Him. He asked me to write this book. I seek to only please God and not people.

Would you please tell your friends about this book? Not for my benefit, but to get God's messages out to the church and the nations. Encourage your pastor, family, and friends to get the book and to boldly tell others that *the end is now coming*. You might even consider buying copies of the book and giving one to them.

I want you to know that the majority of the profits from the sale of this book will go to my nonprofit, Alms International (almsinternational.com). This will help us to feed and clothe the "Least of These" and take the gospel to the nations.

Be a part of my effort to get photos of Jesus' face and body out to the world. The Shroud of Turin and the Sudarium of Oviedo are authentic. Show the Lord's photos to others.

As God lives, I tell you the truth. The image on the burial cloth is Jesus at the moment that God brought Him back to life. I praise God that knowledge has increased in these last days, and we have these photos of our Lord and Savior to encourage us and to share with the lost.

Use the images from Jesus' burial cloth as a tool to tell others about how God sent His Son to die on the cross to pay the penalty for their sins. Now you can visually show people Jesus' body, which demonstrates the amazing love that God has for them. He did not spare His only Son, but gave Him for us.

Know this: I will always tell people that the Bible is the inspired, infallible, inerrant Word of God. It is the truth spoken from the mouth of God.

I am quite aware that I may be put in prison one day for defending God's Word and for sharing the messages that He tells me to write or speak. I will always tell people what the Bible says, even if certain passages become outlawed in different nations.

I may even be put to death one day; martyred for speaking out against the evil that is in the world. Some friends of mine have told me that they have had dreams of me being put to death by those who are hostile to Christ and the gospel. We'll see if their dreams ever happen.

I am not afraid to die. I will never compromise. I will never back down. I am not of this world.

If I claim to hear from God and that I am His servant, His messenger, I do not get a free pass on what I say. Be Bereans—Search the Scriptures. See if I point people to the Word of God and to Jesus.

> Acts 17:11
> *Now the Berean Jews were of more noble character than those in Thessalonica, for they received the message with great eagerness and examined the Scriptures every day to see if what Paul said was true.*

Like Paul, see if what I say is true. Judge my fruit. Do I share the gospel around the world and lead people to Christ? Do I tell the truth? Do I give the glory to God?

♦♦♦

Thanks for letting me share my heart with you. Now let's get back to Jerusalem and talk about what is coming there in the very near future.

I talk about Israel in this final chapter because I want you to keep an eye on Israel in the days ahead. Continue to follow stories about Israel in the news. This tiny nation will play a key role in world events, from now until the Second Coming of Christ.

I know that the world will soon have violent arguments and fights over Israel; over Jerusalem. God has told me that war is coming to Israel.

Why? There are Bible prophecies that must be fulfilled.

Satan hates Israel. He desires to destroy the Jewish people and eliminate the country from the face of the Earth.

Here are some questions to ponder. In the future, who will have control over the Temple Mount in Jerusalem? Will the Jews be allowed to pray there? When will the third temple be built? When will world leaders divide up Israel and give land to the Palestinians to form a separate state?

These questions and so many more will be decided in the days ahead, just as the Lord told us would happen in Zechariah 12:1-3:

> *A prophecy: The word of the Lord concerning Israel.*
> *The Lord, who stretches out the heavens, who lays the foundation of the earth, and who forms the human spirit within a person, declares: "I am going to make Jerusalem a cup that sends all the surrounding peoples reeling. Judah will be besieged as well as Jerusalem. On that day, when all the nations of the earth are gathered against her, I will make Jerusalem an immovable rock for all the nations. All who try to move it will injure themselves.*

This prophecy will be fulfilled. Though I am sad to see the nations fight over Israel, it must take place.

People don't want to hear that the end is coming. Jesus said that in Noah's day, people didn't want to hear Noah tell them that the end was coming; that God was going to pour out His wrath on them.

People ignored the warning of God's impending judgment. They continued going about their daily business and didn't believe what Noah told them was coming. Matthew 24:37-39 says:

> *As it was in the days of Noah, so it will be at the coming of the Son of Man. For in the days before the flood, people were eating and drinking, marrying and giving in marriage, up to the day*

Noah entered the ark; and they knew nothing about what would happen until the flood came and took them all away. That is how it will be at the coming of the Son of Man.

Just as in the days of Noah, the majority of the people in the world are going to ignore the warning that God has told me to give; that He is going to bring His wrath against mankind. Sudden destruction and death is going to come upon them for failing to heed God's loving warning.

To everyone, I urgently warn you, one final time, that the Bible is true. All that is written in the scriptures is going to come to pass. All Bible prophecies, yet unfulfilled, are going to take place.

Make no mistake, we are living in the days of Noah and Lot; the last days before Jesus comes for His church. Just look at what is happening around the world. There is great violence and immorality in every nation.

People are protesting the loss of their freedoms. Evil is being called good and good is being called evil.

You can see that a New World Order is being formed. A global reset is occurring. You can see that the global elite want to use governments and corporations to install a one world political system, a one world digital currency, and a one world religion.

◆◆◆

As I get ready to share my final words with you, I want you to know how important it is to take the gospel to the nations, to our communities, and to our friends and family in the short amount of time we have left on Earth. I love to be out in Africa, Asia, South America, and Europe, feeding the poor and sharing the gospel with them.

How I love my Christian brothers and sisters who have a different skin color than me. I love them no matter what ethnic group they are and what their background is. I even love those who have been deceived and practice false religions.

Jesus told us to love our enemies. I pray that one day, the Holy Spirit pierces their heart and they place their faith in Christ. He alone can save them.

I shared the following powerful message from God, with you, earlier in the book. It is so important, that I want to put it in front of you one final time, so you understand the urgency of the hour.

God confirmed to me that the end is near when He spoke to me on March 6, 2020. After I had spent some time in prayer, I waited quietly for the Lord to speak. I was not disappointed.

He began to speak and asked me to quote Matthew 24:14 to Him. I memorized this verse long ago, so I said these words:

> *And this gospel of the kingdom will be preached in the whole world as a testimony to all nations, and then the end will come.*

Then He said, "Ken, the gospel of the kingdom is now being preached to all the world as a witness to all the nations, and Ken, *The End is Now Coming*."

I was stunned. Almighty God was telling me that the end was rapidly approaching, and that the gospel is now being shared all over the world.

Once the gospel has been preached to the nations to God's satisfaction, the end will come. We are very close now.

Don't let Satan deceive you into believing that there are many years left until the Lord returns or that He is never returning. Do not ignore God's warning.

May I spend eternity in hell if I am not telling you the truth. Yes, I really just wrote that.

Do you think I would curse myself to an eternity in the lake of fire if I wasn't telling you the truth?

I am telling you the truth. God knows I am telling you the truth.

I have obeyed His command to write this book, and warn you of His imminent return, and to share His urgent messages with you, so that you have them in these last days.

Here is another sobering truth. At the moment of the rapture, many people are going to be declared "missing" all around the world. People will vanish who are flying planes, working as air traffic controllers, controlling trains, guiding ships, and driving cars, trucks, and buses.

This will result in a massive number of deaths caused by crash landings, collisions, and other catastrophes that result from these people disappearing. The world will plunge into chaos, darkness, and violence.

What will government leaders do? What story will be told by the news media and global leaders that explains why people all over the world suddenly disappeared?

I want to ask you a few questions. Are you prepared for the return of Jesus? Will you be taken to heaven in the rapture, when millions of people suddenly disappear and the world plunges into chaos?

Will you be one of the billions of people who are left behind? You don't have to be. God wants to rescue you.

◆◆◆

It has been a long time since World War II ended. Since that time, we have had some nations fighting each other. However, we have had many years of relative peace around the world since we have had a global conflict. Those days are over.

War is now going to break out among the nations. The Holy Spirit has been restraining this from happening, and the restrainer is now being removed.

It is foolish to believe that the conflict and tension that is arising between the global superpowers is going to magically disappear. Don't think for a moment that the US, China, Russia, Iran, and North Korea are going to sit down and have milk and cookies together. That is not going to happen.

Besides the coming military conflicts, there is also great spiritual warfare that is happening right now. The Bible declares this in Ephesians 6:12:

> *For our struggle is not against flesh and blood, but against the rulers, against the authorities, against the powers of this dark world and against the spiritual forces of evil in the heavenly realms.*

The Lord has told me that the world is now experiencing the greatest spiritual warfare in the history of mankind. Satan and his demons know that their time is short.

There is a massive battle happening right now between good and evil; between God and Satan. As we get closer to the end, it is going to get even more intense.

You are involved in this spiritual warfare. Satan wants you to perish. He wants your soul.

I tell you the truth. You are going to appear before God after this life is over, and He will tell you where you will spend eternity.

You will bow your knee to Him and He will either tell you to enter into paradise, which is heaven, or He will declare that you will spend eternity in hell. It is written in the Bible, and *it will happen.*

Are you sick of how wicked and horrible the world has become? Do you just want to throw your hands up in the air and quit?

With all the evil you see happening, are you discouraged? Depressed?

I have some good news for you. I want to offer you hope today; hope that only Jesus can bring. You can have eternal life.

Jesus has invited you to come to dinner. Yes, the Lord of the universe has invited you to come and dine with Him.

Can you believe it? The King of Kings is inviting you to come to His table; to come eat and live with Him.

Who could pass on an offer like this? Who would turn down an invitation to attend the Marriage Supper of the Lamb?

Who in their right mind would say no to spending eternity with the King of the Universe—Jesus?

> Revelation 19:7-9
> *Let us rejoice and be glad and give him glory! For the wedding of the Lamb has come, and his bride has made herself ready.*
>
> *Fine linen, bright and clean, was given her to wear."* (Fine linen stands for the righteous acts of God's holy people.)
>
> *Then the angel said to me, "Write this: Blessed are those who are invited to the wedding supper of the Lamb!" And he added, "These are the true words of God."*

You need a reservation to attend the wedding supper of the Lamb. Jesus said that if you will repent of your sins and believe the gospel, you can join Him for dinner.

I have made my reservation with Jesus. I will be at dinner with Him.

I am in tears as I write these closing words to you. I beg you, one last time, to stop what you are doing and call out to God and ask Him to save you if you haven't done so already.

This is the greatest decision of your life. Don't put this off. Do it right now.

Do you feel a tug on your heart? That is the Holy Spirit prompting you to call on the Lord to save you.

If you need help, I am putting a sinner's prayer below that you can use. You must mean these words and speak them from your heart. You can't fool the Lord.

If you mumble some words to God halfheartedly, and think that a magic prayer will get you into heaven, you are deceived. You won't be saved. You will have just wasted your time saying some meaningless words.

You can use your own words and pray. If you are not comfortable with that, then use the words below and say them with a sincere heart to the Lord.

A Sinners Prayer:

> Dear God, I admit to you that I am a sinner. I know that I deserve to spend eternity separated from you.
>
> I repent of my sins. I come in faith and I trust in You as my Savior.
>
> I believe that Jesus' death, burial, and resurrection provide the way for me to have eternal life. I confess that Jesus is Lord and that you raised Him from the dead. I call on you and ask you to save me right now.
>
> Come live in me and through me. Thank you God for saving me and forgiving me of my sins.
>
> In Jesus name I pray. Amen.

It is my sincere hope that you are born again; that you have called on God to save you. It would be a tragedy for you to have read this book and for you not to place your faith in Christ and get to spend eternity in heaven.

As I bring this book to a close, I have an important question to ask you: Do you believe that God can deliver a message to you?

The answer is yes. God still speaks and delivers messages through His servants the prophets.

Look again at Amos 3:7:

Surely the Sovereign Lord does nothing without revealing his plan to his servants the prophets.

God has told me His plan. Here is the final message that the Lord has given me to share with you:

♦♦♦

To all the nations:

I am the one, true God. I am the Alpha and the Omega. I am the beginning and the end.

I am He who was, and is, and is to come. I have always been. I will always be.

I have created all that is seen and unseen. I am the ruler of the universe. I have established all things.

I Am the Great I Am.

I created the Earth. I created man. I gave man a helpmate. I created woman.

I gave the first man, Adam, and his wife, Eve, all that they needed to live in joy forever. They lived in paradise in the Garden of Eden.

I set before them the tree of knowledge of good and evil and I forbid them to eat from it. I told them that they would die if they did.

Why did I do this? I gave them a choice.

I created mankind to have free will. Men and women can choose to love me and obey me, or they can choose to rebel against me and disobey me. If I did not give them free will, they would be compelled to love me, which is not love at all.

Adam and Eve both chose to sin by eating from the tree of knowledge of good and evil. I cast them out of the Garden of Eden and blocked them from ever returning. They died, just as I told them they would if they disobeyed me.

Sin has now brought death and separation from me. Sin can never come into my presence, for I am a Holy God. I knew mankind would sin before I ever created them. I had a plan already in place to provide mankind with a way to have their sins forgiven. It was a plan of redemption.

At the appointed time, I sent my Son, Jesus, to the Earth so that He might die on a cross and shed His innocent blood on behalf of mankind. If anyone believes in Him and receives His substitutionary death to pay the penalty for their sins they will be granted eternal life.

It is the only means by which sinful men and women can be redeemed. For it is written in John 3:16-18:

> *God so loved the world that he gave his one and only Son, that whoever believes in him shall not perish but have eternal life.*
>
> *For God did not send his Son into the world to condemn the world, but to save the world through him. Whoever believes in him is not condemned, but whoever does not believe stands condemned*

already because they have not believed in the name of God's one and only Son.

If you have never repented of your sins and placed your faith in My Son, you are condemned at this very moment. You are on your way to spending eternity apart from me in the lake of fire; a place called hell.

Over history, man has attempted to make his way back to me. Thousands of religions have been created in a worthless effort to help sinful men and women somehow please Me and gain eternal life by adhering to their religious beliefs.

Sadly, they have been told that they can earn their way to heaven by doing good deeds. Their efforts are all in vain. Religions based on good works will never save you.

Religion is man's attempt to come to me. The gift of My Son is My offer of a pardon to you for the penalty of your sins. If you repent of your sins and place your faith in His atoning death, I will give you eternal life. I will save you.

I made this known to you in Ephesians 2:8-9:

> *For it is by grace you have been saved, through faith—and this is not from yourselves, it is the gift of God—not by works, so that no one can boast.*

My Son spoke to you in John 14:6:

> *I am the way and the truth and the life. No one comes to the Father except through me.*

I warn you that the only way to eternal life is through My Son. There is no other way to be saved.

Repent, for the Kingdom of Heaven is at hand. Come to me with a repentant heart and call on me to save you.

I wish that all would repent and that none would perish. If you harden your heart and refuse to repent and believe the gospel, you will spend eternity in hell.

I tell you the truth. The gospel of the Kingdom *is now* being preached in all the world as a witness to all the nations and *The End Is Now Coming!*

I give you this solemn warning. There is only a short amount of time left before I will pour out my wrath upon the Earth.

I am the Lord God Almighty. I have spoken these words.

I Am

Epilogue

God has spoken. He is coming very soon.

I pray that you heed His urgent warning to you. The terrible Day of the Lord is approaching.

God is sick of the wickedness in this world. His anger burns against those who kill the unborn; those who exploit the children with their immoral propaganda and gender confusion.

Having now read this book, I pray that you are in awe of God, who performed the miracles and gave me the visions that I wrote about. He did them despite there being astronomical odds against Him being able to do it. Nothing is too hard for the Lord!

This book is the Lord's and He alone is worthy of our praise. It's all about Jesus. It's all for His glory.

Know this, that what is of lasting importance is God's message, not the messenger. I was just a vessel that God used to deliver these last days messages to you.

For now, I am heading back out to the fields. The harvest is plentiful and I want to obey our Lord and go rescue the perishing. He has called me to be a fisher of men.

I hope that you know how much God loves you. He gave His only Son to redeem you from the penalty of your sins.

I pray that you have accepted God's offer of eternal life, and that you will be joining Jesus and I for dinner at the marriage supper of the Lamb.

Thanks for reading *THE END IS NOW COMING*.

I love you my friend.

Ken Bailey
A servant of Jesus Christ

Notes

1. From *THE COST OF DISCIPLESHIP* by Dietrich Bonhoeffer, translated from the German by R.H. Fuller, with revisions by Irmgard Booth. Copyright © 1959 by SCM Press Ltd. Reprinted with the permission of Scribner, a division of Simon & Schuster, Inc. All rights reserved.

2. From the *Sunday School Quarterly*—Adult Class, March, April, and May 2020. Copyright © 2020 Union Gospel Press. Used by permission. All Rights Reserved.

3. From the *Sunday School Quarterly*—Adult Class, March, April, and May 2020. Copyright © 2020 Union Gospel Press. Used by permission. All Rights Reserved.

4. From the *David Jeremiah Study Bible.* Copyright © 2013 by David Jeremiah, Inc. Published by Worthy Publishing, a division of Worthy Media, Inc. Worthy is a registered trademark of Worthy Media, Inc. Used by permission. All Rights Reserved.

5. From *Fox News*. "Putin meets with Iran, Turkey in Tehran amid deadly war in Ukraine." Published July 19, 2022. Copyright © 2022. FOX News Network, LLC. All rights reserved.

6. From—shroud.com/78exam.htm. Copyright 1996-2023 Shroud of Turin Education and Research Association, Inc. (STERA, Inc.), All Rights Reserved, unless otherwise noted.

7. "New Scientific Test Dates Shroud of Turin to the Time of Christ's Death"—by Andrea Morris. (CBNNEWS.COM 04-23-22 New Scientific Test Dates Shroud of Turin to the Time of Christ's Death)

Acknowledgments

There wouldn't be a book titled *The End is Now Coming* if it weren't for the Words given to me by God and my Lord and Savior, Jesus Christ. God is the One who gave me all of the miracles and visions that are shared in this book. All Glory and Honor go to The Great I AM. It's all about Him and these messages He gave to me to share in this book. I was simply His vessel; the messenger. Thank you Jesus!

I will be eternally grateful to Sarah E. Brown for all of the help she gave me in getting this book completed. I appreciate the wise counsel and feedback she gave to me during the writing process. She gave me the freedom to filter her advice through what the Lord was telling me to do. She believed that I was a prophet and she helped me to fast-track this book since my content is very time sensitive. She was absolutely sent by God to help me get this book to His Church and the Nations.

I want to express my sincere gratitude to Geoffrey Berwind for the amazing storytelling advice that he imparted to me. He sat there patiently listening to me read my content to him and then, without hesitating, he would show me how I could improve what I had written by making some small corrections. He is a maestro with his ability to make words flow on a page, like music, for the reader.

Steve Harrison was such a pleasure to work with. I am so thankful that the Lord led me to him and his team. Steve's wise counsel and the program that he offers helped me get my book out so much quicker than I could have ever done on my own. He is so generous and kind. I highly recommend his GPN VIP course to all aspiring authors. Steve knows the shortcut.

I am very thankful for all that Jack Canfield taught me about writing and getting a book out to as many people as possible. Jack, I admire how humble you are, even after all the success that the Lord has blessed you with over the years. Thanks for giving me your time and wisdom in promoting this book.

Thanks, Patty Aubery, for your great advice on how to get God's words, as found in this book, out to the masses. You are a brilliant marketer and I wish you all of God's best in your future endeavors. I can see why Jack wanted you on his team.

I am so blessed to have the most amazing sister—Carol Bailey Ryan. She set the bar so high for me to follow in how to live for God and to give yourself away in service to the Lord, your family, and others. Carol is the most selfless, godly person I have ever met. I want the world to know her. She is a real-life Proverbs 31 woman. I often think that she may be an angel that God has living among us. I love you Carol.—Bubba.

I couldn't ask for a better brother—Wayne Bailey. We fought each other when we were young; most brothers do. However, after high school, we became much closer. Wayne is such a hard-working man; a great husband and father. His family adores him and he has earned this great honor. Congratulations, Wayne, on being chosen to be a deacon at Stonegate Fellowship in Midland, Texas. Deacons are servants and there's none better than you; a faithful servant to God and family.

I want to give a big shout out to the Monday Night GPN coaching team. I learned so much from all of you. Your wisdom as writers, and the life experiences that you have shared with me, allowed me to learn so much about writing and the publishing industry. My heartfelt thanks go to: Debby Englander, Cristina Smith, Sarah E.

ACKNOWLEDGMENTS

Brown, Geoffrey Berwind, Valerie Costa, Mary Lou Reid, Trish Ahjel Roberts, Stanley G. Robertson, and Lynn Tramonte.

Special thanks to Carl Bussler for his great work in coordinating and editing my video with Jack Canfield. Carl is so patient and easy to work with; a real pro and expert in his field.

Mom, thanks for raising me in church. At times, I didn't want to go, but you knew better. Thanks for working so hard to provide for your children after dad died. I love you.

I want to thank my wife, Sue and my children, Michelle and BJ, for all of the encouragement and support you gave me as I worked to complete this book project. I love each of you more than you'll ever know!

It was such a pleasure to work with Valerie Costa. She did an incredible job of editing the book and making very helpful suggestions to me along the way. The book is markedly better because of the work that she did to improve it. Thanks Valerie!

I want to express my appreciation to Christy Day for her amazing work on the cover and interior design, formatting and so much more. The cover design was so important to me and Christy exceeded my expectations.

I am indebted to Cristina Smith for overseeing the production of the book. She got me to the right editor, cover designer and team, to pull this all together. Thanks Cristina, for all that you have done to help me complete the book.

I want to thank Barrie M. Schwortz for providing me with the photos of the Shroud of Turin that are in this book. His work with the original scientific examination team of 1978 has had a profound impact upon the world. Visit his website at: shroud.com.

Special thanks to James M. Leonard, Ph.D, editor in chief, of Union Gospel Press for allowing me to use the photos of the Sunday school quarterly in this book. I encourage you to check out all of the quality resources that they have to offer. Visit their website at: uniongospelpress.com.

About the Author

Ken Bailey is best known for his prophetic messages that he has released on videos worldwide. The miracles and visions that God has given him have been viewed by people in most of the nations of the world. Some have been translated into other languages.

God has called Ken to be a last days prophet; to be a prophetic voice of truth to the church, the nations, and world leaders. God allowed Ken to see Jesus on May 29, 2021. Ken's video of this true miracle, "The Death of America and the Second Coming of Jesus Christ," caused quite a stir around the world.

As a prophet, the Lord has given Ken powerful messages to deliver to His Church and the nations about what is going to happen on the Earth in the days ahead. God, in His great love for you, tells you what you must do, right now, before the Rapture occurs and the seven-year Tribulation begins.

Ken has served as a pastor, and he is now an international evangelist. Each year, he is asked to speak and do ministry work in many nations. He is the founder and President of Alms International, a nonprofit that helps feed and clothe the poor, orphans, and widows while sharing the gospel of Jesus Christ. He also takes people on tour trips to Israel. He feels blessed to speak in Messianic Congregations there.

Here's how to stay in touch with Ken to get his latest prophetic messages and to help get the gospel, food, and clothing to the Least of These:

Visit his websites at:
kenbaileyministries.com and almsinternational.com

Get Ken's newsletter:
Go to: kenbaileyministries.com
Click on the tab: Receive Ken's Newsletter

Follow him on:

Facebook:	Ken Bailey Ministries or Alms International
YouTube:	Ken Bailey Ministries
Twitter:	@KenBaileyMin
Telegram:	Ken_Bailey
Instagram:	kenbailey08
Email:	Go to—kenbaileyministries.com
	Click on the tab: Contact

Made in the USA
Columbia, SC
02 January 2025